Speaking, Relating, and Learning:

A Study of Hawaiian Children at Home and at School

Stephen T. Boggs
University of Hawaii at Manoa

with the assistance of

Karen Watson-Gegeo

and

Georgia McMillen

ABLEX PUBLISHING CORPORATION
NORWOOD, NEW JERSEY

Cover illustration by Debi Hoeffner.

Printed in the United States of America.

Library of Congress Cataloging in Publication Data

Boggs, Stephen T.
    Speaking, relating, and learning.

    Bibliography: p.
    Includes index.
    1. Native language and education—Hawaii.
2. Hawaiians—Education.   3. Hawaiians—Language.
4. Educational surveys—Hawaii.   I. Title.
LC201.65.H3B64   1985   370′.9969   85–7388
ISBN 0–89391–330–8

Ablex Publishing Corporation
355 Chestnut Street
Norwood, New Jersey 07648

Contents

Acknowledgments

Many ideas gained from others over the years have contributed to the perspective of this book. First was Sir Raymond Firth's focus on studying social structure in the details of everyday life. From Gregory Bateson I have taken the idea of linking social structure to metaphoric communication. Dell Hymes' ideas about social differences in styles of communicating I have tried to apply throughout this study. Bill and Terry Labov further encouraged me in the study of social and situational differences in the fine details of speaking. Ann Peters introduced me to the work of Dan Slobin and his students, which led directly to my recording of children's spontaneous speech. A key concept, that of communicative routine, came to me from John Gumperz' seminar at Berkeley in 1972–73 by way of Karen Watson-Gegeo. Karen's pioneering study of children's narratives was also crucial in reordering my thinking about the performative aspect of narratives and other speech forms. Katherine Luomala introduced me to *ho'opāpā* (see Chapter 2). I am also grateful to my colleagues Alan Howard, Jack Bilmes, and Takie Lebra for several important insights.

I am deeply grateful to the following for the time and financial support which made the research and writing possible: Ron Gallimore and Roland Tharp, then principal investigators of the Kamehameha Early Education Project (KEEP) and the Kamehameha Schools—Bernice P. Bishop Estate which funded the former; and the Department of Anthropology, University of Hawaii at Manoa.

This book would never have been published without the efforts of several persons: Courtney Cazden; Dora Johnson, then at the Center for Applied Linguistics, Washington, D.C.; Shirley Brice Heath; Susan U. Philips; and Cynthia Wallat. I am deeply grateful to them.

Kathy H.P. Au shared many insights about the reading program at KEEP as it developed. Georgia McMillen contributed important ideas to the analysis of the reading lesson in Chapter 10. I am indebted also to Courtney Cazden for critical comments which have affected the content of that chapter.

My indebtedness to those who have taught me so much about the richness of the Hawaiian culture is very great: Mary Lee of Ho'olehua, Moloka'i; Mary Lorenzo of Hana, Maui and O'ahu; Elizabeth Auwae, Violet Lui, and Barbara

Ah Nee of O'ahu. Also the mothers, who helped provide so much information. And to the children. I could not have had more friendly and enthusiastic teachers.

Freda Hellinger typed the examples that appear herein, and also the entire manuscript—twice. I am grateful for her patience and skill.

Finally, I express my warmest aloha to Karen Watson-Gegeo, Ann Peters, and my wife, Joanne Whitehorn Boggs, for their support and encouragement throughout the enterprise.

Acknowledgment is gratefully made to the following authors and/or publishers for permission to quote from the publications cited:

University of Hawaii Press, Honolulu, for Martha Warren Beckwith, *Hawaiian Mythology,* 1970.

Stephen T. Boggs, The meaning of questions and narratives to Hawaiian children, in Courtney B. Cazden, Vera P. John, and Dell Hymes, Editors, *Functions of Language in the Classroom* (1984 reprint edition, Prospect Heights, Illinois: Waveland Press, © 1972 by Teachers College, Columbia University), pp. 301, 304.

East-West Center Publications Office, Honolulu, for K.A. Watson-Gegeo and S.L. Seaton, *Adaptation and Symbolism: Essays on Social Organization,* 1978.

Cambridge University Press, New York, NY, for S.T. Boggs and K. Watson-Gegeo, Interweaving routines: strategies for encompassing a social situation, *Language in Society,* vol. 7, 1978; and S.T. Boggs, The development of verbal disputing in part-Hawaiian children, *ibid.*

A. D. Edwards and V. J. Furlong, *The Language of Teaching: Meaning in Classroom Interaction,* William Heineman, Ltd., London, England, 1978.

George Allen and Unwin, Ltd., Hemel Hempstead, England, for Raymond Firth, *We, The Tikopia,* 1957.

Charles E. Tuttle Co., Inc., Tokyo, Japan, for E.S.C. Handy and M.K. Pukui, *The Polynesian Family System in Ka'u, Hawaii,* 1972.

Alan Howard, *Ain't No Big Thing: Coping Strategies in a Hawaiian-American Community,* University of Hawaii Press, Honolulu, 1974.

Leialoha Apo Perkins, The Aesthetics of Stress in Ōlelo and Oli: Notes toward a Theory of Hawaiian Oral Arts, doctoral dissertation, University of Pennsylvania, 1978.

Karen Watson-Gegeo and S.T. Boggs, From verbal play to talk story: the role of routines in speech events among Hawaiian children, in S. Ervin-Tripp and C. Mitchell-Kernan, *Child Discourse,* Academic Press, New York, 1977.

Ronald Gallimore, Joan W. Boggs, and Cathie Jordan, *Culture, Behavior and Education: A Study of Hawaiian-Americans,* Sage Publications, Beverly Hills, CA, 1974.

This book is affectionately dedicated
to the children—and the children yet to come.

Transcription Key

The following symbols are used whenever the transcript departs from Standard English:

ɜ	constricted high mid-vowel, unrounded
ɛ	as in *bet*
ae	as in *bat*
ə	as in *but* (also written as unstressed final a in words like *mother*)
ʌ	halfway between *pup* and *pop*
ɔ	as in *bought*
ah or ɑ	as in *father*
ö	as in German
ɪ	as in *bit*
ʳ	superscript indicates sound is partially realized or faint
dd	alveolar trill
#	words run together and prolonged
. . .	inaudible or uninterpretable
[	spoken simultaneously with other sounds so marked
'	sound is omitted (this symbol is not used in *mother* because *r* is never used)

CHAPTER 1

Introduction

This book is a case study addressed to the hypothesis that success or failure in school is due in large part to the congruence of or incongruence between ways of speaking learned at home and those required at school. This "match-mismatch" hypothesis is based upon the observation that communicative values and behavior differ in various cultures. Congruence results in children being prepared to interact as the teacher expects them to, with the result that they spend their time productively in learning. A mismatch in ways of speaking, on the other hand, can have grave consequences. As described in this book, for instance, it results in children failing to participate and instead struggling with the teacher for control of the class. One reason for this is that children appear to interpret ordinary recitation as a form of interrogation, portending possible punishment, based upon their past experience, and not as an invitation to dialogue with an adult, as it is in middle-class American culture. Accordingly, they generally refuse to participate in it, rebelling in various ways. Other mismatches occur in responses to teacher's directives, scolding, and other familiar classroom routines. The cumulative consequences include failure to learn to read and eventual alienation from school.

Other investigators have noted mismatches of a similar kind. Gallimore, Boggs, and Jordan, for instance, have described the way in which these children learn to obtain assistance from parents by watching for cues of the adult's receptivity to an approach, while remaining unobtrusive (1974: 223–225). When they enter school, therefore, they tend to use unobtrusive, nonverbal means of obtaining assistance, which are often not recognized by the teacher. Children who use such means more often are not attended to as frequently and regarded, moreover, as less intelligent by their teachers (Gallimore et al. 1974, citing Green 1970: 9, 17–18).

One of the earliest studies to call attention to extensive mismatches between patterns of interacting and communicating at home and school was that of Philips, who describes the way in which Indian children on the Warm Springs Reservation in Oregon learn by observation and testing out their skills in private, followed by supervised practice. In school, they rarely volunteer to answer during recitation because it seems to them foolhardy to speak without having practiced what is being talked about, or having had a prior model at least. Their behavior profoundly affects others' perception of their communicative competence. But when a small group directs their own work, the children talk and work very effectively, because this is a pattern learned at home and in the community (Philips 1972; see also Cazden, John, and Hymes 1972).[1]

There are circumstances, moreover, in which ways of interacting developed in school interfere with important values at home. Sutter, for instance, has vividly described the way in which rural Western Samoan children are socialized as a group to respond to orders given by adults. They are not addressed individually. In school, on the other hand, the child "interacts on a one-to-one basis with an adult who recognizes and instructs him as an individual." As a result, shortly after entering school for the first time, children start behaving more individually at home: calling attention to themselves and not sharing, for example. Family members, in turn, strongly rebuff such behavior. The further consequence of this and other mismatches, Sutter demonstrates, is increased stress revealed in problem behavior, cognitive test results, and catecholamine levels (1980: 148–149). It is noteworthy that the mismatch in this case occurs even though the teachers are themselves Samoan. Apparently, Western based education produces a strong individualizing tendency in Polynesians, as the research of Graves and Graves has demonstrated (1978).

Evidence is accumulating that recitation in schools is based upon patterns specific to Anglo-American middle-class culture which are not found in many other cultures. Recitation has been succinctly described as follows:

> The teacher speaks before and after each pupil contribution. By getting the floor back every other turn, he is able to continue his allocation of turns at speaking. . . . The teacher's comment on each intermediate response indicates that a better answer is still to be attained, either by implicitly repeating the original question or by partly accepting or elaborating what the pupil has said in ways which provide some clue to what that better answer might be. (Edwards and Furlong 1978: 17)

The authors report that this model is overwhelmingly prevalent in English classrooms. Essentially similar descriptions of such "three part sequences" have been presented by Sinclair and Coulthard in England (1975) and Mehan in the U.S. (1979). More recently, the work of Heath has shown that middle-class children in the U.S. are prepared in quite specific ways at home to participate in recitation, while both Black and White working-class children are not (1980, 1982, 1983). Neither are the children described in this book, nor the Athabascan Indian children described by Scollon and Scollon (1979a, 1979b, 1980). Here is a mismatch of great significance. Given the central role of recitation in all kinds of instruction, inability or unwillingness to participate in it probably contributes to failure in learning to read. So does the "decontextualization" of information (Scollon and Scollon 1980), as discussed at the conclusion of this chapter.[2]

Ways of speaking

Ways of speaking are viewed in this study as specific communicative routines and simultaneously as general modes. A communicative routine is a series of exchange sequences in which an utterance by one speaker accompanied by appropriate nonverbal behavior calls forth one of a limited set of responses by one or more others (Hymes 1962, 1971; Sacks, Schegloff, and Jefferson 1974; Berko-Gleason and Weintraub 1976). Each routine follows a sequencing rule in which an utterance of one type must be followed by another of given type(s). Thus Black sounding, for example, follows a rule in which insult must be followed by counter-insult (Labov, Cohen, Robins, and Lewis 1968). Any other type of reply, such as a denial, would not be regarded as sounding. It is important to note that most routines do not consist of memorized units of formulaic speech. Routines vary, from those with nearly fixed content and/or sentence structure, to those with a structure consisting only of a predictable series of speech acts whose content and form may be quite varied (Boggs and Peters 1980). While routines tend to be formulaic when first learned, they evolve with use in order to enable speakers to shift roles, elaborate the internal structure of the routine, and develop greater linguistic competence (see Bruner 1978; Cazden 1979; and Iwamura 1980). Anyone learning a second language has experienced this gradual shift from memorized formulaic speech to variable content and structure (cf. Fillmore 1976). Routines also vary in order to accomplish a variety of interactional goals in specific situations and relationships. Directives, for example, vary in content, type, and specific sequence according to the relative statuses of speaker and addresses (Mitchell-Kernan and Kernan 1977). Similarly, people can dispute about anything, yet disputes have a structure consisting of a predictable series of speech acts (see Boggs 1978b and Brenneis and Lein 1977).

Routines are associated with particular "participant structures" (Philips 1972). Thus, they influence not only what is said to what purpose, but also attitudes about who can say what to whom. Because of associations with specific participant structures communicative routines help to frame, or establish, the relational context for a communication. They also enact, and help to regulate, the relationships of which they are a part (Bilmes and Boggs 1979).

In order to interpret the meaning of a routine used in a particular instance, therefore, one needs to know not only the manifest content, as understood by the speakers, but also other routines that could be used. This is necessary because the meaning involved in the use of the routine is derived in part from its relationship to other routines. It is here that Hymes' concept of the "speech economy" is crucial, for it directs attention precisely to the distribution of particular codes and modes of speech in the various relationships found within a speech community (1974). By knowing this, one is able to understand the use of one routine rather than another in a particular instance.

Modes of speaking, on the other hand, are general features of routines. In this study, the most pertinent modes of speaking are hierarchical and egalitarian. The principles involved in these modes of speaking may be reflected in various languages by lexicon, grammar, style, etc. For instance, some languages have a high, marked rhetoric which contrasts with low rhetoric (again see Hymes 1974 for a discussion of this). By ''hierarchical'' in this study is meant control over the exchange such that the superior has the sole right to initiate, escalate, terminate, and evaluate utterances, whereas the subordinate has the sole obligation to respond or not respond as the case may be. Egalitarian routines are those in which participants share these rights and obligations to a more equal degree. For instance, the punishment routine described in Chapter 5 is a maximally hierarchical routine. Directives are somewhat less hierarchical, allowing a child, for example, to reply with assent, although not to argue. Recitation, as described above, is well on the hierarchical side. Teachers, for instance, have the sole right to evaluate. By contrast, various forms of verbal play, disputing, and narratives, as performed by the children described here, are egalitarian. In an egalitarian mode of speaking, no one owns the interaction, so to speak (Edwards and Furlong 1978: 14, citing Sacks). A striking example of egalitarian speech in story-telling is provided by the Scollons: ''In storytellings, the audience responds at the end of each verse as an indication that the story is being followed. In storytellings that people regard as good, the response of the audience is fuller. The storyteller provides the background information and the audience completes the verse with the verb or even the full fore-grounded clause. In short, the 'listener' tells the story'' (1980: 27).

The argument advanced here is that part-Hawaiian children are prepared by interactional experience with adults and siblings to engage in routines that are clearly hierarchical or relatively egalitarian, and that this experience affects their response to routines in school that appear to them as hierarchical or egalitarian. For example, it is argued in Chapter 9 that the sequencing of directives and scolding by some teachers is perceived by the children as a shift from hierarchical speech to an egalitarian invitation to a discussion. Such a shift would never happen at home. When it happens in school, however, the children eagerly accept the invitation, with the result that intended scoldings have little or no effect. Recitation, on the other hand, is responded to as if it were a maximally hierarchical routine, and accordingly it is resisted by the introduction of egalitarian routines such as verbal play and disputing. The general point is that interpretations such as these are not based upon the children's ability to engage in specific routines, but upon the meaning which modes of speaking have acquired in their speech economy through socialization, added to a specific desire to avoid hierarchical routines and engage in egalitarian ones.

A typology of all of the verbal routines described in the book is presented in Appendix 2, together with a list of illustrations. The modes of speaking are operationally defined in Chapter 7, and discussed further in connection with Appendix Table 2.

Part-Hawaiian children and the KEEP results

Unlike the studies cited above in which mismatch between home and school appears as a cause of academic failure, there is evidence in the case presented here that congruence between ways of speaking at home and school contributes to academic success in a population which has long been at educational risk. The background for this statement is presented in this section.

People born and reared in the 50th state who have some Polynesian ancestry typically consider themselves to be Hawaiian in a sense that distinguishes them from other residents of the State. Comprising from one-sixth to one-fifth of the State's population, these "part-Hawaiians" frequently have incomes below the State average (Alu Like 1976). It is from the population of low income part-Hawaiians that all of the data in this study were obtained, and to which all generalizations are intended to apply. This needs to be emphasized because of the danger of stereotyping all part-Hawaiians, many of whom have achieved higher than average incomes and middle-class status. By focusing upon those part-Hawaiians who have low incomes and ignoring the others, this book, unfortunately, will be seen as adding to the stereotype of all part-Hawaiians as poor, even though that is not intended.

Part-Hawaiians, like others whose ancestors came from other places, retain some traditional cultural patterns which make them differ to some degree. Chapter 2 attempts to describe certain traditional attitudes and relationships that constitute a coherent cultural system among low income part-Hawaiians today. This does not mean, however, that some of the attitudes and patterns of behavior described here and elsewhere in the book are not shared with people whose ancestors came from other places. Indeed, sharing is quite likely, given the widespread intermarriage and adoption of cultural features from others by all ethnic groups in Hawaii. The uniqueness of the part-Hawaiian culture described in this book cannot, therefore, be confirmed. Only comparable information about other local people, which is not available, would allow such a conclusion to be reached.

The information contained in the book was obtained in three communities. One, Aina Pumehana (a pseudonym), is a community containing a Hawaiian Homestead which is located approximately 30 miles outside of Honolulu proper, on the most populated island of O'ahu. Homesteads provide lifetime leases to persons who can prove 50 percent or more Native Hawaiian ancestry. This creates a community in which the great majority claim Hawaiian identity (Gallimore and Howard 1968: 145). It is important to note that Homesteads are not comparable to Indian reservations on the U.S. mainland (except in special cases), because the former are not marked or separated from the larger community of which they are a part in any legal or visible way. Aina Pumehana has a predominantly working-class population, the modal occupational category of both men and women being semi-skilled. Formerly a rural area, the community has grown rapidly since the '60s due to the presence of the Homestead and the availability of relatively low-cost land and housing nearby. The community has a suburban appearance, with many trees and flowering plants along with shaded outdoor areas where much time is spent visiting. Interaction in the community is conspicuously friendly. (For further description, see Gallimore et al. 1974 and Howard 1974.)

In marked contrast, Kalihi, the second community, is a partly industrial area located within Honolulu, adjacent to the old port. Demographically, it is comparable to Aina Pumehana, but the housing is a mixture of multi-family high- and low-rise apartments and single-family houses, and the percentage of Hawaiians is much less. Crowding, traffic, and noise are greater than in Aina Pumehana, and public interaction is noticeably less friendly and frequent. The children who were studied in this community were all from families who were receiving Aid to Families with Dependent Children (AFDC) and many were attending the special demonstration school described below, which was located in the community.

An additional source of information was a group of children studied by Watson-Gegeo in another Hawaiian community (Watson 1972, 1975). This community was comparable to Aina Pumehana in all of the features mentioned, but located in a different part of O'ahu.

The major purpose of the research reported herein was to discover ways to make use of the culture of part-Hawaiian children in the classroom, particularly in order to develop reading skills. The need for such research is great, for there is a very great gap between the desires of parents for their children's education and the results (Alu Like 1976). The dismal facts about the educational problem have long been known (Gallimore and Tharp 1971; Gallimore et al. 1974). Students from low-income, part-Hawaiian communities read at levels well below state and national averages. For instance, in the statewide testing carried out with fourth graders in 1979 and sixth graders in 1980, the schools in Hana, Maui, and Nanakuli, O'ahu, were among those with the lowest Stanford Achievement Test reading scores (SB 11/29/79: F-1; 12/3/80: B-4). They are also among the schools with the highest proportion of part-Hawaiian students from low-income families. Evidence that a problem exists is to be found also in the widespread alienation of part-Hawaiian youth and their parents from the public education that they are receiving. The alienation stems from basic differences between Hawaiian culture and that of the public school classroom, as Hawaiians perceive it (Alu Like 1976). Their perception is supported by the conclusions reached in Chapter 9 of this book.

A teaching method has been developed over the past several years that shows great promise of improving the reading performance of part-Hawaiian children in the first through third grades to levels at or near the national average. As reported by Au and Jordan (1977) and Tharp (1980), these results have been obtained in a research and demonstration school known as KEEP (Kamehameha Early Education Program), which is operated by the Kamehameha Schools and funded by the Bishop Estate—a large trust set up to serve children of Native Hawaiian ancestry.[3] First attempts to transfer the method to public schools have been encouraging.

The principal features of this method, it is argued here, are congruent with a type of speech event referred to in Hawaii as "talk-story." People talk-story using Pidgin, which is referred to as Hawaiian Creole English by linguists (Reinecke 1969, Bickerton and Odo 1976). Both Pidgin itself and talk-story express strongly held egalitarian values, and serve as means for promoting solidarity. As suggested by Doo (1978), talk-story involves a search for, and recognition of, shared feeling. Our observations indicate that this is done by means of a variety of verbal routines, which include recalled events, either personal or folktales, verbal play, joking, and conversing. Any of these verbal routines is very likely to lead to the appearance of others, the resulting speech event constituting talk-story. The term has also been used, however, in a more restricted sense to refer to "a rambling personal experience narrative mixed with folk materials . . . which contrasts with folk-tales of European genre, and [with] sexual teasing" (Watson 1975). These two usages are compatible if viewed as referring to two levels: one a speech event and the other a component routine—story-telling.

Researchers at KEEP were the first to point out resemblances between the reading lessons that had been so successful and features of talking story as described by Watson-Gegeo (Watson 1975; Au and Jordan 1977). Resemblances were seen in the receptive role played by an adult in children's talk-story sessions (Watson-Gegeo and Boggs 1977), the mutual participation characterizing peer teaching/learning interactions (Jordan 1977), and the phenomenon of conarration (Watson-Gegeo and Boggs op. cit.). Further research by Au led her to the conclusion that the major similarity lay in the joint performance typical of the KEEP reading lesson and talk-story sessions outside of school (Watson op. cit., Watson-Gegeo and Boggs op. cit., Au 1980a). Research reported in this book supports this conclusion and expands upon it.

As pointed out by Watson, the stories which appear in talk-story sessions by young children are joint performances, which contrast with story-telling in the Euro-American tradition. Thus, in the latter the roles of story-teller and audience are distinct: it is regarded as impolite for a member of the audience to interrupt frequently or attempt to conarrate a story. In children's story-telling sessions, on the other hand, one or more speakers, aided and occasionally contradicted by members of the audience, jointly developed a story line over a series of exchanges. This structure is described and illustrated in Chapter 7. The KEEP reading lesson is also very much a joint performance, but one in which both teacher and students jointly develop and recapitulate the story in a book and individual stories related to it. As described and analyzed in Chapter 10, this evidence supplements that already provided by Au (1980a). The similarity in participation structure of talk-story and the reading lesson, it is argued, provides a major bridge between the two, enabling the children to participate. But more than that, the contrast between the hierarchical mode of speaking that characterizes recitation and the egalitarian mode of talk-story serves to motivate the children to participate vigorously as well as enabling them to do so. This means that children who are not prepared to engage comfortably in recitation do not have to be trained to recite in order learn how to read. Such a conclusion has potential significance beyond the present case study.

A developmental perspective

Another major theme in the book is that communicative routines develop along with the relationships in which they occur. This is important with regard to school in two ways: first, because these children do not enter school with much experience telling stories and, second, because they are not prepared to accept one another as equals. The latter is important, because it tends to interfere with cooperation among peers in the classroom, and indeed contributes to disorganization of classroom activity as described in Chapter 9. While part-Hawaiian children cooperate with one another in carrying out tasks at home (Gallimore et al. 1974), they do so in an age structured hierarchy (see Chapter 3). Whenever same-aged children interact, however, disputing is endemic. It appears to grow out of a hypersensitivity to assertiveness, as a response to experience in the sibling hierarchy. The normal course of development, as described in Chapters 3 and 4, leads to strict respect for equality among age peers by the time adolescence is reached. Children entering school, however, are at the beginning of this development. The KEEP classroom is organized in such a way as to provide opportunity for children the same age to cooperate among themselves as they do with younger and older siblings at home (Jordan 1977, Jordan and Tharp 1979). Such experiences may help these children to work through peer conflict and learn to accept one another as equals sooner than might otherwise occur. In any event, it is important to know how peer relationships normally develop, since the organization of the classroom may either promote cooperation or exacerbate conflict, thus creating disciplinary problems for the teacher.

Like all children, the children studied here are still in the process of developing the reportative function when they enter school. But unlike the children of teachers, as described by Heath (1980, 1982), these children are not experienced in answering detailed questions about the "there and then" (Sachs 1977; also

Stoel-Gammon and Cabral 1977, and Michaels and Cook-Gumperz 1979). Rather, they appear to develop skills which become part of talking story by learning to relate with a rich variety of verbal routines that include various forms of deliberate distortion, such as punning, alliteration, rhyming, and cospeaking, along with sexual teasing, jingles, and obscenities. Under appropriate conditions, a group of children can use these routines to construct narrative performances that resemble those of adolescents and adults talking story (Watson-Gegeo and Boggs 1977). The role of the adult turns out to be crucial in producing stories in a group of children, as analyzed in Chapter 7.

Together, these facts suggest that story-telling is a skill in the "zone of proximal development" at the time these children enter school (Vygotsky 1978, cited and discussed in Cazden 1979, McNamee 1979). The zone of proximal development consists of those mental processes which a child is not capable of alone, but can accomplish with help. Since narrative performances can be accomplished at a younger age than that at which they usually occur, the necessary skills would appear to fall within this concept. If so, another reason for the success of the KEEP reading lesson may be that it provides an opportunity for children to do something that they are not yet able to do collectively on their own. More important, therefore, than the congruence of verbal routines in and out of school may be the fact that story-telling is still evolving and providing challenges to the child (Cazden op. cit.).

A final point about development: the present study offers evidence that literacy skills develop in a social context. The Scollons have argued that children in middle-class American culture are prepared for Western-style literacy by learning how to "decontextualize," that is, to divorce abstract elements from an immediate context (1979a, 1979b). Heath has described how questions are used to stimulate children to provide decontextualized information in the homes of teachers and at school (1982). As mentioned earlier, the children studied here have not experienced this kind of interrogation at home, and their failure to participate in it is described in Chapter 9. The KEEP reading program, on the other hand, provides a meaningful social context for reading, and this is a major reason for its success, as argued in Chapter 10. Thus it is possible to teach reading without developing the decontextualizing skills typical of middle-class culture. Such a conclusion has important implications for those who insist that instruction in phonics must precede emphasis upon comprehension in the teaching of reading (Chall 1979). Indeed, it may be that the use of questions to extract decontextualized information from children in middle-class homes, as part of conversation, and further reference to information obtained from books, as described by Heath, provides for middle-class children a social context for reading similar to that provided by the KEEP lessons. Such an explanation would help to account for the success of phonics based teaching among middle-class children, along with their participation in recitation, as well as the failure of both among children from many minority cultures.

Fieldwork and methods of collecting data

The information contained in this book was obtained over the period 1966 through 1977 in the three communities identified above. The children studied ranged from about 3 to 12 years of age, although occasional observations were made of older and younger ones. Their approximate number and the hours of speech recorded are given in Appendix Table 1. Two principal methods were used in obtaining information: participant observation and recording of spontaneous speech. While details of these methods are presented in the chapters to which they are relevant, some general considerations are discussed here.

Many months were spent by the author in the company of children in two of the three communities, mostly in school or community playgrounds, occasionally in homes, at public events, and on brief camping trips with boys. This extensive interaction helped to develop a recognition of specific patterns of communicating and ways of relating, which led to noticing similarities among different groups of children in the two communities. The contradicting routine described in Chapter 6, for example, was discovered when children used it jokingly with me, after I had observed it many times used among themselves for serious disputes. The children also forced me to pay attention to their rich variety of verbal play, although not until Watson-Gegeo had discovered that it had a role in her story-telling sessions with groups of children, a development outlined in Chapter 7.

Recording of speech on sound tape and other behavior on video in the case of KEEP was essential for description and analysis of verbal routines and their use in interaction. Conceptually, this was the turning point in the research.[4] Such recordings also have the great advantage of being available to others, so that they can make their own interpretations, as has occurred in the case of the reading lesson analyzed in detail in Chapter 10 (see McMillen, Boggs, and Au 1979; Au 1980a). Moreover, since the recordings were made during naturally occurring events, these data are not subject to the chain of assumptions involved in extrapolating from experimental findings (Cole and Scribner 1974).

Recordings were made with the children's awareness and consent in the case of those over 5 years of age in all but a few instances. Recordings at KEEP were done without the children's awareness that a specific recording was being made. This was part of a continual research monitoring at the school, which is explained and demonstrated to both parents and the children, and carried out with the parents' permission. In the case of children 5 years and younger, mothers recorded the speech of their own children at home. In this way, any influence which an outside observer would have was removed. In these cases, the children never referred to the recorder, except in one instance which was not pursued by others present. The mothers left the recorder running during a wide range of their own interactions with the children, including occasions when they punished the children, and they did not erase such portions, even though they had been invited to do so.[5]

The study has empirical weaknesses which should be acknowledged. The same children were not studied before and after entering school, which would have been a preferable procedure (see Mehan 1979: 202). Data from the three communities have been combined in the analysis as if they had all come from a single group, which may not be justified. Finally, recorded data on preschool children are limited to three families in only one of the communities, although similar interaction was observed in other families in two of the three communities. These limitations warrant caution in accepting the conclusions and generalizing them to all part-Hawaiian children from low-income families.

Epilogue: cui bono?

Any social scientist must ask today whether the results of any research will return as much directly to the people involved as that research contributes to the advancement of knowledge and the rewards that accrue to the researcher as a consequence. This issue is very much in the minds of many Hawaiians, because they have lost so much at the hands of outsiders who have profited by it. Today they no longer welcome research that does not promise important tangible returns. My own purpose for undertaking this research in 1966 was to return something of practical value to the education of part-Hawaiian youth—particularly to the young children who were my first and principal informants and friends. Since they are no longer children, I can, sadly, contribute nothing to their education. My hope, therefore, is that this book will contribute something to their children's education. So let them judge it.

CHAPTER 2

The 'Ohana Past and Present

This chapter examines the principles of relationships that characterized the Hawaiian family in the past, and the role of speech events and oral arts in these relationships. This is necessary in order to learn what may be typically Hawaiian about the culture of part-Hawaiian people today, and also to determine whether the modes of speaking that are hypothesized in the book have a role today as they had in the past.

The analysis to follow indicates that two principles of cardinal importance distinguished family relationships in the past. These principles—hierarchy and equality—are traced to relationships between the Hawaiian *maka'āinana* (commoners) and *ali'i* (chiefs). Absolute obedience to those of high status was required for survival in the past. Offsetting and complementing this was a strong emphasis upon equality among commoners. Above all the sentiment of *aloha,* which has a strong element of equality, provided the basis for the security felt by commoners, as well as the ideal for relationships among everyone.

Certain traditional oral arts described herein served to promote feelings of solidarity and aloha in the past, while others were the primary means of contesting for supremacy. These facts provide a background for subsequent chapters, where we find distinctly different routines in relationships of hierarchy and equality among parents and children. According to the evidence examined in this chapter, both the principles of relationships and the modes of speaking that express them have a basis in the traditional culture of Hawaii.

In the final section the similarities and differences from the past are examined in order to determine what may be Hawaiian in today's part-Hawaiian culture.

The traditional 'ohana

The only sources that we have on the traditional family, or *'ohana,* are the oral traditions of Hawaiians who were raised in rural areas around the turn of the present century. As collected and interpreted by Mary Kawena Pukui, the most comprehensive account of these traditions appears in *The Polynesian Family System in Ka'u, Hawaii* (Handy and Pukui 1953, here cited as 1972). It is this work that provides the principal information for this section, in which we hope to analyze the principles of social relationships that characterized the *'ohana* in earlier times. Until recently, one could not safely assume that the description drawn by Pukui applied outside the Ka'u district of the island of Hawaii, where the information was obtained. Studies of contemporary families carried out in the past decade indicate, however, that the basic principles described by Pukui survive in families which originated on each of the islands. Hence, these principles must have been general. These studies are reviewed in the final section of this chapter.

We find it useful to organize this account of the traditional family according to the perspective provided by Homans' concepts of the *external and internal systems*. The external system, according to Homans, is that behavior of a group which allows it to survive in its environment. It includes "sentiments, activities, and interactions" and their interrelations (1950: 90). The internal system is, approximately, the "expression of the sentiments towards one another developed by the members of the group in the course of their life together" (p. 110). Like him, we recognize that these systems are concretely a single system, one action or feature usually serving both to adapt to external forces and to meet internal needs. Thus, any principles inferred on the basis of described sentiments and practices must make sense both in terms of adapting the *'ohana* to its total environment, and its members to one another, within this context. This point is particularly important in the discussion of authority below. These concepts are useful, furthermore, in analyzing the culture of the *maka'āinana,* because these folk can be seen as adapting to both a physical and societal environment—the latter comprised of the ruling chiefly class.

Physically, the *'ohana* was a network comprising all of those persons who recognized one another as "relatives by blood, marriage, and adoption" (Handy and Pukui 1972: 2). Linking relatives could be of either sex. Thus, persons who had any relative in common, whether ancestor, collateral, or descendant, were potentially part of the same *'ohana* (op. cit.: 69–70). In practice, however, the *'ohana* was limited to those who lived in the same locality. According to Pukui, it was "concentrated geographically in and tied by ancestry, birth and sentiment to a particular locality which was termed the *'āina*" (op. cit.: 2; but see Pukui, Haertig, and Lee 1972: 170).

The tie that bound members of the *'ohana* to one another was the sentiment of *aloha*.[6] It is difficult to stress sufficiently the cardinal importance of this sentiment in Hawaiian social organization. A conference of 53 Hawaiian elders held in May 1980, and conducted entirely in Hawaiian, concluded that the first value taught to them by their *kūpuna* (elders) was "love one another" (Conference 1980). Aloha was the basis of the security felt by traditional Hawaiians. Security could not be based upon tenure of land, because this could be taken away by the *ali'i moku,* or ruling chief (Goldman 1970; Handy, Handy, and Pukui 1972). Only personal ties guaranteed one support, a welcome, and a sense of personal identity (see Perkins 1978: 205). Perhaps a consequence of this, aloha was a master symbol (Firth 1973). In addition to affection, fondness, and commitment, this word in Hawaiian connoted hospitality (*ho'okipa*), meeting other's needs, mutual sharing (*ha'awi*), cooperation in work (*laulima*), feasting, and incorporation into the *'ohana* (traditional adoption of adults as well as infants and children).

Each of these meanings reflects the adaptation of the *'ohana* to its environment, thus demonstrating the adaptive significance of aloha. Sharing, for instance, was based upon ecological factors. Because the principal protein and carbohydrate foods were obtained at the shore and in the uplands, respectively, exchange was a necessity for basic subsistence. The Hawaiians arranged this exchange by means of the concept of *'ohana,* which included those who dwelt inland and near the sea (Handy and Pukui 1972: 2). Even inland areas had ecological variations, however. Thus informants from different types of areas all report sharing within the *'ohana* (Boggs 1977). Thus, from a practical, functional perspective, the *'ohana* was the basic unit of production and distribution.

The *'ohana* was also the source of labor for any task demanding a large amount of labor. Hence the practice of *laulima.* Since the *'ohana* was also the labor pool upon which everyone depended, commoners and chiefs alike, it was to everyone's advantage, so long as resources were available, to encourage newcomers to join it. That apparently was what was done:

> The people of Ka'u married mostly within their own district and discouraged marriages to those of the outside district or islands. If there was a marriage with one outside of the district, that person was encouraged to remain as one of them. (Handy and Pukui 1972: 110)

The principle of incorporation is reflected also in the reckoning of kinship bilaterally, recognizing ties through marriage as well as birth, the cementing of ties through the birth of children and many different forms of adopting adults as well as children (op. cit.: 73–74, Pukui et al. 1972: 167).

Hospitality is virtually synonymous with aloha, and often served as the initial step in incorporation. Thus:

> A total stranger may come and be welcomed in somebody's house. . . . A bond of aloha has been accepted, and by acceptance becomes enduring if cherished. *Ho'omakamaka* means to make friends by extending hospitality (Ibid.: 73–74)

Since first contact Hawaiians have been renowned for their hospitality (ibid.: 170). Greetings (ibid.: 172–173), food, and lodging (ibid.: 186–187) were offered freely to all comers at any time of the day or night, no matter how little there was to share. To deny hospitality was a cause for scandal (ibid.: 187, 191). While such unrestrained hospitality was not offered for any purpose other than aloha, it often created such deep aloha in return that incorporation resulted.

So far, all of this is intended to apply only to the Hawaiian commoners—the *maka'āinana*. Their way of life concerns us almost exclusively in this book, because their descendants make up by far the largest proportion of the part-Hawaiian population today. Consideration must be given to the entire social structure of ancient Hawaii, however, because it affected the culture of the *maka'āinana* profoundly, we believe. Put simply, the *ali'i* can be regarded as part of the environment to which the *'ohana* of the commoners was adapted. What was this structure, and how did the *'ohana* adapt to it?

Excellent descriptions are available of Hawaiian social structure immediately before contact, and of the relations between *ali'i* and *maka'āinana* in the works of Malo (1951), Kepelino (Beckwith 1932), Kamakau (1961, 1964), I'i (1951), Fornander (1969), and Beckwith (1970), among others. Perhaps the best analysis of these materials has been provided by Goldman (1970). Drawing upon the latter, one can state briefly that Hawaiians in theory owed everything to the chiefs—their loyalty, service, obedience, and even life itself—in return for prosperity, protection in war, and tenure of the land on which the *'ohana* lived. From an objective, materialistic point of view, the chiefs were much more dependent upon the commoners than vice-versa. But the cosmology enshrined in chiefly genealogies, together with the doctrine of *mana* reversed this, so that commoners in ideology derived from chiefs the basis of their existence. Customary rights of access to use of land, water, and sea exerted some check upon the arbitrary exercise of chiefly power (e.g., Nakuina 1893), but still a single *'ohana* confronted the power of a ruling chief (*ali'i moku*) much as it did a force of nature. Both had immanent power of life and death over the individual to a degree that was unmatched elsewhere in Polynesia (Goldman 1970).

How did the commoners adapt to such fearsome power? This question has been given very little attention in the literature on Hawaii, so we can only speculate about it. One way to adapt to absolute and threatening power is to be absolutely and compulsively submissive. Extreme examples of this in other societies are the concentration camp inmates described by Bettelheim and the villagers of feudal Japan confronted by samurai. In these cases, disobedience, or even the slightest sign of disrespect at the wrong moment, could and did bring death. When faced with this possibility, attitudes of obedience and respect for authority, Elkins (1968) has argued, had to be built into the personality at a deep level. Does such an analysis apply to the Hawaiian commoner in precontact times? In personality, the commoner did not resemble either the inmate or the Japanese peasant. Hawaiian commoners were strong, autonomous individuals within the *'ohana* when not in the presence of the *ali'i moku*. Being far removed from the court of the latter gave them a certain protection. So, while attitudes of obedience and respect were present at all times, continual suppression of contradictory impulses was not necessary. It seems likely to me, therefore, that the subservience manifested in the presence of the latter was a situational adaptation, rather than a trait of character.

Respect for constituted authority, and intense dislike of rebellious behavior both within the family and society at large, are stressed by informants of every age today. While this emphasis today may be in part a consequence of missionary teaching during the nineteenth century, as discussed below, it could also represent an adaptation to the threat posed by the power of the *ali'i moku* in the past. Accordingly, we hypothesize that children had to be taught strict obedience before they had any contact with *ali'i* as adults, for their own protection and that of the whole family.[7]

By tying the members of the *'ohana* together in a lasting commitment, aloha provided the basis for its internal system. Demonstrations of aloha began at birth and continued throughout childhood. Handy and Pukui put it, "Perhaps the first expression of what the Hawaiians termed aloha was between mother and child" (op. cit.: 165). The feelings involved are well expressed by the term *'a'a:*

> "An ejaculation." A demonstration of joy at the sight of a person who is loved. When a child extends his arms eagerly, makes an audible sound of joy or other demonstrations at the sight of a home-coming parent, that is *'a'a.* (op. cit.: 165)

"Constancy of devotion between *'ohana* from infancy to old age" was the principal goal of life. Aloha was also shown by how well parents provided. One cannot overstress the importance and significance attached to the role of provider:

> "The main post." Said of a person on whom others depended. . . . (op. cit.: 174)

Contributing services to the family was also important. When we examine the modern household, we will see that it is a cardinal principle in its internal organization. In the past, each person, child as well as adult, had his or her own *kuleana,* or responsibility, in carrying out various household tasks.

Hierarchy was a major principle of the internal structure and organization of the traditional *'ohana.* It was manifested in several ways:

> Horizontally, the family is stratified by generations: grandparents, parents, brothers and sisters, sons and daughters, grandchildren.
>
> Precedence or status was determined by genealogical seniority, not by generation or age, or by sex: persons stemming from a genealogically elder branch outrank older generations of junior branches. (op. cit.: 43)

"The pivot of the *'ohana* was the *haku* (master, director), the elder male of the senior branch of the whole *'ohana*" (op. cit.: 6). The *haku* directed all regular, as well as extraordinary, activities involving several households; acted as ritual head; and represented the family before visiting *ali'i* (ibid.). The first-born to each couple was their *hiapo.* The male *hiapo* of the senior lineage became, ideally, the *haku* (op. cit.: 47). But the principle of genealogical seniority applied to each set of siblings and cousins as well. This was reflected in the concepts of *hānau mua,* another term for the first child; *poki'i,* younger brothers, sisters, and cousins; and *hanau muli,* the youngest of the family, or of each sex (op. cit.: 46). Highest status was accorded the oldest, but the youngest was often elevated to high status because of endearment. He or she might be "playfully called *haku* because the elders like to carry the little one around on their shoulders, which ceremonially was an honor accorded to the first-born" (ibid.). This very much resembles the playful egalitarian interaction with young children to be analyzed in Chapter 7.

The kinship terminology likewise reflected the genealogical principle of seniority. One term was applied to elder siblings of the same sex, while a different term was used for younger. This same set was used to distinguish first cousins who were children of older or younger siblings of one's parents, respectively— not those who were older or younger in age (op. cit.: 67). Attitudes and behavior were consistent with these distinctions. As stated in *Nānā I Ke Kumu,* "younger siblings obeyed elder" (Pukui et al. 1972: 170).

As in other hierarchical systems, acting as if you were of higher status than you were was resented: "trying to be the equal of one's superiors was to be *pi'ikoi* (straining to ascend) and a person who did this was regarded with scorn" (op. cit.: 190).

> To fail to heed the teachings of parents and grandparents and to be wilful and headstrong, was called *ho'oki'eki'e,* to elevate oneself above others.[8] (Ibid.)

The respect accorded those of higher status was mitigated, however, in the relationship of grandparent and grandchild, which was one of "intimate attachment" (op. cit.: 177), for, in addition to respect, the grandchild shared a reciprocity with the grandparent, returning indulgence with affection. Grandparents, moreover, had license to show favoritism for individuals, thus overriding other status relations (op. cit.: 46). This is similar to the transforming of affection for the youngest into respect, as noted above.

It is of great significance to education to consider that it was in the grandparent-grandchild relationship that intellectual growth was to be nourished. Affection, in fact, was conceived to grow out of the teaching of grandchild by grandparent (op. cit.: 177). The transmission of the most abstract knowledge, that which lacked immediate and concrete observation, was not expected to occur in relationships marked by a stricter hierarchy—those between parents and children or between older and younger children—but in one marked by indulgence and reciprocity. This point is central to our consideration of modes of speaking, and their impact upon teaching and learning, later in this book.

There was a principle of equality in Hawaiian social structure also, although much less attention is given to it. It appears in respect for individuality. This has been forcefully stated by Pukui: "From the prenatal period, throughout life and

beyond death the individual is regarded as a free, whole, independent entity"
(op. cit.: 75). Individualism was reflected in the relationship of adults within the
'ohana. For example:

> The *haku* headed the councils of the *'ohana;* he was the revered leader; but the old
> folk, men and women, of strong character were extremely independent in speech
> and action; consequently the *haku* was no dictator. . . . (Handy and Pukui 1972: 7)

Also in the conduct of *ho'oponopono,* a family council that was called when
something threatened the unity and well-being of the *'ohana,* ordinary statuses,
such as parent and child, were to be set aside during the proceedings (Apoliona
1979). As Turner has pointed out, all structured, differentiated status systems
have an antistructural phase in which community or equality overrules status
differentiation (1968). This was true in traditional Hawaii, we believe. Again,
aloha provided the master sentiment which linked the structural and antistructural
phases together. Thus, the setting aside of everyday statuses in *ho'oponopono* (to
the extent that it occurred) was done "for aloha" and the well-being of the
'ohana (which are synonymous: see Pukui et al. 1972). Likewise, punishment,
the primary metaphor of strict hierarchy and subordination, is typically followed,
according to my observations, by the mutual expression of feelings and recon-
ciliation. The tribute which the *maka'āinana* gave to the *ali'i* was given as an
expression of aloha (Handy et al. 1972: 326; Kamakau 1964: 19), while chiefs
were seen as motivated by aloha to protect and provide prosperity to their
followers. It is on the basis of such evidence that we said in the introduction to
this chapter that aloha provided the ideal for all relationships. Situationally,
behavior varied from hierarchical to egalitarian, and each way of relating had its
values, but aloha was believed to underlie all relationships, except, of course,
that between warring equals.

A digression is necessary here in order to mention briefly relations between
Hawaiians and non-Hawaiians with respect to aloha today. As noted in Chapter 9
and throughout much of this book, children of Samoan and other ethnic backgrounds participate easily in speech events in predominantly Hawaiian peer
groups. This is not due to their sharing the ideology of aloha, but rather to their
striving for equality, which is common to children everywhere. Aloha is not a
sentiment reciprocated fully by many other ethnic groups in Hawaii although
each group has sentiments which overlap with it, such as generosity, reciprocity
in gift-giving, etc. Thus, in inter-ethnic relations today, Hawaiians typically feel
that other groups do not really understand aloha. My observations and experience
support their view. As I have argued here, aloha makes full sense only in the
traditional external and internal systems of the *'ohana,* where it served as the
primary means of incorporation and commitment, as we have sketched above.

Sex differences provided the objective basis for another principle, that of
ritual sexual segregation.

The *Mua* or men's eating house was a sacred place from which women were excluded. It was the place where the men and older boys ate their meals and where the head of the family offered the daily offerings of *'awa* to the family *'aumakua*. Here men and family gods ate together, and that was why women, who were periodically unclean, were not allowed to enter here. (Handy and Pukui 1972: 9)

It was in the *mua,* starting about age 5 years, that boys traditionally learned by daily example how to practice masculine skills and to become men (op. cit.: 9). The removal of the *mua* from Hawaiian life, a consequence of the overthrow of the *kapu* system in 1819, left boys in the company of women throughout childhood. We think that this change in circumstances may have affected the formation of masculine personality during historic times. In Chapter 4 it is suggested that hazing of younger boys by older ones teaches the former not to express antagonism under genuine provocation. This is the kind of development that could be expected to come about by constant association in activities within the men's house.

Speech events and oral arts

Hawaiians in the past developed oral expression to a high art. Some forms of this art resembled the routines that are labelled "verbal play" in Chapter 7. Evidence indicates also that verbal play and narrative were interwoven in speech events that today would be referred to as "talking story" (see Chapter 1). Finally, verbal play was also an essential part of contests for supremacy.

Handy and Pukui illustrate the importance attached to the interweaving of narrative and other verbal routines with an anecdote:

Te Rangi Hiroa (Dr. Peter H. Buck) once described how, in his early days as a Public Health Officer visiting Maori communities, it often was necessary to explain to the assembled elders of a tribe the reasons for some regulation or medical measure that he had to enforce. His careful exposition of the dry facts of the situation without recourse to a chant or an anecdote or a story to flavour and enliven his discourse, would be interrupted by some friendly old fellow calling out: *Te vai! Te vai!* ("Water! Water!"). (Handy and Pukui 1972: 160)

The interweaving of chant, anecdote, or a story to "enliven . . . discourse" also appeared at feasts:

While the merry-makers were eating there was much banter, joking, relating of anecdotes, matching wits. . . . The feasting and jollification roused some to rise here and there to dance a *hula,* as someone chanted a *mele* (op. cit.: 115)

There were particular named skills involved in this "banter" which resemble the routines involved in verbal play today. Thus:

A person skilled in humorous expressions and witty remarks (*'ōlelo ho'oka'au*), in the use of figurative speech and in making similies (*'ōlelo ho'opilipili*), was always well liked. How I remember listening to the Hawaiians of my childhood! Skilled were they in using the *'ōlelo ho'opilipili* to make their conversation or their sermon interesting and comprehensive. Such choice of words! Poetic and beautiful and never offensive—even when directed at a person's faults. . . . In the olden days, a wit, who had humor and wisdom, found his way to the court of the chief. (op. cit.: 186)

Luomala has described, citing Beckwith, the high development of oral arts in the courts of the *ali'i* during the time she calls "the Golden Age." These skills were also present and appreciated among the *maka'āinana* (see also Perkins 1978). The *ali'i*, according to Luomala, were always looking for men skilled in oral arts, word play, and narratives, even among those of humble birth. It was a risky life, for it involved contests of wit and knowledge, termed *ho'opāpā*, in which property, and even life, were wagered. The term itself was used to express "the play of words back and forth in a debate," or "riddling contest" (Beckwith 1970: 455). There were clear rules for these contests.

In more homely usage the art consists in betting on a riddle to be guessed, in a brag upon which the opponent has been induced to put up a bet, or in merely playing with language in a way to entangle the opponent with contradictory and seemingly impossible meanings. Puns were delighted in as a way of matching an opponent or fulfilling a brag. Taunts . . . must be met with a jibe more bitter. (Beckwith 1970: 455)

While formal contests were common in Polynesia, according to Luomala, only Hawaiians gambled so heavily upon them. New riddles were eagerly sought and devised. The contests involved word play, alliteration, and other devices. Proverbs might be cited in exchanges, sometimes insulting. Such contests could lead to battle, which, appropriately enough, began with boasts, wisecracks, and gestures. The names of famous oral artists were remembered in genealogies and narrative chants (Luomala 1979).

Many of these routines are echoed in the speech of the children and families described in this book. Thus Watson-Gegeo, citing Perkins (1978), states:

Word play was very common in traditional Hawaiian oral arts, much of it being sound substitutions or metathesis, or shift in stress, all of which were done to suggest a different meaning (perhaps even mocking) to the hearer. Some such alterations added greatly to poetic imagery, and others touched *ka'ona* (hidden meaning of the religious or philosophical type). (personal communication, February 3, 1979)

She quotes Perkins:

. . . slight changes alter the meaning of the words yet keep the suggestions of the meanings of the former words, Hawaiian, for example, may shift its stress: *li'i li'i*, small, or *lili'i*, tiny; or *lili*, jealous; or *li'ili'i*, petty. (1978: 354)

While such changes perhaps cannot occur as easily in Hawaiian Creole English (Pidgin), similar processes appear in speech cited in Chapter 7.

Moreover, specific routines occur today in the same kind of relationships as they did in the past. Thus, verbal play and narrative occurred during feasting, which involved reciprocity and equality, and verbal dueling involved competition for status. Neither appeared in the context of a superior addressing a subordinate, that is, in an unrelieved hierarchical relationship. In subsequent chapters, evidence is presented to indicate that children link verbal play and narrative, that both express the principle of equality in opposition to that of hierarchy, and that verbal play and humor develop as a means of overcoming incessant conflicts over status. Thus, features of the traditional speech economy seem to resemble those today.

The *'ohana today*

In this final section, we review studies of the Hawaiian *'ohana* today in order to determine how similar or different it is to that of the past. We find that, despite the weakening of ties between households, which has resulted from loss of the *'āina*, individual households retain the obligatory sharing within, and incorporation of members from outside the nuclear family that were typical of the traditional *'ohana*. The expression of unrestrained aloha for infants is still very noticeable. The emphasis upon contribution of services by all, and care-taking by siblings in particular, sets up a hierarchy among children that has far-reaching consequences for the development of social relationships, as described in later chapters. The hierarchical principle also pervades relations between parents and children in matters pertaining to nurturance, punishment, and discipline. Children growing up seek to establish equalitarian relationships among peers, thus reinforcing in adults the strong value placed upon equality in the culture. These points can be discerned in recent studies of Hawaiian families. They are to be seen again in our analysis of verbal routines in subsequent chapters.[9]

Families still tend to incorporate broadly. Relatives are still recognized through links of marriage and adoption, as well as blood, through both sides of the family, as in the past (Rosco 1977; Heighton 1971: 30; Howard 1971: 63). The birth of children still cements ties between in-laws. As a consequence, a Hawaiian *'ohana* today can be quite large. Rosco reports at least 266 persons recognized as *'ohana* by her informants, who limited their identification even so to persons descended from common ancestors four generations prior. One hundred and six of the persons recognized were in ego's generation. The *'ohana* can be so large because membership is not determined by residence in a specific *'āina*. Instead, members are scattered throughout an urban society, including even the U.S. mainland. The change is due to the fact that most families have lost their land, and others no longer live on the land even if they have it. Thus, Rosco reports that her principal informants still possess the family *'āina,* but that only one member resides on it. This appears in Heighton's data also. He reports that, although some informants traced their genealogy for the sake of establishing claims to a share in family land, and many still associate their families with a specific *'āina* (1971: 30, 31), only one member stayed on and used the land (op. cit.: 52).

The typical household in Aina Pumehana, one of the communities studied, is large and contains persons who are not members of a single nuclear family. The average size was 6.5 (Gallimore et al. 1974: 51). Women over 30 years of age had borne an average of 6.3 children (ibid.: 104). Nonnuclear households outnumbered nuclear ones by a slight margin (Howard 1974: 20). In a sample of families of pre-school children, nearly half had adults other than parents caring for them regularly, in addition to parents (Gallimore et al. 1974: 128). When only households with children under 5 years old are considered, there were 9.7 persons residing in the household (Howard 1971: 36). Thus, the composition of the traditional *'ohana* is still reflected within the typical household in this community.

Aloha is still the force uniting the *'ohana.* It is valued above property by many Hawaiians:

> Hawaiian-Americans generally choose to honor commitments to friends, provide aid to a person in need, and seek to engage in situations of cooperative fellowship, even when it requires material deprivation for themselves and their families. Individuals with this value orientation tend to dissipate resources as fast as they accumulate, for resources are seen as a *means* to maintaining and expanding interpersonal networks rather than as an *end* in themselves. (Howard 1974: 25–26)

Sharing between households is also very frequent. Rosco (1977) reports it as an ideal still honored within the *'ohana.* Heighton states that it is obligatory, and carried out for the sake of expressing commitment (op. cit.: 45–48). The Alu Like survey found that 89 percent of 2,366 households throughout the State reported sharing some food with other households (1976).

Within the household, the contribution of labor or income by all is still a rule without exceptions, according to Gallimore et al. and Howard (see below). Once again, as in the principle of incorporation into the household, it appears that traditional *'ohana* values are still intact within the household, and this despite pressures for individual achievement which have reduced the strength of such values in other cultures. The practice of adoption is likewise still very evident. Thus, in Aina Pumehana 32.5 percent of all households had an average of 1.8 adopted children (*hanai, luhi,* or legally adopted) while a number of other homestead communities had percentages about as high (Howard, Heighton, Jordan and Gallimore 1970). Moreover, adults not related by blood or marriage are still found in five percent of the households there (Howard 1971: T.3), and they are often referred to as *hanai* (field notes).

In sum, compared to the traditional *'ohana* described earlier, the *'ohana* of today remains strongest within the household, which is still large, extended in many cases, often incorporating children and occasionally even adults by adoption, and bound together by obligatory sharing. The extended *'ohana* comprised of many households is no longer the major unit of production and distribution that it once was, having lost its *'āina*. As a consequence, it is scattered and no longer corporate.

Turning now to the internal structure of the *'ohana,* there is today a marked emphasis upon the demonstration of unrestrained affection for babies, just as in the past:

> At large social gatherings such as luaus, babies are often passed around among the women who take turns holding and playing with them, the older women having priority. . . . when a women was playing with a baby, any male in the vicinity was likely to be as occupied and entertained by the child as she was. (Gallimore et al. 1974: 107)*

> The pleasure of interacting with infants . . . appears to come from the smile or laugh or contentment of the infant as he responds to the cuddling, jiggling, chin-chucking, or verbalizations directed towards him. . . . babies respond tirelessly. Children have often been observed, "pumping" babies for smiles by bringing their faces very close and repeatedly and vigorously chucking the baby's cheeks, chin, and lips. (Ibid.: 108)

The similarity with *'a'a* of old is obvious. The style of verbalization which accompanies this interaction has a continuity in specific verbal routines that occur throughout childhood, adolescence, and adult life, as described in Chapter 7.

Parents are still regarded primarily as providers. No function is regarded as more important by the men of Aina Pumehana. Wives, however, also act as providers, fully 90 percent having worked at some point in their married lives, and around half are working at a given time, despite having young children (Boggs and Gallimore 1968). It is noteworthy that contributions are discussed by parents and adolescents alike in terms of *kōkua,* aloha, family feeling, the importance of all family members helping out (*laulima*), the need to work together, the virtues of helpfulness and generosity, and the feelings of affection, intimacy, and loyalty. Moreover, shifts and exchanges of tasks, and pitching in together on the same task, "enhance the family feelings of solidarity" (Gallimore et al. 1974: 84–87).

---

*Ronald Gallimore, Joan Whitehorn Boggs, and Cathie Jordan, "Socialization: Infants and the Solidarity Function of Children," pp. 103–116, in *Culture, Behavior and Education: A Study of Hawaiian-Americans.* Copyright © 1974 by Sage Publications, Inc. Reprinted by permission of Sage Publications, Inc.

Performing tasks sets up a regular and predictable role-structure within the family:

> The division of labor . . . in which boys care for the car and yard and girls are responsible for housework is typical. It is also common that younger siblings are a work crew for an older sibling who is responsible to the parents for keeping the place clean. (Ibid.: 69)

Overall, girls contribute more tasks than boys, and older children more than younger. There are no differences by birth order (ibid.: 74). These data strongly suggest that younger children take over tasks from older siblings as they mature, a key point in the analysis of the sibling hierarchy in Chapter 3.

Sibling care-taking and the sibling hierarchy are stressed by these authors. Thus, in 56 percent of the Aina Pumehana sample households at least one older child, usually a girl, supervised the tasks of younger siblings in the mother's absence (ibid.: 128), Three-fourths of the households reported one or more child-care tasks performed on a regular basis by siblings (ibid.: 127).

Older children assume a quasi-parental role in caring for younger siblings (ibid.: 78–81). Howard states, "Older siblings have authority over them and have powers to reward and punish. . . ." He believes that older children are likely to be more erratic in meting out punishment, but also more easily distracted than parents by joking and play on the part of younger ones (1974: 44). Evidence is presented in Chapter 3 of arbitrary behavior by older care-takers, but our findings do not support the view that younger ones distract older ones with joking and play. In our observations younger children learn early not to challenge their older siblings by play or otherwise.

Turning to the question of authority within the household, Howard presents some findings that give a clue to one possible source of the emphasis upon obedience mentioned earlier. When asked, "What do you think is the most important thing in raising children?" answers fell in three main categories: care and affection, training, and obedience. Those who stressed obedience as the most important thing reported a lower degree of Hawaiian ancestry, had lower scores on a test of Hawaiian language, and were more involved in Christian religion. Those stressing care and affection, by contrast, had the opposite characteristics, and they also felt more confident in their role as providers. We would agree with Howard that this suggests that the emphasis upon care and affection has a Hawaiian cultural origin (Howard 1974: 172–175), but we would add that the emphasis upon obedience may have originated in part at least in the teachings of nineteenth-century Christian missionaries (cf. Johnson 1977). All regard care and affection as important, however, and it is the combination of these values that is significant, rather than either alone. Gallimore et al. have put it well:

> Parents hope to appear both powerful and generous, so as to stimulate helpfulness, obedience, and harmony. . . . authoritarian control is most successful when it is

least in evidence—when the children are willingly and spontaneously assuming and sharing responsibilities. (1974: 93)

Nurturance can thus serve a dual purpose, reinforcing obedience and rendering occasional punishment more dramatic and impressive.

Both nurturance and punishment derive from hierarchy—the clear recognition of the paramount rights and prerogatives of the parent and the subordination of the child. The principle of hierarchy makes sense out of the ''shift,'' which many observers have written about. The ''shift'' constitutes a withdrawal of nurturance from children between the third and fourth years of life:

As children become increasingly mobile and verbal, parental indulgence begins to give way to irritation and a lack of tolerance for insistent demands. The birth of a subsequent child is generally sufficient to create a marked shift in this direction, but even though no new infant (arrives), a distinct change in parent behavior is notice-able as a child matures. (Howard 1974: 42)

Howard interprets the underlying reasons for this as follows:

attention-seeking behavior is apt to be seen as an attempt to intrude and control. It is therefore an assault on the privileges of rank, for only the senior-ranking indi-vidual in an interaction has the *right* to make demands. By responding harshly parents are therefore socializing their children to respect the privileges of rank. (loc. cit.)

Following onset of the shift insistent demands for parental attention, such as whining, tugging, trying to climb on the parent's lap, etc., draw increasingly harsh punishment. So children gradually learn to wait until the parent initiates interaction, such as asking a child to fetch something or do some chore (ibid.: 43). Following performance of the task, the child is likely to receive attention and requests may be granted, or at least registered at a favorable time. Thus, *laulima* becomes for older children an occasion for receiving favorable attention from parents.

The prerogatives of status are also impressively symbolized by the way in which punishment is administered. Thus, parents may become angry over any sign of ''hesitation or question about their requests'' (Gallimore et al. 1974: 91). ''Talking back'' when given an order, indeed any discussion of it, is regarded by parent and child alike as disrespect, and likely to be severely punished. So children avoid it. When they do not want to obey they withdraw, do not listen, or otherwise avoid the situation (ibid.: 153–154). In fact, those Hawaiian fathers who say that they are willing to negotiate with their children are more identified with Caucasian culture (Howard 1974: 191).

One final feature of disciplining is also consistent with the maintenance of adult prerogatives. That is the strong, conscious dislike of ''rewarding'' children individually for their behavior, or "bribing" as it is commonly called (field notes). As Howard points out:

> It is as though parents realize that if they made rewards contingent (upon the child's behavior at a particular time) they would be opening themselves to manipulation, and in effect yielding some control of the relationship to their children (op. cit.: 59–60)

Further evidence of these points is provided in the actual interactions of parents and children reported in Chapter 5. We conclude that a wide range of parental behavior relating to nurturance, punishment, and discipline within the contemporary Hawaiian household can be derived from the traditional principle of "respect for rank and authority within the family." In fact, we believe this to be more basic than emphasis upon obedience, per se, which may have a partly exogenous origin, as suggested above.

The grandparent–grandchild relationship, unfortunately, is not touched on in either of these books, nor the present book. This is due in part to an ethnocentric preoccupation with the parent–child relationship, and to the fact that the households we worked with lacked grandparents.

There is a strong emphasis upon equality within the community of Aina Pumehana (Howard 1974: 28; Gallimore et al. 1974: 174–175; Heighton 1971: 48–50). Heighton points out that resentment is expressed about any allegation of *ali'i* ancestry, unless the person involved has attempted to keep it hidden (loc. cit.). This is just the attitude that one would have expected among *maka'āinana* in the past. The principle of equality appears clearly in relationships among adolescents. Here it complements hierarchy within family relationships:

> The sharp contrasts between the experience of youth in the peer group and in the family partly explain the high value attached by young people to the privilege of "going out." In the peer group, the norm is spontaneous, lighthearted interaction without the intrusions of superior status and power of the kind they must accept from elders. (Gallimore et al. 1974: 167)

Among adolescents, equality is manifested in ready acceptance of everyone (op. cit.: 168), and in "strong dislike for those 'who think they are better than you' " (op. cit.: 169), an exact mirror of the traditional attitude toward those who act superior when they are not. Adolescents like peers who are friendly and helpful and do not presume to tell others what to do (op. cit.: 170). Attempts to influence one another are avoided, but when they occur, are responded to "by refusing to take them seriously," i.e., by treating them as jokes (op. cit.: 172).

In this chapter, we have presented evidence from oral tradition that the *'ohana* of the past was organized by the principles of aloha, hierarchy, equality, and sexual segregation. Only the last of these has not been emphasized in recently conducted studies of the modern *'ohana,* whereas many of the detailed expressions of the other three principles in the daily lives of commoners before are likewise described in families of today. In the following three chapters, evidence provided by the spontaneous verbal behavior of parents and children is presented in order to demonstrate the ways in which hierarchy develops and is reinforced and the struggle for equality is waged and finally resolved. Beginning with the third of these chapters, attention is also paid to the form and structure of the verbal routines which constitute the hierarchical mode of speaking. The subsequent two chapters then take up two forms of the egalitarian mode of speaking: disputing and talking story in its broadest sense. The routines involved in disputing and talking story, it is believed, bear a meaningful resemblance to the speech events and oral arts described in this chapter.

CHAPTER 3

Relationships between Children within the *'Ohana*

In this chapter, we begin to examine the way in which the hierarchical mode of speaking develops. Although both modes of speaking are first experienced and acquire their fundamental meaning in relations with parents, the examination begins with relations among children. There are several reasons for this, the foremost being that this experience within the family sets the stage for the struggle over equality among children the same age which is encountered when children leave home and enter school, as analyzed in the next chapter. Another reason is to demonstrate that the verbal routines used by children when playing house, playing with, and caring for younger ones resemble and clearly derive from the routines that parents use with children, which are described in Chapter 5. It would come as no surprise that parent–child relations are hierarchical. But it needs to be demonstrated, particularly to those of American culture, that hierarchy is firmly built into relationships between children of different ages, and reinforced daily. In this and the next chapter, moreover, we analyze the development of relationships. Beginning with Chapter 5, attention shifts to the structure and function of routines and the structure of meaning which they acquire within the speech economy.

Brothers and sisters relate to one another while carrying out tasks for the family and taking care of younger siblings. Care-taking itself starts when playing with infants and young children, and is gradually extended by the addition of responsibility, supervised by parents, for their amusement and welfare. In the course of carrying out such activities day by day, children learn the verbal routines, attitudes, and values that characterize relations among children within the *'ohana*. These relationships are clearly hierarchical.

The information that follows derives from several sources: stories told to the author during many sessions with the children, a few spontaneous dramatizations while "playing house," and sound recordings of interactions at home which were made by three mothers of young children.

Playing house

A prototype of the perceptions and verbal routines involved in doing chores and caring for infants was provided by a spontaneous dramatization performed by a group of about six kindergarten children which occurred in the "doll corner" of the school conducted by the Kamehameha Early Education Program (KEEP).[10]

Example 3.1. (Carmen, group leader: Ela, Loke, Malia, girls: Moke, boy) (Note to readers: In this and the examples that follow throughout the book the text is presented in the first section. In the second section, translations and comments are presented in parentheses, with glosses in quotes: Overlapping speech is bracketed.)

Roles:	Mother	Mother's lieutenant	Children
C : 1	Hey, daughta, you gotta change da baby's clothes, daughta.		
E : 2		Not me, her.	
L : 3			Ho! Evrytime I have to do tha-at!
C : 4	Change it! [firm, matter-of-fact]		
Ma: 5			...her washing clothes, das why. (excuses E, answers L)
C : 6	...an you make--I gon wash the dish an you make the two babies go [hums].		
? : 7			And I gon make the lunch.
? : 8			I gon iron da clothes. ...Her'z baby's clothes --ahyr-r.
E : 9		...Mommy! Dis goes down fo wash?	
C : 10	Yes, you... wash...		
E : 11		Aw diis goin down fo a wash	
Mo:12			...even you' muu-muu you didn' take care of.
? :13			went down fo wash you know.
? :14			Hurry up, you guys, wash da clothes.
C : 15	Wash da clothes. Girl, you betta wash da clothes, eh?		

C : 1	(Hey, daughter, you have to change the baby's clothes, daughter.) (commands, frames play)		
E : 2		(Not me, her.) (evades, attempts to shift task)	
L : 3			(Ho! Everytime I have to do tha-at!) (complains)
C : 4	(Change it!) (unmoved, repeats)		
Ma: 5			(She's washing clothes, that's why.) (excuses E, answers L)

continued

Example 3.1. *continued*

Roles:	Mother	Mother's lieutenant	Children
C : 6	(...and you make-- I'm going to wash the dish and you make the two babies go [hums].) (commands, explains)		
? : 7			(And I'm going to make the lunch.) (claims task)
? : 8			(I'm going to iron the clothes. ... Here's the baby's clothes--ahyr-r.)
E : 9		(...Mommy! "This is to be washed?") (requests directive)	(claims task, task noise)
C :10	(Yes, you...wash ...) (answers request, directs)		
E :11		(All this "is to be washed") (follows up C's directive)	
Mo:12			("You didn't take care of your dress either.") (complains)
? :13			("It was supposed to be washed." (justifies self)
? :14			(Hurry up, you guys, wash the clothes.) (urges others on)
C :15	(Wash the clothes. Girl, you better wash the clothes!) (command, reminds ? of her status)		

The lines were delivered in a register that clearly imitated their models at home, thus indicating that it was a drama. We cannot assume that it reflects the actors' actual roles at home or the actors' attitudes toward them, however. To determine these things, the dialogue will be compared later with recordings and observations of actual interaction at home. The drama does indicate, however, the children's positive motivation to perform such roles, since they were free to pursue a wide range of other play with the materials available, and it indicates their perception of the roles they have experienced.

The actors apparently perceive their roles when playing house as involving the following verbal routines (see 2.1.1 in Appendix 2):

Mother, as portrayed by Carmen, the group's real leader, assigns tasks by means of commands:

1 "Hey daughta, you gotta change da baby's clothes. . . ."
6 "you make the two babies go [hums]."

She answers requests for directions and explains:

10 "Yes, you . . . wash . . ."
6 "—I gon wash the dish . . ."

and insists on obedience to her direction by means of commands, remaining unmoved by complaints and arguments:

4 "Change it!"
15 "Wash da clothes. Girl, you betta wash da clothes, eh?"

Despite her directiveness and domination, mother does not initiate every exchange. When engaged in doing chores it is appropriate to ask her for direction, although not to challenge her authority—not even in play.

Children claim their own tasks when mother is assigning them (lines 7,8), complain about the specific task assigned to them (line 3), complain about and make excuses for their own and one another's lack of compliance with orders (lines 3,5,12,13), and carry out orders, presumably.

Mother's lieutenant is another role, which will appear more clearly in actual behavior at home. Note Ela's participation. She shifts an order from mother to another child (line 2), requests direction from mother (line 9) and then follows up on it (line 11).

These roles and the associated verbal routines, as we shall see in Chapter 5, are typical of the hierarchical relationships between mother, older sister, and younger siblings at home. To judge from this and many other examples, such verbal routines and their associated attitudes have become part of the children's repertoire by 5 years of age.

Carrying out tasks

The emphasis that parents place upon children doing their share of work results in a high degree of motivation for doing it, an internalization of the value of work before pleasure, and a desire to assume the tasks of older brother or sister. Any attempt to take over an elder's task, however, results in interaction which teaches the younger to stay in their place and thus reinforces the hierarchy that already exists among siblings based upon older caring for younger. Evidence for these points is presented in this section.

Both boys and girls are expected to do chores, starting at an early age. This appeared when I asked Pila, 7 years old, what they called him at home, meaning his name. He replied, quoting:

Example 3.2.

P: "Empty the wubbish can!"
me: [surprised] Izzat how dey say it!?
P: [pleased] "Honey Boy! Pila! Empty da slop." [imitating]

The emphasis placed upon doing these tasks is reflected in the children's description of them. For instance:

Example 3.3. (Shari, age 6 yrs)

me: Do you have anything you gotta do at your house? [material deleted]

S: . . . one has to wash da dishes, Tricia—an one, um—an one, um—one has to clean da house— A' [all] da time when d'-dey say, "Oh!" n my mudda say, "Wash da dishes," n den one a say, "Wash da dishes m gon clean da—dem ah-furnitures n a' [all]." Ooh, ha'd werk we 'ave to do man! ("Whenever they say, 'Oh!' my mother says, 'Wash da dishes,' and when one will say, '[You] wash da dishes, I'm going to clean the furniture and all.' Ooh, hard work we have to do man!")

The quoted speech in this example is nearly identical with that of the children playing house in Example 3.1, although it was spoken by different children in a different community. Thus it is clearly a verbal routine.

Young children are quite impressed with the emphasis that parents place upon doing their chores. Thus, a 7-year-old girl recounted:

Example 3.4.

G: When my fada come home [he] get mad because my sista no clean the house.

me: What does he say then?

G: "Give dem lickin. Wait till you mudda comes home you folks goin get a lickin." I gotta clean the counta, if I no clean the counta good my fada goin give me a lickin, too.

This was an accurate reflection of the fact that she was not allowed to go out until the chores had been done by all, as I observed. The emphasis upon doing chores results in children internalizing the rule: work before play. As stated by Pila, "I don't play, I work. When I *pau* [finished] I go play."

Not all of the tasks dramatized in Example 3.1 are typically performed by children as young as 5 or 6 at home, however. Thus, interviews indicate that children this young do not change diapers, but in Example 3.1 a child complained when told to change the baby's clothes in play. In real life, 4- and 5-year-olds are eager to do it, the very reverse of their dramatized behavior. This bit of fantasy, then, reveals the fact that children eagerly anticipate taking on the tasks which older children perform, and even mimic their attitudes towards these tasks, when given an opportunity to do so.

Evidence of the desire to take on the tasks of older siblings can be seen in claims to know how to do them. Thus, the same girl in Example 3.4 said:

Example 3.5.

G: When my sista dem was in Honolulu I had [to] wash and wipe. I know how to wash an wipe! Sista Shalene (aged 12) and my sista Mary (aged 10) they take turns and my brudda Fred and Kahe they gotta take turns sweeping and mopping. . . . My sister Mary she everytime get moody because I help my sista Shalene wash the dishes.

me: When you get big like your sistas, do you want to clean up the house?

G: I like watch TV, I going be lazy.

The last comment assumes the ambivalent attitude of the older sister, enabling the girl to feel more grown up. Note that when she takes over older sister Mary's task, the latter "gets moody." This resentment leads to reinforcement of the heirarchy, as we shall see.

Since older boys are expected to be less responsible in household chores, they become less responsible. Reflecting this, a 7-year-old girl said, "My mudda no like one boy, he go play, he do nutting." A 7-year-old boy explained to me that he did not do his work because "I no like, a la-azy." Despite this, I found boys on camping trips eager to help with the cooking, sweeping, and setting up of camp (washing dishes was less popular). One of the surest ways to create moodiness, in fact, was to deny a boy a chance to do one of these tasks. Apparently, the value of helping is strong in boys outside of home, suggesting that their roles at home do not fully utilize it.

Sibling care-taking

Children begin caring for younger ones by playing with the new baby within the first weeks of the infant's life. This experience is full of delight and excitement, which shows in the voices of the children as they describe it:

Example 3.6. (Leilani, 6 yrs)

L: When my baby was—when my mother was in—in the doctor, she had one baby. And our baby had teeth for real! My daddy everytime put his finger inside the mouth, and bite hard, for real!

me: Oh boy! Were you scared?

L: Yes, he scare somebody. And then she let—my mother let us play with her, and then we all go put our two fingers inside, she go bite us, and then we go say "Ow!", that's what we say.

me: I'll bet that was fun.

L: Yeah, good. Good fun.

As the infant grows into a young child, playful fighting replaces gentler forms of play:

Example 3.7. (same as Ex. 3.6)

L: And our baby going come big. My baby name one Maxer, one girl. She going come big, she going rascal us. Even my brother Jeffrey (younger than L), he know how to fight my brother them, for real. And then my brother go—hego—he go hit Jeffrey around. Then my big brother, he—he go fall down, Jeffrey scared.
("And our baby is getting big. My baby's name is Maxer, [she is] a girl. When she gets bigger she is going to rascal us. My brother Jeffrey also knows how to really fight his [older] brothers.")

It is interesting to note that Leilani gave a name to this play: "rascal us." One mother called her similar play "laughing it up with the kids" (see 1.1.2 in Appendix 2).

Parents faced with many demands upon their time and attention in large households seek to encourage their children to assume responsibility for supervising younger ones nearby. When this happens, a clear hierarchy appears with specific roles and verbal routines (see 2.5 in Appendix 2). This is illustrated in the following episode, which was recorded by one of the mothers at home.

Example 3.8. (S̲halene, 5 yrs; M̲olly, 4 yrs; J̲unya, boy, 3 yrs; P̲am, 2 yrs; L̲ei, 11 months)

Roles: Older sister	Lieutenant	Children
S : 1 You an an Pam, an-- Lei go on da bed. I gotta ᵍsomeplace. [interruption]		
2 Hurry ah-ahp! 'o [go] take Lei on deah-ah!		
	[unrelated material deleted]	Le: 3 [murmers]
	M : 4 Shalene! Lei no like!	
S : 5 Dis coverum. [pause] 6 ...Let me, ʸae 7 ...An don' drop her.		
[interruption]		
8 Now I gon put dis blanket--		
	M : 9 Stop. Do-on't! [steady, high pitch]	
	10 [yell]	
S : 11 Get that...out!		
	[dispute and crying]	Le: 12 [crying]
S·: 13 Come on to-op!		
	M : 14 Baby look! Carnᵊbu', carnbaw, carnᵊbul. Carnᵊbul.	
S : 15 Go get Lei! [shout] 'oh 'oh, bəp. 16 Stop!		
		Le: 17 [gurgling]
	[comments on baby's movements deleted]	
	M : 18 We'z Lei going?	
S : 19 On hiyah. All you folks, ceyz I gon get right oyᵊ hiya. [pause]		
S : 20 Oh, 'oh [crooning]		
		Le: 21 [babbling]
S : 22 Aiy yo, hel lo [chant] 23 Now Junyᵊ Boy, get o-ff! Look you droppin the cookies.		
		J : 24 Like dis?
S : 25 Sit down! Gᵇ all the way back. [pause]		

Example 3.8. *continued*

Older sister	Lieutenant	Children
26 Si' ahp! Sit like di-is! [pause] An cross yo' leg --nobo'+noⁿ+like see you' peepee.		
		J : 27 Not! [matter of fact] Is fo' it.
		? : 28 ŋaŋ, ŋaŋ, ŋaŋ, ŋaŋ.
S : 29 Come Moll'! Get off dat blan- ket.	M : 30 I a- am! Shalene, what if Lei fa-all?	
S : 31 [silence]		
	[interaction between M and J]	
	M : 32 Sha! Shalene, Jyə knock down ouʳ kine, box!	
S : 33 Get out! Punk! Get ou-ut! [pause]		
		J : 34 ᵐdis free yea's ow'. [retreating]

Older sister	Lieutenant	Children
S : 1 (You and Pam, and --Lei go on the bed. I have to go someplace.)		
2 (Hurry up! Go take Lei on there!) (commands, explains)		Le: 3 [murmurs]
	M : 4 (Shalene! "Lei doesn't want to!") (reports)	
S : 5 (Just cover her. 6 [pause] ...Let me, yeah? 7 ...And don't drop her.) (commands, takes over, cautions)		
8 (Now I'm going to put this blanket--) (demonstrates)	M : 9 (Stop. Don't!) (interdicts someone) 10 [yell]	
S :11 (Get that...out!) (commands offender)		Le:12 [crying]
	[dispute and crying]	
S :13 (Come on top!) (commands, in- structs)	M :14 (Baby look! Carnival...) (seeks to amuse, word play)	
S :15 (Go get Lei! 'oh 'oh baby. 16 Stop!) (commands, word play, interdicts)		Le:17 [gurgling] (satisfied)
	M :18 (Where's Lei going?) (requests in- formation)	
S :19 (On here. All of you, because I'm going to get right over here.) (replies, directs, explains)		

continued

Example 3.8. *continued*

Older sister	Lieutenant	Children
S :20 (Oh, 'oh [crooning]) (word play with baby)		
		Le:21 [babbling] (joins in)
S :22 (<u>Hello</u> [chant] Now Junior Boy, get <u>off</u>! Look you're dropping the <u>cookies</u>.) (word play, inter- dicts, corrects J: "You can't do anything right.")		
		J :24 (Like this?) (requests approval)
S :25 (Sit down! Go all the way back. [pause]		
26 Sit up! Sit like this! [pause] And cross your leg. "Nobody likes to see your penis.") (disapproves, com- mands, directs demonstrates, corrects, insults)		
		J :27 (Not! <u>Is</u> for it.) (defends self, meaning obscure)
		? :28 (ŋaŋ...) (word play with baby)
S :26 (Come Molly! Get off of that <u>blan- ket</u>.)		
	M :30 (I a- am! Shalene, what if Lei <u>fall</u>?)	
S :31 [silence] (ignores verbally)	(complies, anti- cipates diffi- culty)	
	M :32 (<u>Sha</u>--! Shalene, Junior knocked down "the <u>box</u> we were using!") (reports diffi- culty)	
S :33 (Get out! <u>Punk</u>! Get <u>out</u>! [pause]) (interdicts, insults)		
		J :34 ("I'm just three years old.") (defends self)

L_____I   indicates overlapping speech

In this episode, Shalene, the older sister, issues commands like those of the mother in Example 3.1. The commands include:

1 "you and Pam and Lei go on da bed."

2 "[Go] take Lei on <u>deah-ah</u>!"

11 "Get that . . . out!"

13 "Come on <u>to-op</u>!"

15 "Go get Lei! [shout]"

16 "Stop!"

29 "Get off dat <u>blanket</u>."

She also revises commands to her younger sister, Molly:

5   "Dis coverum."

She issues permission directives to her also:

6   "Let me, ʸae?" (the tag in a question is a mitigating form)

She cautions her:

7   "An don't drop her."

Demonstrates for her:

8   "Now I gon put dis blanket—"

Responds to her younger sister's requests for information and explains:

19   "On hiyah . . . ceyz [because] I gon get right oyᵊ hiya."

And corrects:

29   "Come Moll'!"

The younger sister in this episode, Molly, acts as *lieutenant*. She informs her older sister:

4   "Shalene! Lei no like!"
32   "Shalene, [Junya] knock down ouʳ kine box!"

and requests information and advice:

18   "We'z Lei going?"
30   "What if Lei fa-all?"

They share tasks, each substituting for the other within the limits of their respective abilities.

It is striking that the brother, although only a year younger than Molly, in no way shares the same kind of relationship with the older sister. Instead he is insulted (lines 26,33), corrected scornfully (lines 23,26), ignored when he objects (lines 27,34), and in general treated as if he lacked any competence. There is reason to believe that such treatment is accorded to boys, regardless of age (see Chapter 4, p. 51).

An immediate consequence of experience in the hierarchy is that children consistently pay attention to relative age. Another is that older children feel pride at being able to do more things than their younger siblings and cousins can do.

So, when a younger child claims to be able to do what an older one can do, he or she faces the elder's scorn:

Example 3.9 (Shari, age 7 yrs)

> S: My cousin a small shrimp. My cousin she say next year she going to school [scornfully]. . . .
> Even my other cousins . . . they small, they can hardly walk, and they said they can ride my
> cousin's—their sister's bike.
> ("My other cousins also, they are so small that they can hardly walk, and they said. . .".)

The older care-taker also feels resentment and frustration when the younger one makes demands and cannot keep up with the elder's activities:

Example 3.10. (Girl, 7 years old

> G: That's my mudda's baby gon follow me, then I go lick em and my smaw brudda carry em
> home, then I wen run play.

As the last report indicates, young children may be subjected to a certain amount of punishment by their older care-takers. But this cannot happen often, because parents take an extremely stern view of any neglect of their responsibility to look out for the younger (see Example 5.10). The attitude of the elder is no doubt made clear to the younger, nonetheless. Added to the scorn which the elder expresses when the younger tries to act above his age, this leads the younger to accept a subordinate status, and not challenge the elder directly. There are no such challenges in my data.

When children grow up in such a hierarchy, they demonstrate a tendency to treat younger ones as they have been treated by older children. This results in something like hazing, which occurs among girls taking care of younger brothers, as above, and also between adolescent boys and somewhat younger boys in their families, as described in Chapter 4. In these ways, then, children learn respect for seniority—not to act above their age.

This account of care-taking has given more attention to the role of girls than to that of boys. The reason for this is that girls more frequently act as care-takers. An occasional boy acts as chief care-taker, but this is not frequent. Thus, it is no accident that most of the informants above are girls. Further attention is given to boys' relationships to the family, and to one another, in the next chapter.

To summarize, playing with babies develops into responsibility for their care, particularly with girls. Parents encourage and supervise this. As children grow older, the care provided by older ones sets up the hierarchy among children within the family which is marked by clearly differentiated roles and specific verbal routines. The desire of younger children to claim the tasks and knowledge of older ones is rebuffed by the latter, as a consequence of which children learn respect for seniority. This value is internalized with great effectiveness. We encountered no evidence that it is subject to challenge or joking within the sibling relationship.

CHAPTER 4

Relations with Peers

This chapter analyzes the struggle for equality that occupies so much time among children of approximately the same age. In these relations, children learn gradually how to treat one another as equals, something they do not learn in the hierarchical relationship among siblings at home. Verbal disputes (2.3 in Appendix 2) both aggravate and express relationships among peers throughout much of childhood, while verbal humor (2.2.6 in Appendix 2) plays an increasing part in resolving disputes as children grow older. This development, as we shall see, depends upon other experiences as well. From 10 to 12 years of age, a change in peer relations occurs. On the one hand, children develop means for resolving conflicts, such as negotiating rules for games and activities. On the other hand, their expression of antagonistic feeling when frustrated diminishes, so that they appear less sensitive to behavior that earlier they reacted to as assertive. This transformation in boys appears to be related to a kind of hazing which younger boys are subjected to. The overall consequence of these changes is a scrupulous respect for equality among adolescents.

The data in this chapter are primarily verbal behavior in natural situations, but they are supplemented by my own observations. Both were obtained by hanging out with groups of boys for many days over a period of several years on school and neighborhood playgrounds, as well as on camping trips, and with groups of girls at school and around their home neighborhoods. While most of the recordings illustrated here were made on camping trips with the boys, observations covered a broader range of settings. The behavior analyzed below was found in all of these settings.

Activities

Preferred activities are those that do not require much coordination, influencing, or individual competition, all of which give rise to frequent disputes. As described in this section, disputes are so frequent that circumstances alone, however, cannot explain them.

After they start school at age 5, children spend increasing amounts of time with other children outside their households, although they are not isolated from such contact earlier. This is especially true of boys, since they obtain permission to leave the house more easily than girls do. Thus, when arranging trips, I discovered that every girl had to make special arrangements about her chores before being allowed to leave, whereas only two of more than twenty boys had to. Added to this, there is some evidence in the boys' talk that they experience a push away from home. For example, several 11 to 12-year-old boys told how their sisters, only half-jokingly, told them not to come home as the boys prepared to leave on a camping trip with me. This report led to accounts of brothers and fathers who slept outside under the house when young. By adolescence, many if not most boys devote almost all of their time and interest to their peers.

The activities of children from 8 to 12 years of age are similar to those of children who have access to the outdoors and the shore anywhere, but the most popular activities in my observations were those in which each was free to participate on his or her own terms. For example:

Example 4.1. (Kono and Kevin, 10 yrs) (Overlapping speech shown by brackets across lines.)

Ke: You know da bike? Had the big tree, uh, behine? Um, you know da taiə [tire], a-an da rope, uh? W-we go swing-g+y'know?

me: Uh hm.

Ke: M-ma bike ⌈ da buggah bʌs ahp [bust up].
Ko: ⌊ M-m-m
     da sɛng+go [the thing go].

Ke: Ride um, uh? An jump off da buggah go, straight in da bushes. Crack up.

(I.e., they would ride a bike, jump off onto a tire-swing, and the bike would crash into the bushes.)

One of the most popular activities on camping trips was going to the beach at night with flashlights to catch "sand turtles." These small, soft-shelled animals can be spotted burrowing into the sand as a wave retreats. While one boy held the light, others would pounce on them, dig them up, and store them in a pail. Although the whole group kept count of how many they had, and asked me how many other groups had caught, they did not keep individual score. Although disputes were otherwise frequent, there were none here. Such loosely-structured activities, carried out with an audience, but lacking close coordination and individual competition, were preferred by the boys whenever they had an opportunity to choose.

Keeping score in a competitive game, by contrast, was certain to produce a great number of verbal disputes. Thus:

Example 4.2. (Donnie, Damien, John, Manny, Fiti and about six other 9-10-year-olds were playing a pick-up game, divided into two teams and keeping score. Their manner was hard and aggressive on the court, matching their verbal tone.)
For explanation of columns, see Chapter 6, p. 81.

Initiation	Reply	Escalation
? :1 Get twenny, ae?		
	Do:2 Yeah, twenny	
		Da:3 Y'have to get twenny a'redy! [scornful]

Example 4.2. *continued*

Initiation	Reply	Escalation
	? :4 Not!	
	? :5 Us fa-as'!	
		? :6 Ae-ae-ae!
		sev:7 You guys--you guys--
		Da: 8 You guys--you *dda one cheat!
		? :9 Ae-ae-ae.
? :1 ("We have twenty, yeah?") (requests confirmation)	Do:2 (Yeah, twenty.) (confirms)	Da:3 ("You have to get twenty--show-off!") (sour grapes)
	? :4 (Not!) (contradicts accusation)	
	? :5 ("We're just fast!") (justifies)	?:6 (Ae-ae-ae!) (derides)
		sev:7 (You guys--you guys--) (accusation, insult)
		Da:8 (You guys are the ones who cheat!) (counter-accusation)
		? :9 (Ae-ae-ae.) (derides)

*dd is an alveolar trill.

Almost any claim to being first in something, no matter how trivial, was likely to be disputed:

Example 4.3. (Fiti, Andrew, Kevin, and another 10-year-old were arguing about who got into the car first the day before.)

Initiation	Reply	Escalation
Fi:1 I was da firs one came inside a cah', man		
	A :2 No' [not]. I ⌈was--	
	Fi:3 ⌊Secon' Da time we ⌈g -	
	T :4 ⌊sᵊgᵊ yeah, you was secon' bᵊkˢ--you know da time I jis--I'm-- I'm rʌn inside... ova hiah.	
	A :5 Not! I was da firs' one ⌈--	
	Ke:6 ⌊Den came--I.	

continued

Example 4.3. *continued*

Initiation	Reply	Escalation
	A :7 an I wn go out so you come <u>in</u>!	
	Fi:8 I wn stay--I wantshyu to go <u>iin</u>. De' [den] I wn <u>siit</u> down, den--den--den an then you was ova <u>dea</u>! An wich person you <u>knew</u>, uh, T?	Shii evytime you lie because you blackie.

Initiation	Reply	Escalation
Fi: 1 (I was the <u>first</u> "to get into the car", man.") (claims)		
	A : 2 (Not, I was--) (contradicts, counterclaim)	
	Fi: 3 (You were second. The time we--) (alleges contrary, expands)	
	T : 4 (Seco-- Yeah, you were second because --you know the time I just ran inside...over here.) (supports Fi, argues)	
	A : 5 (Not! I was the <u>first</u>--) (repeats claim)	
	Ke: 6 (Then I came in.) (claims)	
	A : 7 (and "I made room for <u>you</u>!") (argues)	
	Fi: 8 ("I waited for you to get in, then I sat down" and you were over <u>there</u>! "T, you know which one, yeah?" (counter argues, appeals to T)	Shii--you always lie, "you nigger.") (accuses, insults)

Attempts to influence another's way of doing something also caused sharp disputes, as in the following instance, when a 10-year-old boy attempted to direct a girl making string figures:

Example 4.4. (<u>M</u>alia, <u>L</u>en, <u>R</u>uby, and others, 10 yrs)

Initiation	Reply	Evaluation/escalation
L :1 oh-h, I do um.		
	? :2 O.k. me an you.	L :3 Whatchu <u>doin</u>?
	? :4 Malia, me an you-- aw!	

Example 4.4. *continued*

Initiation	Reply	Evaluation/escalation
		L :5 Wah-aht? I do it. I know how.
	M :6 No-o-o. Jus' about to draw you pull my han' awɛ-ɛ'!	
	L :7 Make um good!	[pause] Wrong!
	R :8 You pull? [pause] You can do um any way, Len!	[pause] Wrong!

Initiation	Reply	Evaluation/escalation
L :1 (Oh, I do it.) (claims task)	? :2 (O.k. me and you.) (offers to share)	L :3 (What're you doing?) (challenges M)
	? :4 (Malia, me an you --aw!) (repeats offer, exclaims)	L :5 (What? I do it. I know how.) (challenges, claims knowledge)
	M :6 (No. When I'm just about to draw you pull my hand away!) (contradicts, com- plains to L)	
	L :7 ("Do it right!") (directs)	[pause] Wrong! [pause] Wrong!)
	R :8 (Do you pull? [pause] You can do it any way, Len!) (requests informa- tion, argues, jus- tifies M)	(accuses)

And so it continued through two dozen more exchanges.
Even having to wait for another brought accusations and disputes.

Example 4.5. (Cha'lie, Fiti, and Ray, 12 yrs. Fiti is Samoan)

Initiation	Reply	Escalation
		C :1 Stink! Samoin. Why you neva hi' [hear] us, eh? Let um go --shi-ish!
	Fi:2 Shi-iz!	
	C :3 You call um--hundred times he no come. T'ree hundred times he no come.	
	R :4 Four t'ousan' times! An he come.	

continued

Example 4.5. *continued*

Initiation	Reply	Escalation
		C :1 (Stink! You Samoan. "Why don't you ever listen to us, ey? Ignore him"--shiish!) (insult, accusation, directs)
	Fi:2 ("Shiish!") (mimics C)	
	C :3 (You call him-- hundred <u>times</u> he doesn't come. Three hundred times he doesn't come.)	
	(accuses, jokes)	
	R :4 (Four thousand times! Then he comes.) (jokes)	

The use of scarce objects and the sharing of treats were also likely to cause disputes. Why were children as old as 10 years apparently so unwilling to share with their peers in light of the great emphasis which Hawaiian culture puts upon sharing? This contradiction, together with the great number of different circumstances giving rise to disputes, suggested that something besides immediate circumstances were involved in producing disputes. To this we now turn.

Sensitivity to assertiveness

Sometimes, the boys appeared to regard another's behavior as assertive when no such intention seemed reasonable. For instance, a 12-year-old boy wearing an arm cast was accosted by another in the following way:

Example 4.6.

2:   Trow da' [that] dumb thing away!

1:   No can! [hotly]

3:   He like everybody know he was in da hospitu.

Incidents such as this suggested that boys were extraordinarily sensitive to assertiveness. That they had a highly developed scorn for assertiveness was revealed in the following story, which concerned a local wrestler named Ripper Collins. It produced rapt attention when told by a group of 10- and 11-year-olds.

Example 4.7. (<u>A</u>tta, <u>B</u>obby, <u>Fr</u>ank, and <u>Fa</u>tau) For an explanation of columns, see Chapter 7, pp. 106ff.

Summons/proposition	Response/corroboration	Mediation
A : 1 You kno' we saw him at da zoo. ...membə da time we aescursion, ae? we saw 'im at da zoo.		

Example 4.7. *continued*

Summons/proposition	Response/corroboration	Mediation
	B : 2 Yah, at da zoo he git+teu [go tell]	
	A : 3 Yeah, he wa' tellin as	"Get da <u>heu</u>' outa hiyə, kiids!"
A : 4 He--we tell um why, "Get da hell outa hiyə..."		[gruffly]
	B : 5 Was Reginal', some-tin li' dat... (orients)	
Fr: 6 One man 'i punch 'im, you neva see um?		
	B : 7 [pause] What?	
Fr: 8 He tol+the son get ...his ass outa dea. Us guys lookin at the leper^d.		
	B : 9 Owen [when]?	
Fr:10 Wh--when we+^w as in t--uh, secon' grade. [pause] Mem'a we+en go zoo?		
	B :11 Yeah.	
Fr:12 He go punch um-- he awmos^t--make like dat to da kid [gestures] an tol the kid go+wɛ'. So da fa--da	? :13 Yeah, he go hit	di<u>x</u>--[da kid] (x is velar fricative, emotional emphasis)
		Fr:14 fadə come ova dea, "whoo-oom!"
	Fa:15 Da <u>fadə</u> when hit um?	Fr:16 Da fada wen hit um fo B :17 Yeah, da bugga <u>had</u> it! Fr:18 slappin da <u>son</u>.
		[pause]
		A :19 Cause he tink he da king!

A : 1 (You know we saw him at the zoo. ...Remember the time we went on excursion? we saw him at the zoo.) (formal opener, orients)		
	B : 2*(Yeah, at the zoo he "said:"	"Get the <u>hell</u> out of here, kids!") (enactment)
	A : 3 (Yeah, he was tell-ing <u>us</u> (affirm, narrative clause)	
A : 4 (He--"we asked him why he said 'Get the hell out of here...'") (new narrative clause)		
	B : 5 (It was Reginald, something like that...) (orients)	
Fr: 6 (A man punched him, didn't you see?) (new narrative clause)		
	B : 7 [pause](What?) (requests infor-mation)	
Fr: 8 (He told the son to "beat it," when we were looking at the leopard.) (new narrative clause, orients)		
	B : 9 (When?) (requests infor-mation)	

continued

Example 4.7. *continued*

Summons/proposition	Response/corroboration	Mediation
Fr:10 (When we were in t---uh, second grade. [pause] You remember going to the zoo?) (orients)	B :11 (Yeah.) (affirms)	
Fr:12 (He punched him--he almost--"did that to the kid" [gestures] an told the kid to go away. So the fa--ther-) (resumes narrative, new narrative clause	? :13 (Yeah, he hit the kid.) (affirms, adds emotional expression)	the kid.) emotional expression)
		Fr:14 (father came over and went "Whoom!") (enactment)
	Fa:15 (The father hit him?) (requests information)	
		Fr:16 (The father hit him for)
		B :17 (Yeah the bugger had it!)
		Fr:18 (slapping the son.)
		[pause]
	A :19 (Because he thinks he is the king!) (states moral of the story)	

* also new narrative clause, thus proposes.

I.e., on a trip to the zoo when they were in second grade, Ripper Collins—allegedly—told them "to get the hell out of there," gesturing—as if(?)—to slap a boy. The boy's father thereupon "let him—the wrestler—have it," because of the latter's arrogance in "slapping" the son.

Boys routinely explain fights as the result of assertive behavior. Thus:

Example 4.8. (Fiti, Ray, Donnie and several others, 12 yrs old, are discussing a disliked boy.)

Summons/proposition	Response/corroboration	Mediation
me: 1 Hey, why is Danny so --why is--why is he such a big shot?	R : 2 *He walk on his--|	
	? : 3 †Hey, yeah! 'Iy is	
†?: 4 Yeah I sawn Danny one day--	? : 5 How he walk?	
?: 6 In Pualei [with Pualei].	D : 7 When Pualei goes in da back of our yard--	
	? : 8 I's the gir^u with the--	
		? : 9 He was hol'ing her--her han'.
		? :10 Oh dah siick.
		Fi:11 'Sa sick guy!
		? :12 'As a one she go --he go wiit.

Example 4.8. *continued*

Summons/proposition	Response/Corroboration	Mediation
me: 1 (Hey, <u>why</u> is Danny so--why is he such a big shot?) (request for information)	R : 2 *(He walks on his--) (begins report, supplies information)	
	? : 3 †(Hey, yeah! He <u>is</u>.) (agrees)	
†?: 4 (Yeah I saw Danny one day---) (new narrative clause)	D : 5 (How does he walk?) (request for information)	
? : 6 (With Pua<u>lei</u>.) (replies, new narrative clause)	D : 7 (When Pua<u>lei</u> goes into the <u>back</u> of our yard--)	
	? : 8 (It's the girl with the--) (orients)	? : 9 (He was holding her--her <u>hand</u>.)
		? :10 ("He's really <u>sick</u>.")
		Fi:11 (He's a sick <u>guy</u>!) (evaluations)
		? :12 (That's the one he go--he go <u>with</u>.) (explains)

* **also proposes**
† **same speaker**

In other words Danny was judged to be a big shot because of the way he walked, holding a girl by the hand in public.

Example 4.9. (<u>Faa</u>tau, <u>Frank</u>, <u>Alan</u>, and <u>Atta</u> are discussing fighting with Michael.)

Summons/proposition	Response/Corroboration	Mediation
At:1 Y'memba the time, uh --Micha' wa' playing hookey, εh? An we+'as eatin lunch an he wa' walkin to da ^bweach?		
	Fa:2 Yeah, he ^wgon make troubu to [with] da haole.	
Fa:3 Den we stah't fight, n den we fight.		
	Fr:4 Us guys dive in press him by da neck	"Get out!" [laugh]
[further narrative omitted]		
		Al:5 I <u>hate</u> Michaels!
	Fa:6 He act when walkin...	
		At:7 An las' yi' [year] went <u>steal</u> um.

continued

Example 4.9. *continued*

Summons/proposition	Response/Corroboration	Mediation
At:1 (You remember the time Michael was playing hookey, yeah? And we were eating lunch and he was walking to the beach?) (formal opener, orients)	Fa: 2 (Yeah, he was going to make trouble with the haole.) (affirm, orients)	
Fa:3 (Then we started to fight and then we fight.) (new narrative clause)	Fa: 4 (We dive in and press him by the neck. (adds detail)	"Get out!" [we said]. [laugh]) (emotional emphasis)
		Al:5 (I <u>hate</u> Michael!) (evaluation)
	Fa: 6 (He acts when walking...) (orients)	At:7 (And last year he <u>stole</u> something.) (evaluation)

Thus the way Michael walked while "going to make trouble with the haole" is cited to justify the fight. The fact that he also stole is thrown in for good measure. Both incidents have in common that a boy is seen as assertive.

Why should these children be so likely to perceive their peers as assertive, whether or not it is intended? I suggest that it is a result of the hierarchical relationships experienced with siblings. As we have seen in Chapter 3, children grow up in a system in which "older is better," and younger ones learn that they cannot challenge older ones successfully. They learn also that the only way out of a lower status is to take the role of an older child with someone younger. They presumably bring these attitudes with them when they start interacting with others the same age. But there a dilemma is posed: who is to play the role of the older? One could suppose that equality would resolve the dilemma, and indeed we believe that it does eventually. But before children have much experience with peers outside the family, they do not know how to behave as equals. In this case, it appears to be learned in part as a result of hazing, which causes children to inhibit their antagonistic reactions to one another when frustrated. Other experiences also lead to the same result.

The inhibition of antagonism

Hazing consists of a deliberate attempt to arouse a stong feeling of anger in a younger boy, and then to force the latter to suppress any expression of it. The routine is often initiated by the older boy with a shove, a teasing remark, or the epithet "*punk!*" This is a fighting insult, as we shall see. It proceeds with the older one trying "to get a rise out of" the younger, i.e., to make him show some sign of resistance. But if he does, the older one will hit him quite hard on the upper arm, and this intent is communicated nonverbally. All of this occurs along with cues indicating strong, controlled emotion.

Example 4.10.

I watched Harow (15 yrs) tease Kimo (9 yrs), his cousin, at the luau. I first noticed it after an exchange of challenging remarks, which sounded serious. Harow passed Kimo and did something to him which I could not see. Kimo immediately scowled and said, "Punk!" (attempting to reverse the roles). They started arm-wrestling, but it was not good-natured. Harow continued to threaten, nonverbally, but did not touch Kimo. Kimo was backed up against a car, scowling, back very straight, not moving in the slightest. This exchange of gestures continued for almost 15 minutes, although nothing else happened.

In being hazed, the younger boy is put in a double-bind. By not resisting, he proves the charge, because a punk is someone who won't fight when provoked. But if he does attempt to fight, he cannot expect to win. This likewise proves that he is no fighter, hence a punk, and this adds to the derision that is communicated by his tormenter.

Younger boys do not appear to enjoy this experience at all. This may be one reason why boys in adolescence do not associate with those who are more than a year older, unless they are related. Teenage boys regularly refer to younger boys as "punk kids." This reflects, of course, the way that they were regarded. In so doing, they are moving up the hierarchy, exactly as children do in the family.

The only way out of the hazing bind for the younger boy is "to play it cool," that is, to suppress any show of his own feelings and thus not provoke his tormenter. As boys learn not to express their antagonism under genuine provocation, it becomes easier for them to mitigate such expression in the disputes that mark their relations with peers.

In passing, it should be noted that boys have to experience hazing before they haze younger ones. Before age 12, approximately, boys were never observed scapegoating, or acting in an overbearing way, with young children. Quite the reverse—they show a tender concern for them.

Learning not to show resentment when provoked is the result of hazing. That this learning is carried over into peer relations can be seen in the fact that boys of about the same age haze one another, using the same words and acts that older boys use with them, except that they do it in a good-natured, although teasing, manner. For example:

Example 4.11. (Fiti, Ray, Bobby, and Donnie, 12 yrs old, are watching girls at the beach from about 100 feet away.

Initiation	Reply	Escalation
me: 1 [Where] dat girl goin wid 'er boards?		
(carrying body- surfing boards)	? : 2 [yell]	
	? : 3 [whistle]	

continued

Example 4.11. *continued*

Initiation	Reply	Escalation
Fi:4 One mo <u>time</u>, Mista St--		
	R : 5 Shut <u>ʌp</u>! [laughs]	
		B : 6 'Ey, <u>punk</u>!
[a little later]		
D :7 Ah do' know what she ...		

Fi:8 Djyou like
    da blue on [one]
    las iis?		

	B : 9 What da' [dat] word?	
		Fi: 10 [punches B in friendly fashion]
	B :11 <u>Ou-uch</u>!	
	[Fi and B pound one an- other good naturedly]	
	R :12 Nanakuli Awstah' [laugh]	
	[more good natured pounding, laughing, joking complaints]	

me: 1 (Where is that
    girl going with
    her boards?)
    (calling atten-
    tion, instigat-
    ing)		

		? : 2 [yell]
		? : 3 [whistle] (joking approach)

Fi: 4 ("let's go, Mista
    St--"
    (joking sugges-
    tion to approach)
	R : 5 (Shut up! [laughs])
	    (interdict, jokes)	

		B : 6 ('Ey, punk!) (insult, joke)
D : 7 (I don't know what she...)		

Fi: 8 ("Would you want the
    blue one like this?")
    (joke, requests in-
    formation, distorts
    speech)		

	B : 9 (What's that word?) (challenge, jokes)	

		Fi:10 [punches B in
		    friendly fashion]
		    (blow, joke)

	B :11 (Ouch!) (exclamation)	

	R :12 (Nanakuli Allstars
	    i.e., "tough guys")
	    (allegation, joke)	

Note that each time a boy replies assertively:

R: 5 Shut ʌp!
B: 9 What da' [dat] word?

another responds with an insult or a blow, but couples it with a laugh. The message thus communicated is to "laugh it off" when provoked by assertiveness—at least when the relationship is friendly.

   Boys often become friends despite fighting with one another, and in some instances·even because of it. One reason for this may be that they become more tolerant of one another's assertiveness, or learn to avoid showing such quick resentment of it.

The above analysis has referred to boys throughout. Yet girls dispute as readily as boys do (see Chapter 6 for examples), and they seem to be as sensitive to assertiveness on the part of peers. While girls do not seem to undergo hazing like boys experience, they develop similar equalitarian attitudes by mid-adolescence. How does this come about? Data to answer this question are lacking. One can speculate that as a girl moves through the hierarchy, taking on the roles of older sibling and even parent, she experiences different status relationships, so that she is not as anxious to avoid inferior status as boys are, and thus more tolerant of assertiveness in peers. Boys, however, do not move out of an inferior status as long as they remain in the family (see Chapter 3). This happens only outside in the peer group. There, fighting and disputing appear to be a necessary part of learning to be equal.

Learning to negotiate rules

Another development which appears to have a similar result is the collective ability to negotiate rules for structuring competitive situations. In early childhood, rules, if mentioned at all in competitive circumstances, are simply asserted and compliance is demanded or violations are charged, which only intensifies the dispute. Rules are not suggested in a mitigating manner, or seriously debated. By age 12, however, the boys were negotiating rules on occasion, and in the process inventing games. It happened this way. On the last camping trip, I brought along a toy that the boys had not seen before: a Time Bomb. When wound up, this toy ticked loudly until it suddenly made a loud explosive noise. Without any instructions, it suggested a game: throwing it to another so that it would go off in another boy's hands. The boys started out with this game. They derided losers, and the resulting disputes were frequent and typical. But this time they kept playing for an hour or more at a time. Over a day or so, several individuals discovered how to anticipate exactly when the thing would go off, so that they never lost. This relieved some of the tension and increased the pleasure. Next they decided to form teams, and to roll the thing back and forth, so that now teams were winning and losing, rather than individuals. In the process they suggested, articulated, and eventually agreed upon a set of rules for conducting the game and counting score. I was appealed to during disputes over application of these rules, but refused to arbitrate. By the last morning, they were playing the new game amicably and with enjoyment. It was only then that I realized the significance of what had happened. I realized then that other rules had been suggested to me on that trip—for instance, that those who had not had a turn to help me cook be allowed to help at the next meal. Even when I suggested such rules on earlier trips, they had been ignored. Now the boys were suggesting them, instead of me.

Situational joking

The third development that helps to produce an egalitarian relationship by the time adolescence is reached relates to the way verbal disputing itself is carried out. As detailed in Chapter 6, verbal disputing typically escalates rapidly from simple assertion and contradiction to argument, challenge, and insult. This happens because of the sensitivity to assertiveness discussed earlier. While a few disputes end in a fight, or blows, most terminate with grumbling and moodiness—sometimes on the loser's part, sometimes mutually. Once a verbal dispute has broken out, children seem to have no means of resolving it to the satisfaction of both parties. Between 10 and 12 years of age, however, an increasing number of disputes ended in laughter by all concerned (see Chapter 6). This was brought about by another kind of verbal routine, which is labelled *situational joking*. An example:

Example 4.12.

At one point in the afternoon, David and Kono, then 10 years old, were on a losing team. They got very angry at one another, especially David, who did a lot of yelling and sulked for a long time. That evening, to make matters worse, prizes were handed out to the winning team. David, not receiving a prize, got raging mad. He was given a share by one of the winners, whereupon Kono demanded a share from David. The latter refused, and Kono began raging at him. As his anger rose, he began to threaten, "Hɛ'—you wait, I goⁿ git my temp'rə' (temper up)" and he followed this with a dramatic cry, "Woo-oo-oo!" which ended in a high falsetto. Then, with a tone of ultimate exasperation, he hurled at David, "*Piss* in da *ass!*" This brought everyone down with roars of laughter. Eighteen months later, the boys were still telling the story.

It is interesting to note the typical elements which appear in this episode: conflict over sharing, arrogance on both sides, refusal to accept the rule about awarding prizes, and the insult itself, which was equivalent to calling David a *punk*. The style of Kono's performance, which triggered the laughter that terminated the dispute, was unique, however.

Kono was a verbal leader, as Fiti later became. The former was often ridiculed and insulted with impunity, because every boy knew that he could not fight. Fiti, however, was a fighter. But by the age of 12, it made no difference: both could achieve more by joking than by fighting, as we shall see in Chapter 6. Among adolescents, the most popular boys are those who are known as *sha'p ta'kə's*.

This development reflects the fact that humor displaces serious disputing in adolescence, for all but the most serious matters. In fact, much joking among adolescents celebrates their equality by making a parody of adult directives. Gallimore et al. point out:

Peer interactions we observed seemed to celebrate by constant joking the absence of intrusive adult authority or of responsibility to supervise younger siblings. . . . Harsh criticism and threats are followed by laughter. In some groups, nothing seems too outrageous to say, as long as it is not taken as a serious attempt to evaluate or influence. (1974: 171)

Humor thus helps to produce equality, and to symbolize it as well. Hence it is natural for parents to contradict their young children when playing with them—as described in Chapter 6.

In this chapter, we have seen that loosely structured activities are preferred by boys whenever they have an opportunity to choose. Claims of any kind, attempts to influence, and sharing, on the other hand, are all so likely to occasion disputes as to suggest that something else underlies the ubiquitous disputing among peers. It is hypothesized that a basic cause of frequent disputing is a sensitivity to perceived assertiveness in peers, which results from past experience in hierarchical relationships among siblings. By adolescence, however, both girls and boys have come to accept peers as equals. In the case of boys, this outcome appears to result from a change in ways of relating. Younger boys learn from being hazed not to show resentment when provoked. Peers develop an ability to negotiate rules for competing. Along with these developments, situational joking comes to resolve serious disputes, as described in greater detail in Chapter 6. Adolescents, it has been noted, celebrate their equality by joking about assertiveness.

Taken with the conclusions of Chapter 3, these findings confirm the argument of Chapter 2 that hierarchy and equality are organizing principles of the 'ohana and demonstrate the way in which both are internalized as children grow up. The development of equality has implications for schooling as well, since the analysis presented here indicates that children are just beginning to deal with assertiveness in peers when they enter school. The resulting tendency to dispute can have a disorganizing effect upon classrooms, as we shall see in Chapter 9. In Chapter 10, it is suggested that opportunities can be afforded children in school to learn how to resolve disputes at an earlier age than appears to be usual.

CHAPTER 5

Relations with Parents: The Rhetoric of Authority

Beginning with the present chapter, the focus shifts from relationships to the form and structure of the routines that occur in them and the meaning which these routines acquire in use. By analyzing the verbal routines that parents use in commanding and punishing children (1.5 and 1.6.1 in Appendix 2), responding to children's requests (1.4.1 and 1.4.2), and questioning children (1.6.2) and children's responses to them, we hope to show something of the meaning that one-sided, adult-controlled speech events and routines acquire. The negative attitude towards such routines contrasts significantly with the positive attitudes developed in egalitarian routines, which are likewise experienced in relations with parents. The latter are analyzed in Chapters 6 and 7. The argument to be developed later on is that the contrast in meaning between these two modes of speaking carries over to the classroom, and that this helps to account for the striking differential response that children demonstrate in recitation (Chapter 9) as compared with the reading lessons conducted at KEEP (Chapter 10).

The relationship between form and meaning in use is referred to as "rhetoric." For instance, when a child questions a parent about whether the family is going to the beach (see Example 5.3 below) it may be an innocent request for information, or an indirect request to go to the beach (see Ervin-Tripp 1977; Mitchell-Kernan and Kernan 1977). These are two different routines, although their forms are identical. Routines are used to accomplish particular purposes in interaction. They are not structures which automatically direct behavior according to certain rules. More correctly, routines are forms by means of which the meanings of interaction are arrived at (see Bilmes and Boggs 1979; Mehan 1979). Moreover, meanings are not invariably shared by participants. For instance, in Example 5.9 below, a parent appears to be requesting information for no ulterior purpose, while the children respond as if they were being trapped into incriminating themselves.

The rhetoric of authority, as analyzed in this chapter, appears in the parents' unrestricted right to question children, and in the fact that children can only question, or make requests of parents, in subdued fashion. It appears in the parents' right to issue arbitrary and corrective commands and the child's obligation to obey without "talking back." It appears most dramatically when an angry parent punishes a child for disobedience. From experiencing the consequences of parental directives and punishment, children appear to develop a general negative attitude toward answering direct questions asked by an adult. The implication of this attitude for classroom behavior is discussed in concluding the chapter.

Approaching and negotiating with parents

In Chapter 2, it was argued that the traditional principle of respect for rank and authority within the family meant that parents and not children had the right to initiate interaction between them. This principle included requests for information, expressed in the general rule: observe, do not ask questions (cf. Handy and Pukui 1972: 91). In each of the families where recordings were made, it was observed that whenever children address, request, or attempt to negotiate with a parent, the latter, usually a mother, does not respond verbally right away, and in most cases ultimately does not provide what was sought, while in a few instances the child is scolded for the overture.

The children involved are at the age, 2½ to 5 years, when intrusive demands upon parents are supposed to be punished, according to the "shift" hypothesis (see Chapter 2, page 25). Our data, however, fail to provide any instances of demands upon parents that we would judge at all intrusive, even by children as young as 2½ years. In fact, the only difference noted between the older and younger children in this age range is that the older ones repeat their questions less often, apparently realizing sooner that they will not prevail. Hence, we conclude that children learn very early not to be intrusive or to make demands. While the major reason for this may be punishment, our data would suggest that nonreinforcement of requests also plays a part. The parent's nonresponse has the added effect of tesing the child's motivation—either extinguishing it, making the child more self-reliant, or encouraging patience.

Along with the inhibition of demanding behavior goes greater dependence upon the sibling hierarchy (see Chapter 3). In our view, the "shift" is less sudden and dramatic than has been described in the literature. In any event, such training appears to succeed, for children can be observed both at home and school waiting patiently for an opportunity to ask a question of an adult, asking repeatedly but modestly, and persisting when ignored.

The two common purposes for children's questions appear to be obtaining information or requesting permission or assistance from the parent. In requesting information, children typically ask a question several times, reformulate it, and perhaps speculate, while waiting patiently for a reply (see Examples 5.1 and 5.2). The parent typically does not reply right away, if replying at all. In these and the following examples, requests are classified as "initiation" (see Chapter 6 for general definition of "initiation," "reply," and "escalation"). In these examples, escalation consists of any increased urgency on the child's part, or an interdiction, other command, or challenge on the mother's part. In the first two examples, there is no escalation by either, and initiations are unsuccessful in obtaining any verbal response from the mother.

Example 5.1. (Junya, 3 yrs, and Mother)

Initiation	Reply	Escalation
J : Go ^{s}shool, yah, Mom? [pause] Mommy, you, you 'koo$^\vartheta$?		
	M: [silence]	
[later] J : Mommy, you like ah(?) go schoo'?		
	M: [silence]	
J : ("Asking if he have to go school, "M's gloss.) (reformulates, repeats q.)		
	M: (no reply)	
[later] J : ("Mommy you want me to go to school?")		
	M: (no reply)	

Example 5.2. (Molly, 4 yrs, and Mother, same family)

Mol: Some--Mommy, ...ony me gon come bi-ig, yeah? Now Sha' gon come 'maw aftə diis. [pause] An her grow up herseu'f.		
	M: [silence]	
Mol: ("I'm going to get bigger and Sharlene [older sister] is going to get smaller. She will grow up, too.") (requests information, speculates)		
	M: (no reply)	

In the following episode, there are 10 attempts to question the mother by various children compared with a single reply from the mother. In behavioral theory, such a reinforcement schedule would tend to promote patience and persistence—and that seems to be borne out by this episode. The distortions as they ask are worth noting. While 4-year-old's use of "t" for "k" in "kind" (lines 20, 26) is not unusual among speakers of all ages, the "d" for "g" in "go wear this one" (line 28) is unusual, and so is "wɛri" for "wear." The three-year-old's "cuu', ah 'ohᵈ diis?" (line 23) is definitely a distortion, as he usually speaks more clearly. Such use of distortion in hierarchical speech events is discussed in Chapter 7.

Example 5.3. (Charlene, 5 yrs; Molly, 4 yrs; Junya, 3 yrs; Pam, 2 yrs; and Mother)

Initiation	Reply	Escalation
J : 1 Mommy! Mommy-- [appealing]		
	Mol: 2 I know--fo' o'clock.	
J : 3 Um--		
	C : 4 Fo' tirty.	
J : tomo'ow	Mol: 5 I know fo' o'clock fo' thirty.	
	C : 6 Aeⁿ.	
J : beach?	Mol: 7 One a clock!	
		J : 8 Beach!
	C : 9 Aeh--six o'clock, an a eight a clock.	
	Mol: 10 Na-aht!	
	C : 11 Et is.	
	M : 12 [silence]	

[4 unrelated turns of talk in which M participates omitted]

Mol: 13 Mommy,		
	M : 14 [silence]	
[later]		
Mol: 15 Mommy, ding wear wiidə? da white one, wid da blue one?		
	M : 16 [silence]	
P : 17 Momma?		
J : 18 Oh, got two bucket'		
C : 19 Mommy! [resigned]		
Mol: 20 Mommy tan use dis tai'?		
	M : 21 [silence]	
J : 22 Das ou' buckε' [chanting]		
23 C'we-- cuu', ah 'oh, 'ow^d diis?	M : 24 Yes.	
	M : 25 [silence]	

[4 unrelated turns of talk in which M participates omitted]

Mol: 26 Mommy, dis tain'?		
	M : 27 [silence]	
[later]		
Mol: 28 Mommy, dow wεri dis one?		
	M : 29 [silence]	

J : 1 (Mommy! Mommy--) (calls attention to ask question)		
	Mol: 2 (I know--four o'clock.)	
J : 3 (Um-- ("are we going tomorrow-	C : 4 (Four-thirty.) (corrects Mol)	
	Mol: 5 ("I know--either four or four-thirty.")	
	C : 6 (Aeⁿ.) (rejects Mol's claim to know)	
J : 3 to the beach?") (M's gloss)	Mol: 7 (One o'clock!) (speculates)	J : 8 (Beach!) (anticipates eagerly)
	C : 9 (Aeh-- "six or eight o'clock.") (contradicts Mol)	
	Mol: 10 (No-ot!) (contradicts C)	
	C : 11 (It is!) (reaffirms self)	
	M : 12 (no reply)	

[4 turns of talk omitted]

Mol: 13 (Mommy,) (calls attention to ask question) [later]		
	M : 14 (no reply)	

continued

Example 5.3. *continued*

Initiation	Reply	Escalation
Mol: 15 (Mommy, "what do I wear with it? The white one with the blue one?") (asks what to wear to the beach)	M : 16 (no reply)	
P : 17 (Momma?)		
J : 18 (Oh, got two buckets!) (soliloquy to herself)		
C : 19 (Mommy! [resigned]) (beginning to give up)		
Mol: 20 (Mommy can use this kind?) (referent unclear)	M : 21 (no reply)	
J : 22 (That's our bucket! [chanting]) (soliloquy)		
23 (Could we-- <u>could</u> I hold this?)	M : 24 (Yes you can.) (replies to Mol) M : 25 (no reply to J)	
[4 turns of talk omitted]		
Mol: 26 (Mommy, this kind?) (repeats request)	M : 27 (no reply)	
[later] Mol: 28 (Mommy, I go wear this one?) (repeats request)	M : 29 (no reply)	

On a very few occasions, information was willingly provided by a parent. In the following episode, the children were attempting to understand remarks that they had overheard about a threatened teacher's strike. This topic drew the mother's interest, and she responded with more than the information requested. The mother's explanations (lines 8, 12, 14, 16) are categorized as "mediation," by analogy with the role of mediation in narrative (Watson 1972). Lika's "bull shit!" (line 7) is an evaluation, which is also part of mediation, as is mother's argument as to why they have to go to school (lines 26, 28—see Chapter 7 for definitions).

Example 5.4. (<u>B</u>oy, 5 yrs; <u>L</u>ika, 4 yrs; <u>H</u>oward, 3 yrs, and <u>M</u>other)

Initiation	Reply	Mediation
	M : 1 What?	
L : 2 Teachers going, strike?		
	M : 3 Strike?	
L : 4 Yae.		
	M : 5 Yaeum.	
B : 6 Misə Wan stri', yeah?		
		L : 7 "Bull <u>shit!</u>" M : 8 'As why yō mo' schoo' today.
	L : 9 Yeah.	
L : 10 Us...going, ya?	H : 11 Miss Wan...s'rite?	
		M : 12 No, today a <u>ho</u>liday.
	L : 13 <u>Ho</u>liday	
		M : 14 [yawning] Tomorrow get schoo'.
	L : 15 Oh, yeah? [surprised]	
		M : 16 You gotta go back schoo'.
H : 17 I yai yɪt.		

Example 5.4. *continued*

Initiation	Reply	Mediation
L : 18 I miss schoo, yeh, Mommy?		
	M : 19 You...you get tomorrow.	
	L : 20 Yeah.	
	H : 21 Bu' I no moə.	
	M : 22 Ge-et! ...	
L : 23 I no n'like schoo.		
	M : 24 You no like schoo'?	
L : 25 Yeah.		
		M : 26 Well, stay <u>home</u>, den.
	L : 27 No-<u>o</u>!	
		M : 28 You go' stay home an get d^mb?...
	L : 29 Hunh?	
[Mother is distracted momentarily] [later]		
	H : 30 I-I s'ay home. I s'ay home, I get gum.	

	M : 1 (What?)	
L : 2 (Teachers going, strike?) (request for info)		
	M : 3 (Strike?)	
L : 4 (Yae.)		
	M : 5 ("That's right.:)	
B : 6 (Missuz Wan strike, yeah?)		
		L : 7 ("Bu<u>ll</u> <u>shit</u>!") (quotes popular comment on strike)
		M : 8 ("That's why you don't have school today.")* (explains their staying home)
	L : 9 (Yeah.)	
L : 10 (Us...going, ya?)	H : 11 (Miss <u>Wan</u>...strike?) (imitates B's q.)†	
		M : 12 (No, today a <u>holi</u>day.) (reply to L, changes explanation)
	L : 13 (<u>Holi</u>day.) (imitates M)†	
		M : 14 ([yawning] Tomorrow you have school.)
	L : 15 (Oh, yeah? [surprised])	
		M : 16 (You gotta go back to school.) (reaffirms correct explanation)
H : 17 (I like it.) (self report)		
L : 18 ("I can miss school?") (request)		
	M : 19 (You have school tomorrow.) (contradicts L)	
	L : 20 (Yeah.)	
	H : 21 ("But not me.") (echoes L)	
	M : 22 ("You do!") (contradicts H)	
L : 23 I don't like school. (self report)	M : 24 (You don't like school?)	
L : 25 Yeah.		
		M : 26 (Well, stay <u>home</u>, then.) (suggests, non-serious)
	L : 27 (No-<u>o</u>!) (rejects suggestion)	
		M : 28 ("Do you want to stay home and be dumb?") (argues)
	L : 29 (Hunh?) (doesn't understand)	
[Mother is distracted momentarily] [later]		
	H : 30 (I stay home. If I stay home I'll get gum.)	

---

* "yo mo'" is a reduction of "y'no mo'". "~" indicates nasalization

† Imitations not part of new routines are considered "replies." (See Chapter 6 for definitions.)

When children request something tangible from parents, they usually receive a reply more quickly than they do when requesting information, even though it be a denial. When refusing, however, parents often give an explanation. This suggests that parents regard requests for legitimate needs as permissible, provided they are not demanding. A limited right to initiate interaction is accorded children in this circumstance.

Requests for tangibles, such as food or drink, are typically made in subdued fashion. A very young child simply pronounces the name of what is wanted with a unique falling pitch, suggestive of an appeal to pity: e.g., "*Jù-úice.*"[11] Somewhat older children will express a desire by saying, "I like *sʌ́-ʌ́m*," with a similar intonation. Another tactic is to report or predict what they would like to have happen. This might be classified as a hint (see Chapter 9). An interesting sidelight is that older boys frequently interpreted my statements about possible future events as suggestions, when they wanted to make requests. E.g.,

me: Tomorrow I go to town.
boy: Okay, we go.

Similarly, adolescents typically make group decisions by throwing out such hints and waiting to see if they are picked up.

Children, when refused, repeat requests in a variety of forms. "Nagging," as this is called, is frequently reported by parents. Often, several children will each take a turn, trying to get the same thing, younger ones succeeding older. For instance, in the following, the children were trying to get their mother to take them to the beach:

Example 5.5. (Boy, 5 yrs; Lika, 4 yrs; Howard, 3 yrs; and Mother)

Initiation	Reply	Escalation/Mediation
L : 1 Mommy, I going.		
	M : 2 Going whea?	
	L : 3 I'm going swimming.	
	M : 4 No, we cannot go swimming today.	
L : 5 Bəəmby yeh, Mommy?		
		M : 6 Daddy gotta go play music, 'as why.
	L : 7 Muswik.	
	M : 8 Not "muswik."	
B : 9 'Wimming.	Music.	
ˢwimming.		
	L :10 Wivii.	
B : 11 Wimming [sung]		
	L :12 Not.	
	M :13 Not.	
	"wiviin," music.	
	L :14 Miswi	
	B :15 Not.	
	M :16 Music	
	B :17 Not.	
	Not.	
H : 18 We go swimming. Yeh, Mummi? Yeh, Mummi?		
	L :19 No moah swimmi'...	
B : 20 ...yeah, Mommy?		
21 Swimmin!	M :22 No moah.	
22 Mommy I'm get down dea-ah.		
[altercation]		
H : 23 Wheə that goes?		
		M : 24 What? [rising]
	H :25 Put on my shoeˢ.	
		M : 26 Fo what?

Example 5.5. *continued*

Initiation	Reply	Escalation/Mediation
	H :27 Put on my shoe-e. [fading]	
		M : 28 We not goi' <u>no</u> place. Jis take it off Turn off dat light.
L : 1 (Mommy, I going.) (suggestion)	M : 2 (Going where?) (requests information) L : 3 (I'm going swimming.) (repeats, clarifies suggestion)	
	M : 4 (No, we cannot go swimming today.) (refusal)	
L : 5 (Later yeah, Mommy?) (prediction)		M : 6 (Because Daddy has to go play music.) (explains refusal)*
	L : 7 (Muswik.) (imitates M) M : 8 (Not "muswik." Music.) (corrects L's pro- nunciation)	
B : 9 ('Wimming. ^Swimming.) (word play, suggests going swimming) B : 11 (Wimming [sung])	L :10 (Wivii.) (word play or imitation) L :12 ⌈(Not swimming.) (contradicts B) ⌊(Not "wiviin," <u>mus</u>ic.) (corrects L)	
	L :14 ⌈Miswi (attempts to imitate M) B :15 ⌊(Not music.) (contradicts M) M :16 ⌈Music. (repeats) B :17 ⌊Not. Not (repeats)	
H : 18 (We go swimming. Yeh, Mummi? Yeh, Mummi?) (suggests) B : 20 (...yeah, Mommy?) (unclear) H : 21 (Swimming! 22 Mommy, I'm going to get down there.) (exclaims, suggests) [altercation]	L :19 ("There will be no swimming...") (takes M's role) M :22 ("There won't be any.")	
H : 23 (Where does that go?) (requests information)	H :25 (Put on my <u>shoes</u>.) (clarifies, suggests) H :27 (Put on my shoe-e, [fading]) (de-escalates suggestion)	M : 24 (What? [rising]) (challenges) M : 26 (What for?) (challenges) M : 28 (We're not going <u>any</u> place. Just take it off. And turn off that light.) (cancels suggestion, interdicts, commands)

*Mediation, see explanation preceding Example 5.4.

The above episode illustrates several characteristic features of the rhetoric of authority. First, the nagging: the 4 year old begins with suggestions (lines 1,5), the older brother picks it up in the form of word play (line 9), and finally the 3-

year-old continues it (lines 18, 21)—all attempts to elicit a response from mother. When Howard persists and makes a direct request for information (line 23), he is challenged, interdicted, and commanded to do something unrelated by mother—all escalations (lines 24,26,28). Clearly, the mother has had enough—perhaps the altercation added to her response—and she reasserts her authority. However, the use of unrelated, corrective commands to reassert authority and perhaps also to distract is characteristic.[12] Another feature is the use of questions to challenge, which is discussed further below.

The older boy's use of word play, and the pronounced contrapuntal nature of the dialogue at that point (see Note 19), suggest that the boy is trying to shift the relationship to a more egalitarian one, since hierarchical relationships between parent and child can be changed by playful teasing, as we shall see in Chapter 7. But it does not succeed here in diverting mother from her ultimate refusal.

We can see in this episode that the rhetoric of authority is being learned when the 4 year old takes the mother's role, after he has been refused, saying to his younger brother, "No *mo*ah swimmi'. . ." (line 19). One can surmise that children who are equals could easily misinterpret simple assertions as intended imperatives. Note in this regard how an identical form of speech has different meaning when it comes from a superior, rather than a subordinate. The child's report, "I going," (line 1) functions as a suggestion (or hint), whereas the mother's report, "We not going *no* place," (line 28) has the force of a command. It is the framing aspect of the objective relationship which renders assertions ambiguous between age peers.

As mentioned above, children can only make requests for things in subdued fashion. Subsequent requests, therefore, are never escalated in urgency. Rather, the reverse occurs: they sound less serious, and may even diminish to a whisper.[13] This is illustrated in the following episode. Here the 3 year old is asking for more drink and being refused until he eats what is on his plate:

Example 5.6. (Charlene, 5 yrs; her friend, Sharilyn, 8 yrs; Molly, 4 yrs; Junya, 3 yrs; Pam, 2 yrs, and Mother)

Initiation	Reply	Escalation
J : Mommy!		
	M : Yes, Bɔ	
[unrelated conversation]		
J : I like some mo-oah.		
	M : Eat first.	
[pause]		
P : Pa-au!		
		Mol: Pa-a-ah
		ca-ahdit out!
		S : You' motha said eat all you' foo-ood.
		P : Ea-eat! [yell]
J : Mommy-y I no wan i-i [whine]		S : Dats right.

Example 5.6. *continued*

Initiation	Reply	Escalation
		C : No! Junya+Boy, eat!
		S,C: [... Baəmby you cannot eat.
		C : O' you comin, real skinny an you no can eat all.
S : [begins narrative to support her point]		C : Yeah, an...mo' 'kinny if you no eat a^wll.
[9 turns of narrative omitted]		
P : Pa-au!		
P : I ea-eat!		
[J and P interact for several turns, spanking and crying follow]		
		M : Now stop it!
J : Maimi-i! I want mo-oah! [repeats 3 times, subsiding]		

Initiation	Reply	Escalation
J : (Mommy!)	M : (Yes, Boy.)	
[unrelated conversation]		
J : ("I want more to drink.")	M : (Eat first.) (refusal)	
[pause]		
P : (Finished!)		
		Mol: (Bo-o-oy cu-ut it out!)
		S : (Your mother said eat all of your foo-ood.) (interdict, argue)
		P : (Ea-eat! [yell]) (command)
J : (Mommy-y I don't want i-i [whine] (pleads)		S : (Dat's right) (supports P)
		C : (No! Junya Boy, eat!) (rejects plea, commands)
		S : [start simultaneously
		C : then stop]
		S : (later you cannot eat.)
		C : ("Or you'll become real skinny and won't be able to eat everything.") (argue to support command)
S : [begins narrative to support her point]		C : ("yeah, and then you'll be more skinny if you don't eat everything."
[9 turns of narrative omitted]		
P : (Finished!)		
P : (I ate it all!)		
[J and P interact for several turns, spanking and crying follow]		
		M : (Now stop it!) (command)
J : (Maimi-i! I want more!) [repeats 3 times, subsiding]		

One never hears a demand addressed to a parent by a child over 2½ years of age on these tapes—nor have I observed any elsewhere—nor a complaint after being turned down. Either type of utterance would be regarded as "talking back," which is the worst offense a child can commit. The rhetoric of authority is so deeply imbedded in Hawaiian parents that they are visibly uncomfortable when Caucasian children make demands in their presence. Note further in Example 5.6 the way in which the girls take on this rhetoric and exercise it on behalf of the mother—even the boy's little sister, age 2 years, and an older friend of the family. All of them train their guns on the boy, sometimes simultaneously—a good example of the use of a verbal routine.

The persistence of children's requests for tangible things suggests that there is some probability, however small, that parents will grant the requests. After all, ignoring or refusing a request goes against a major value in Hawaiian culture. Thus, parents frequently report that "nagging" makes them uncomfortable, particularly when it occurs in public, and they have a hard time not giving in, although they may punish the child instead.

Children have a limited right to initiate interaction with parents when making certain requests, as we have seen. They have a practically unlimited right to initiate talk, however, when they report the misbehavior of siblings. While parents typically respond to these reports as they do to requests for information: long-delayed or not at all, they regard them as legitimate. This is reflected in the confident tone of the children's reports, unlike the tone when requesting information. Children, incidentally, do not reproach one another for these reports, they only try to defend themselves. There is no concept of "tattling." Such a concept presupposes that children regard it as legitimate to evade adult authority without detection, and these children have no such idea. In this, they clearly indicate their acceptance of parental authority. If you get caught, you *should* get caught.

Parental directives and punishment

The rhetoric of authority is enacted most dramatically in punishment. At the opposite in every way from the words which greet the baby are the words of an angry parent who is about to punish a young child. Any act by a baby brings a delighted response, as described in Chapter 7. But a child being punished behaves as if any act would be dangerous, so the child stands meek, silent, and downcast before the angry parent. The precursors to punishment usually follow a routine and predictable course. Certain of its features engrain upon a child's mind a wariness to confrontation and to direct questions that last a lifetime.

Punishment ordinarily results from failure to obey a command issued at some earlier time. When parents first try to get children to do something, they typically issue a series of commands. Children either ignore these or comply only verbally at the start. For instance, in the following, mother was half-heartedly trying to get the children to go outside:

Example 5.7. (Boy, 5 yrs; Lika, 4 yrs; Howard, 3 yrs; Kini, girl, 2 yrs; and Mother)

Initiation	Reply	Escalation
M : Boy!		
	B : Whae'? [rising]	
M : Get out hiyah!		
	B : Okay+wait.	
		M : Get out hi-ir!
	L : Come on, Ba-a. Dis way out.	
		M : Ba-a!
	B : 'Kay [matter of fact]	
		K : Ba-a gaegə.
	H : Out'ide dea.	
	B : You too, yeah?	
	L : Yeah.	
[B continues playing, growling]		
M : Boy, come hiyah!		
	B : Hae?	
M : [silence]		
	B : Whae'?	
M : Put that down.		
	B : Hae? Whea? 'Bout dis one?	
M : Taell Lika get out a hiya.		
	B : Lɪ-ɪta ge yauyi 'ahyah [sloppy].	
[playing continues]		

Initiation	Reply	Escalation
M : (Boy!)		
	B : (What? [insincere])	
M : (Get out of here!) (command)		
	B : (Okay wait.) (accepts, requests)	
		M : (Get out of here!) (repeats, emphasizes)
	L : (Come on, Boy. This way out.) (urges compliance)	
		M : (Bo-oy!) (emphasizes)
	B : (Okay.) (accepts, mollifies)	K : (Bo-oy is shit.) (insults B)
	H : (Outside there.) (suggests compliance)	
	B : (You too, yeah?) (to L)	
	L : (Yeah.)	
M : (Boy, come here!) (modest command, de-escalates)		
	B : (Huh?)	
M : (nonverbal command)		
	B : (What?)	
M : (Put that down.) (repeats command)		
	B : (Huh? Where? This?) (requests clarification)	
M : (Tell Lika to get out of here.) (command)		
	B : (Lika, get out of here.) (complies, distorts, insincere)	
[playing continues]		

Throughout the above incident, it is obvious that Boy knows that he does not have to obey, despite Mother's emphasis. Something about her tone or the situation must have communicated this to him, while the mother confirms it by de-escalating and ignoring noncompliance several times. Firth has given a similar account of such behavior in Tikopia, which is likewise a Polynesian society:

Since promises of punishment are much more frequent than the act itself children, knowing this, are apt to stand their ground despite all commands made to them. Though these be uttered in most peremptory tones the youngsters merely smile. Repetition is necessary to produce any effect, and so much is this a habit that most orders are given automatically three times over at the start! Much talk and little obedience is the impression gained of family discipline in questions of ordinary restraint. (1957: 156)

The parents in these families initially repeat commands numerous times, escalating only by verbal emphasis, complaints, and routinely delivered threats, e.g., "You guys gon git it." In this ritual escalation, no genuine anger is expressed, however, and no punishments follow without signs of genuine anger. This fact contributes to noncompliance, as in the above episode.

Before a child is punished, however, there is usually a definite series of additional cues from the parent: unmistakable signs of anger, specification of the circumstances in which punishment will be meted out, e.g., "If you not pau when I come in dea," and finally a confrontation. The scenario for the final confrontation calls for specification of the command that was violated, followed by accusation and the presentation of evidence. The incriminating evidence is usually elicited by means of a direct question to the accused. Judgment is then announced, often in the form of an insult, e.g., "Stupid!" Punishment follows immediately. While a scolding may be substituted at the last moment, the drama does not appear to be diminished by such a substitution. This general sequence is illustrated in detail by the following episode.

Example 5.8. (<u>B</u>oy, 5 yrs; <u>L</u>ika, 4 yrs; <u>H</u>oward, 3 yrs; <u>Mi</u>chael, cousin, 5 yrs; and <u>M</u>other)

Initiation	Reply	Escalation
M : Boy, you heard what I <u>told</u> you, you keep it ahp an you gon git <u>lickin</u>. I gon make you stay home, Boy!		
[irrelevant material deleted]		
M : You like--you like ^tstay <u>home</u> I tink, dat kiid. [angry]		
[irrelevant material deleted]		
	H : S'ay <u>home</u>.	M : Where's 'a comb? [angry, sharp]
		M : Where's 'a comb?! [rising, high]
[irrelevant material deleted]		
M : Who's go' a comb hurry ahp?		
	Sev: <u>Hiya</u>!	
	L : Mommy I no ba-abe [whine] ...Mo-om	M : Come on, babe! [angry]
[irrelevant material deleted]		
		M : I told you open um and put um inside dea, go on. You open da mout you gon git <u>lickin</u>, Boy, fr nae'.
	B : [silence]	

Example 5.8. *continued*

Initiation	Reply	Escalation
	[from this point all children but H speak in hushed voices]	
		M : If you not pau putting on yo' pants by da time I get tru combing Michel's heya, Bɔ, you gon git good lickin from <u>me</u> an I <u>mean</u> it!
[irrelevant material deleted]		
		M : <u>You</u> betta hurry up, Bɔ! From now on you kids go ^tsleep seven o'clock, instead of <u>nine</u>. Dammit you.
[pause]		
	H : Oh Mommy I do' wɛ-ɛ^ə 'aik <u>diis</u>. [whine]	
	M : [silence]	
? : Lookit Boy. [whisper]		
[irrelevant material deleted]		
M : 'Kay, look ahp, come hiya. [murmur]		
	B : Whe' izat going?	
		M : : Get over here, Bɔ.
	Mi : Yeah, you going?	
	B : Going down dɛz^s, an get Daddy. [murmur]	
		M : Whe's yo' <u>pocket</u>, Bɔ?
	B : [inaudible voice]	
		M : Whe's a pocket fo' dis pan's?
	B : [silence]	
		M : [inspires sharply] Look on yo' <u>pants</u> if get pocket, look+look+look+ look. Izat how you suppose a put on yo' clothes?
	B : [silence]	
		M : Hae? stupid! [slap] Go on an open dat clothes, hurry up.
	B : [silence]	
	M : You gotta go on an open it.	
	B : [a single sob]	
		M : Boy, you try cry.

M : (Boy, you heard what I told you, you keep it up and you're going to get a lickin. I'm going to make you stay home, Boy!) (accuses, warns)		
[irrelevant material deleted]		
M : (You like to stay home, I think--that kid.) [angry] (grumbles, starts to get angry)		
[irrelevant material deleted]		
		M : (Where's that comb?) [angry, sharp] (anger escalates)
	H : (Stay home.) (imitates M)	M : (<u>Where's that comb</u>?!) [rising, high] (impatience increased)
[irrelevant material deleted]		

continued

Example 5.8. *continued*

Initiation	Reply	Escalation
M : ("C'mon who's got a comb?") (ordinary tone, de- escalates)		
	Sev: (<u>Here</u>!)	
		M : (Come on, babe!) [angry] (command, escalates)
	L : (Mommy I'm not a baby! [whine] ...Mo-om) (pleads)	
[irrelevant material deleted]		
		M : ("I told you to take them off and put them inside there. Do it. If you open your mouth you're going to get a <u>lickin</u>, Boy, for that.") (accuses, directs, commands, threatens)
	B : (no reply)	
	[from this point all children but H speak in hushed voices]	
		M : (If you're not finished putting on your pants by the time I get through combing Michael's hair, Boy, you're going to get a good lickin from <u>me</u> and I <u>mean</u> it!) (threatens, specifies circumstances, emphasizes)
[irrelevant material deleted]		
		M : (<u>You</u> better hurry up, Boy! From now on you kids are going to sleep at seven o'clock, instead of <u>nine</u>. Dammit you.) (reminds, threatens, expresses anger)
[pause]		
	H : (Oh Mommy I don't wear [it] like this [whine].) (complains)	
	M : (no reply)	
A : (Lookit Boy.) [whisper]		
[irrelevant material deleted]		
M : (Okay, look up, come here.) [murmur] (announces end of task, end is approaching)		
	B : (Where does that go?) (requests information)	
		M : (Get over here, Boy.) (command, the moment specified has come)
	Mi: (Yeah, are you going?)* (requests information)	
	B : (I'm going downstairs, and get Daddy.) [murmur]	
	B : [inaudible voice] (attempts to avoid incriminating self)	M : (Where's your <u>pocket</u>, Boy?) (accuses, interrupts)
	B : (no reply)	M : (Where's the pocket for these pants?) (repeats--pants are inside out) M : [inspires sharply] ("Look at your <u>pants</u> and see if you have pockets. <u>Look</u>! Is that how you are supposed to put on your clothes?") (mobilizes, calls attention to evidence, accuses with question)
	B : (no reply)	M : (Huh? stupid! [slap] "Go on and take em off, and hurry.") (announces judgment, punishes, commands)
	B : (no reply)	

Example 5.8. *continued*

Initiation	Reply	Escalation
	M : ("You have to go on and take them off.") (admonishes, de-escalating)	
	B : [a single sob] (expresses feeling)	M : (Boy, "just you cry.") (warns)

* This and the following utterance are considered replies because the boys are trying to escape from the punishment to come by avoiding attention.

Although the occasion for the mother's anger is not entirely clear (it probably had to do with his pants being inside out), she makes her mood abundantly clear before taking any action. When it is apparent that she is angry, the children immediately become silent, or speak in subdued fashion, except for the youngest present, who may not know any better. The rest of the episode follows the general description above. Another illustration is provided in Example 5.10 below. I have seen similar enactments in other families also.

Questioning children

As we have just seen, direct questions are used when a parent is about to punish in order to accuse a child of wrong-doing, and to extract from the child's own lips the incriminating evidence. Earlier, in Example 5.5, we saw how the same mother challenged her children by asking questions. It is because of experiences such as these, we believe, that children answer minimally and warily whenever they are questioned directly, even when the parent has no intention of accusing. Consider the following episode in comparison with Examples 5.8 and 5.10.

Example 5.9. (Boy, 5 yrs; Lika, 4 yrs; Howard, 3 yrs; and Mother)

Initiation	Reply	Mediation
M : You guys wen go play downstεiz?		
	B : Yeah.	
M : Not too long, dow, eh?		
	B : [silence]	
M : What you guys was doin?		
	B : Play+ball.	
	L : Fauwa.	
M : Play? Flowa? Whe'+you +guys+ʷgo+pick+up+all+ da+flowers+o'de'? [fast]		
	L : In schoo' [sounds suspicious]	
M : No-ot!		
	L : Yeah!	
M : 'Aei downstεiz?	B : Yeah	
	jes+'ch⌈ool	
	H : ⌊Not 'idahnjahn	
	L : No-ot.	
	M : Shua-ah.	
	L : No-aht!	B : Momma Da'y got dεzdεz?
	M : [silence]	
		B : Dad+go' zdεzdεz?

continued

Example 5.9. *continued*

Initiation	Reply	Mediation
	M : Daddy stay downstɛiz? No, he stay ahpstɛiz. B : Not. H : Dahp'tairs. Up'tairs. B : Not. L : Um hm [affirmative].	

		B : He iit dahctah.
		L : Dɛ'iis--. Yeah,
		    Mummy? De' g'o--
		    go up'tairs, yah?
		    Uptɛ-ɛiz[s]?

M : [ə]guys go see Lani?		
	B : ⎡Yeah. L : ⎣Yeah.	
M : Whea?		
	L : In, Gramma house. M : M-m-m.	
L : Get plaen[s]--get two[s], get plen'y.		
[at this point B and L begin their own conversation]		
M : You guys gon see again?		
	B : ⎡Yeah. [wary] L : ⎣Yeah.	

M : When?
B : Outsi-ide... Y'ahik?
    M-m?
    I goi' outside. Can?		

	L : Ah goii...[whisper]	

M : (Were you guys playing
    downstairs?)
    (requests information)
	B : (Yeah.)
	    (one word reply)	

M : (Not too long, though,
    eh?)
    (comments with q.)
	B : (no reply)	

M : (What were you guys
    doing?)
    (requests information)
	B : (Playing ball.)
	L : (Flowers.)
	    (one word replies,
	    distorted)	

M : (Playing? Flowers?
    Where did you go pick
    all of those flowers?)
    [fast]
    (requests information,
    friendly style)
	L : (At school [sounds
	    suspicious].)	

M : (No-ot!)
    (contradicts, teases)
M : (Is Daddy downstairs?)
    (trick q., see below)
	L : (Yeah! [at school])
	    (minimal reply)
	B : (Yeah
	    just at sch-)
	    (both re-affirm)
	L : ⎡(-ool)
	H : ⎣("He's not downstairs.")
	    (contradicts M,
	    distorts, M's gloss)
	L : (no-ot [downstairs])
	    (contradicts M)
	M : (Su-ure.)
	    (re-affirms)
	L : (No-aht!)
	    (repeats, distorts)
		B : (Momma
		    "is Daddy down-
		    stairs?")
		    (challenges with q.)

	M : (no reply)	B : ("Is Daddy down-
		    stairs?")
		    (repeats, same distortion)

	M : ("Is Daddy downstairs?
	    No, he's upstairs.")
	    (repeats B's q., admits
	    the truth)
	B : (Not.)
	    (contradicts M)
	H : (Upstairs. Upstairs.)
	    (imitates M)	

Example 5.9. *continued*

Initiation	Reply	Mediation
	B : (Not.) (repeats contradiction) L : (Um hm [affirmative]) (joins in affirming)	
		B : ("He's at the doctor.") (argues to support contradiction, dis- torts)
		L : ("Daddy is-- Yeah, Mummy? Daddy went upstairs, yah? Upstairs?") (appeals for confirma- tion of his affirmation)
M : (You guys going to see Lani?) (changes subject, known answer q.)	B : ⌈(Yeah.) L : ⌊(Yeah.) (both give expected answer in unison)	
M : (Where?) (another known answer q.)	L : (At, Granma's house.) (gives expected ans.) M : (M-m-m) (nonverbal comment)	
L : (There's plenty.) (volunteers report)		
[at this point B and L begin their own conversation]		
M : (You guys going to see her again?) (resumes known answer q.)	B : ⌈(Yeah.) [wary] L : ⌊(Yeah.) (both give expected answer in unison)	
M : (When?) (M knows answer better than they do)	B : (no reply) L : (no reply)	
B : (Outside... "You want to go?" M-m? I'm going outside. Can I?) (suggests to L, requests permission)	L : (I'm going... [whisper]) (doesn't wait for M's reply)	

This is one of the longest parent-child conversations on the tapes. Note that Mother initiates and controls the dialogue. She changes subjects and routines unpredictably, while her known answer questions, by calling for known answers, control the children's replies. In these circumstances, they respond warily and almost as minimally as they would during punishment. The one time a child volunteers any information is when the mother ceases her questioning and says, ''mm.'' Their attitude is also revealed by the fact that they withdraw from the situation before the mother is finished. Individual children's replies to direct questions during friendly conversations with me were similarly brief, compared to their utterances when I was not questioning, as reported earlier (Boggs 1972). It is clear from evidence such as this that children are not accustomed to the use of questions by adults as an invitation to conversation. The absence of conversational questions in speech addressed to infants bears this out (see Chapter 7). Questions come to be associated, therefore, primarily with interrogation, which occurs in a hierarchical mode of speaking. The use of questions in punishment, as the following episode indicates, is nearly identical with their use in the foregoing conversation. The family in this case was different.

Example 5.10. (Charlene, 5 yrs, and Father)

Initiation	Reply	Escalation
		F : ...An who said you $^{\partial z}$gonna run away? Huh? Whe? Whe' you was?
	C : Downstairs [low].	
		F : Whea?
	C : Playin in da fron'.	
		F : What you doin in da front, I say you had to go in da back?
	C : [silence]	
		F : One mo; time, Cha'lene, I find you-u run away from you' sista dem, you gon come home, you gonna git good licking, good, good lickin, Cha'lene, I know you need a ʁcod lickin. Dis stick gon break from cross--right across ova hiya.
		F : ("...and who gave you permission to run away? Huh? Where were you? Where?") (accuses with q.)
	C : (Downstairs) [low] (provides information)	
		F : ("Where downstairs?") (requests incriminating information)
	C : (Playing in the front.) (provides it)	
		F : (What were you doing in the front when I told you to go in the back?) (accuses with q., specifies command that was violated)
	C : (no reply) (no reply possible)	
		F : (One more time, Charlene, "if I find that you ran away from your brother and sisters, you're going to get a good licking, a real good licking, Charlene. Because I know that you need a good licking. This stick is going to break right here on you.") (threatens, specifies circumstances, emphasizes, scolds)

In the above episode and the foregoing conversation, direct questions are used to obtain information about the child's whereabouts and activities. In both, the adult is also directing and controlling what is said. Children apparently see such events as similar, for they response with similar caution.

This analysis has some implications for education. As Gumperz has pointed out, and we have noted in discussing recitation in Chapter 1, teaching frequently involves adult-controlled, one-sided speech events:

(The teacher) sees the activity as . . . one in which the relevance of utterances is determined by her alone, and children's production is almost entirely in response to her elicitation. The entire episode takes the form of a sequence of questions and answers. The teacher's implicit authority is reflected in the fact that she assumes the right to continue questioning even in the face of no response. (Gumperz and Herasmchuk 1972: 118)

Under circumstances such as these, one would predict that these Hawaiian children would respond warily, and probably therefore less well intellectually, than they would in a freer exchange. This is one reason why they rebel in typical classroom recitations, as suggested in Chapter 9.

This analysis suggests that teachers not attempt to control verbal production, but instead respond more to the initiative of students in discussion. The results of such an attempt, as practiced at KEEP, are presented in Chapter 10. At KEEP, the technique appears to increase involvement in teacher-student dialogue during reading lessons, and thus leads to greater intellectual involvement in learning to read.

In conclusion, evidence presented in this chapter indicates that the rhetoric of authority is expressed in parents' right to question, command, and correct and the child's obligation to make requests in a subdued fashion. When challenged, the full weight of authority is brought to bear upon the culprit in punishment that totally inhibits his or her slightest reaction. The results of such authority appear to be deep, early, and long-lasting. Children as young as 3 years of age refrain from making demands, and request in subdued and indirect ways. They are patient and persistent in requesting. Children become sensitive to one-sided, adult-controlled speech events, and particularly to direct questioning in such an event.

Older children appear to imitate the rhetoric of parental authority with younger children, particularly girls speaking to younger boys (see Example 5.6, and Chapter 3). But when children the same age interact, this same rhetoric does not work. Relative status is not fixed, yet each perceives the other to be speaking in a hierarchical mode and resists. The result is the rhetoric of conflict, to which we now turn.

CHAPTER 6

Contradicting: The Rhetoric of Conflict

Part-Hawaiian children can frequently be observed to use a forceful "Not!" as an outright contradiction of another speaker. This is the most easily recognized element of a routine that is here termed the "contradicting routine" (2.3 in Appendix 2). This routine provides the form for the rhetoric of conflict. This chapter describes the form and functions of this routine as it develops from early childhood to adolescence. While the routine is not limited to part-Hawaiians by any means, their use of it concerns us here because of the unique role that it plays in the development of the egalitarian principle in Hawaiian culture.

We have already seen in Chapter 4 that disputing is endemic in relations among same-aged peers. It accompanies a hypersensitivity to assertiveness, which grows out of experience in hierarchical relationships among siblings. Such sensitivity is enhanced when children transfer the rhetoric of authority, which is copied from parents and applied in sibling relations, to their relationship with same-aged peers. Use of the rhetoric of authority contributes to the tendency to perceive even simple allegations as assertiveness, i.e., as claims to have, know, or have experienced some particular thing. Contradicting is a natural response to perceived assertiveness. But the contradicting routine itself originates in a startlingly different manner. Children are inducted into this routine by parents and other adults as a means of playful teasing in which adult and child act as equals (1.1.3 in Appendix 2). In form, the routine thus originates in the rhetoric of equality, not in true conflict.

As children grow older and experience many unresolved and dissatisfying disputes with their peers, another change occurs. As mentioned in Chapter 4, humor (2.2.6 in Appendix 2) appears to intrude more often or more successfully into circumstances that occasion disputing, so as to resolve or prevent it. By adolescence, "Not!" has become a metaphor for childish dispute, itself a joke. The contradicting routine, at least this form of it, thus regains its original place as part of the rhetoric of equality. Since it has a playful meaning to adults, it is natural for them to introduce it into playful episodes with their children. This helps us to understand why parents who are so concerned about hierarchy should introduce the rhetoric of equality to their children.[14] There is no evidence that versions of verbal play such as those described in Chapter 2 were used with children in the past. The analysis presented here would lead one to expect that they were.

In this chapter, we first examine the social significance of the contradicting routine as it is originally experienced by the very young child in the parent-child relationship and with older siblings. We then examine its formal pattern and functions among age peers from 4 to 12 years of age. We shall see here that the routine lacks the power to transform serious disputing about assertiveness into play. The humor that finally helps to resolve this impasse comes not from contradicting, it turns out, but from various forms of verbal play.

Initial experience of the routine

Children engage in the contradicting routine with parents from a very young age. The parent initiates with a patently false statement, threat, or insult, which the child then contradicts. Repetitions typically lead into taunting, playful threats, challenges, and mock fighting (1.1.2 in Appendix 2, illustrated in Chapter 7). For example, in one family, an infant grandchild has been brought to visit. Everyone's attention is immediately focused on the baby, and, after warm greetings, much laughter, and excited talk by all, the following occurs.

Example 6.1. (Ellen, 8 yrs; Lupe, cousin, 5 yrs; and Fa, grandfather)

Initiation	Reply	Escalation
Fa: Shut up you guys. Me the king!		
	L : No! yer not the ki-ing!	
	Fa: Yeh, me the king.	
	E : The baby is the king.	
	L : The baby is the king.	
		Fa: Ah, all you fela git lickin, ds why.
	L : No-ot!	
[as tape runs out Fa says: "What!"]		
Fa: (Shut up you guys. I'm the king!) (joking claim, inviting contradiction)		
	L : (No! you're not the ki-ing!) (contradicts)	
	Fa: (Yeh, I'm the king.) (re-affirms)	
	E : (The baby is the king.) (counter-alleges)	
	L : (The baby is the king.) (imitates E)	Fa: ("Ah, I'm the king because I give the lickins.")
	L : (No-ot!)	(joking threat)

It is obvious in this case that the grandfather deliberately provoked the children into disputing his claim. It is interesting that the younger of the two girls is the first to pick it up and that she, rather than the older one, continues it. She may take it more seriously than the older one, who is more familiar with the routine.

Parents deliberately tease their young children in play by contradicting them, and they in turn tease the parent in the same way. The following occurred in another family. In this case the routine was initiated by the child.

Example 6.2. (Boy, 5 yrs; Lika 4 yrs; and Mother) (M has just ordered L to leave the tape recorder alone. He responds by announcing his intention to do something that M has to participate in.)

Initiation	Reply	Escalation
L : I call ə' gramma.		
		M : You call gramma your neck.
B : Ne^{y}k.		
	M : You' neck.	
	B : Your neck.	
		M : Skinny!
	B : Skinny.	
	M : You! Skin-ny$^\varepsilon$!	
	B : Bwa-a!	
	M : Bwa-a skinny [taunting].	
	L : ...'kinny, Bwa-a	
M : Leave dat phone alone. You heard me!?		sik-⏌ [moves to pick up phone]
	L : Whoa-at!?	
M : Leave um alo-one! Oh-h boy [sigh]. You wats out dat phone faw down 'n broke you guys gon get it.		
	B : Yeah, get it [affected].	
	L : Yaes? You too, Mommy?	
B : zum zum [hum]		
	M : Yu-^{ow}!	
	L : Yu-^{ow}!	
	B : Yu-^{ow}!	
	M : Shut ap.	
	B : Yu-^{ow}!	
	L : Yu-^{ow}!	
	M : Yu-^{ow}!	
	all repeat again	
L : (I call up gramma.) (announces)		
		M : ("You do and it'll be your neck.") (joking threat)
B : Ne^{y}k. (word play)		
	M : (Your neck.) (contradicts B)	
	B : (Your neck.) (contradicts M)	
		M : ("Shrimp" or "little penis") (insults)
	B : (Skinny.) (imitates M)	

Example 6.2. *continued*

Initiation	Reply	Escalation
	M : (You are skinny!) (contradicts, stylistic emphasis)	
	B : (Bo-oy!) ("I'm Bo-oy!")	
	M : ("Boy is a shrimp [taunting].")	
	L : ("...skinny. Boy is--	
M : (Leave that phone alone You heard me!?) (ritual interdict, warning)	(imitates M)	ski-" [moves to pick up phone]) (teases while engaging in routine)
	L : ("You're not serious.")*	
M : (Leave it alo-one! Oh-h boy [sigh]. You watch out if that phone falls and breaks you guys are going to get it.) (repeats interdict and warning, grumbles)†		
	B : ("I'll bet.")	
	L : ("Oh yeah? What about you? You'll get it, too.") ("Yes" is sassy.)	
B : zum zum [hum] (significance not known--music to sass by?)		
	M : ("Not me. You.") (contradicts both)	
	L : (You.)	
	B : (You.)	
	M : (Shut up.) (interdicts)	
	[contradicting continues for 6 turns]	

*Mother typically indicates disbelief with "What?"—see Example 5.5.

†for a comparable instance see Example 5.5.

It is noteworthy that the disobedience and sassiness expressed by both boys in this exchange, particularly after the mother's order to leave the phone alone, would have brought a slap if the mother had not been joking. The boys, however, read her mood correctly. Note also the use of word play by Boy to provoke her into the routine. He may have tried the same ploy in Example 5.5, as suggested there. A little later on the same tape, the mother initiates the routine herself:

Example 6.3. (Lika, 4 yrs; Howard, 3 yrs; and Mother)

[M has just lured all four of her children into a wrestling match with her. After much laughter, delighted squeals, etc.:]

M: [sigh] You ugəly, yeah?

L: You galy.

M: You!

L: Youə!

M: You ugəly.

continued

Example 6.3. *continued*

L: You galy.

M: You loo' lai'ᵊ monkey [laugh].

L: Jis die, man, ʰu monkey [laugh].

M: You-u [breaks up laughing] ⌈look like

L: ⌊You!

M: one monkey, <u>you</u>

L: You-u!

(M tries to draw Boy into it, accuses him of looking like a donkey, Dracula, and Monster. L and H imitate her and Boy laughs and wrestles. She also threatens to "twist you guys' head [penis] like the snake." She also calls them "skinny" and "puka" [vagina]. Finally:)

M: Guys drivin me ap da <u>wa</u>-all.

H: Wa-aw.

M: Oh, my brains is going ʌp in diɛ-ɛᵊz [airs].

L: In dɛ-ɛᵊ.

M: In d'ɛ-ɛrz!

L: Dᵊ ɛ-ɛᵊz. Ma <u>pocket</u>.

M: Yo-oa pockˡ, yo' pockˡ is turn inside out like your brai<u>n-nz</u>!*

L: Yaes, Mommy!

M: <u>Yu</u>-ᵒʷ!

───

*For meaning of this see Example 5.8.

This incident illustrates particularly well the playful mood of the contradicting routine when children are relating to parents.[15]

The formal pattern and its consequences among peers

Despite its salience, "Not!" occurs less often than other forms of contradiction, such as denial, correction, and counter-claim (20 compared to 40). There are no differences in function of the different forms of contradiction, however, so we regard them as equivalent. The contradicting routine typically begins with an assertion, claim, or allegation which is contradicted. From that point, the original assertion, etc., may be repeated, or a supporting allegation, argument, or appeal to authority may be introduced. The former is illustrated by Example 6.1 above, and by Exchange 1 in Example 6.8 and Exchanges 1 and 2 in Example 6.7 below. The latter is illustrated by Example 6.4. Either way, a challenge is likely to follow in the form of an objection or question, which is answered by a supporting allegation, argument, or appeal to authority, as in Examples 6.5 and 6.6. The routine may escalate at any point to insult, followed by counter-insult, threat, or trial, as in Example 6.7. A threat or trial may be verbal and/or nonverbal, as in Example 6.8.

Example 6.4. (Manny and Fiti, 10 yrs)

Initiation	Reply	Escalation
M : Ge' one hole in da back ...an dey sneak in too. [material deleted]		
	F : Not get one hole in da back!	
	M : Yes	
		...an dey come by da steps.
M : (There is a hole in the back...and they sneak in too.) (reports) [material deleted]		
	F : (There is not a hole in the back!) (contradicts)	
	M : (Yes (contradicts)	(...and they come to the steps.) (argues with sup- porting report)

Example 6.5. (Tui, Manny, and Warren, 10 yrs)

Initiation	Reply	Escalation
		T : Yeah, Mister Steve,
T : nobody never write the words on the rock, yeah?		
	? : Not!	
	W : Some guys did. Ma fren' did.	
		M : Who-o?
	W : Ma fren' Homa-a. Dey bring up de' car and dey wipe da kine--dey spray da paint. Sprayed it on top da waw'.	
		T : (Yeah, Mister Steve, (appeals to authority)
T : nobody wrote the words on the rock, yeah?) (alleges fact)		
	? : (Not!) (contradicts)	
	W : (Some guys did. My* friend did.) (argues with sup- porting report)	
		M : (Who-o?) (challenges with q.)
	W : (My friend Homer. They brought up their car and they wiped that-- they sprayed the paint. Sprayed it on the wall.) (argues with supporting report)	

* Argument follows an appeal to authority, hence is not escalating
according to the rules set forth below.

Example 6.6. (continued from Example 6.4: M̲anny and F̲iti)

Initiation	Reply	Escalation
	F : [hotly] I know mo ... than you̲.	
	M : I knew̲, I knew long time.	
		F : I be+chu! [pause] Who wen broke dat?
	M : [pause] Who̲-o? [rising and falling intonation]	
	F : Who wen broke dat? [matter of fact]	
	M : I do' know but. ...somebody tow' me dat [low].	
	F : ([hotly] I know more* ...than you̲.) (argues with supporting claim to know)	
	M : (I knew̲, I knew for a long time.) (argues with counter-claim)	
		F : (I bet you̲! [pause] Who broke that [board]?) (challenges with trial and q.)
	M : [pause] ("Are you asking me who?" [rising and falling intonation]) (counter-challenge)	
	F : ("That's right," who broke that?) (repeats challenge)	
	M : ("I'm not sure." Somebody told me that [low].) (surrenders, while appealing to authority)	

* Note "th" in text, which is rare.

Example 6.7. (L̲inton and W̲arren, 12 yrs)

Initiation	Reply	Escalation
Exchange 1		
		L : Ey! Mista Steve,
L : you se' dis is ten times campin?		
	W : T'ird.	
	L : Ten! Y-you said ten.	
Exchange 2		
	W : I said third̲, man̲! [loud]	
	L : Ten.	
Exchange 3		
		W : You stinky,
	W : I said third!	
		L : You get stink mout,
	L : you said ten.	
		W : You get stink bo̲to
		[continue with more insults]

Example 6.7. *continued*

Initiation	Reply	Escalation
Exchange 1		
		L : (Ey! Mister Steven, (requests confirmation of claim by W)
L : you said this is the tenth time you went camping?) (reports claim by W)		
	W : (Third.) (contradicts, corrects L)	
	L : (Ten! You said ten.) (repeats report)	
Exchange 2		
	W : (I said <u>third</u>, <u>man</u>!* [loud]) (repeats correction, stylistic emphasis)	
	L : (Ten.) (repeats report)	
Exchange 3		
		W : (You stinky, (insults)
	W : I said third!) (repeats correction)	
		L : (You have a stink mouth, (returns insult)
	L : you said ten.) (repeats report)	
		W : (You have a stink penis.) (returns insult)
		[continue with more insults]

* Note "th" in text--rare.

There is a tendency for disputes to escalate: a challenge or insult cannot be strongly answered by repeating a prior assertion, claim, or allegation. An interdiction, e.g., "shut up," "stop that," may occur at any point in the routine. Speakers appear to use it unpredictably when they cannot think immediately of an adequate reply, so as not to be left without a reply.[16]

The examples of disputing presented above and throughout the book show which utterances were regarded as "initiation," "reply," or "escalation." Wherever used, an "initiation" is an utterance containing reference to a given topic which is not preceded by another utterance in the same routine and topic. "Replies" and "escalations" are utterances which are relevant and predictable following a preceding utterance in a given routine and topic. In the contradicting routine, escalations consist of supporting arguments, allegations, or appeals to authority following contradiction, introduction of a challenge following a supporting argument, etc., and introduction of insult (or accusation), counter-insult, etc., following any utterance. Otherwise they are replies.[17]

Disputes are most likely to end following any sequence with both parties "grumbling," i.e., complaining about one another, often recalling past grievances. Occasionally, blows may be exchanged, but in any event once a dispute has begun it is rarely resolved to the mutual satisfaction of the participants. There do not appear to be any means of resolving disputes once begun. This is partly

Table 6.1. Age and Functions of Contradiction

	Age	
	5–8 years	10–12 years
Function	Number of instances	
To claim object, age, status; or to shift blame.	11	11
Directions to another.	4	2
To deny allegations and report.	5	22
To defend self in discourse.	1	4
Totals	21	39

Source: All contradictions occurring in the contradicting routine (2.3 in Appendix 2) classified according to single most salient function.

due to the lack of any forms of mitigation. Requests for confirmation of assertions from peers, for example, are rare. Most allegations, not to mention other utterances in disputes, are posed in a direct, forceful form. This tends to generate a perception of the speaker as assertive. And this may in fact be the case, since each is trying to assert his or her equality.

What are the functions of contradiction among age peers? Among children 5 to 8 years of age, contradiction is used most often to contest another's claim to such things as objects, age, or other status (including roles in play); to shift blame; and to dispute directions. It is used less often to contest claims of knowledge or simple allegations of fact, as indicated in Table 6.1.

A contest over age is illustrated in the following, which is the longest dispute recorded at any age. It occurred between siblings who were only 1 year apart in age. It is interesting to note that the two rarely disputed. Usually, the younger acted as the cooperative lieutenant, as described in Chapter 3.

Example 6.8. (Charlene, 5 yrs; Molly, 4 yrs; and Sharilyn, friend, 8 yrs)

Initiation	Reply	Escalation
Exchange 1		
C : ...Momma, how o'd--	M : Five.	
	C : [to S] Her fo'.	
	M : No, I five.	
Exchange 2		
		C : I five.
	M : I five.	
Exchange 3		
	C : I'm five [fast].	
		M : T^{ry} ask Mommy.
	C : [silence]	
		M : T^{r}a'k Mommy!

Example 6.8. *continued*

Initiation	Reply	Escalation
Exchange 4		
	M : 'ai Mommy sɛ' me^{y}an you-u fi-ive!	
	C : 'm'm [mouth closed]	
	M : Da Mommy, Mommy sɛ' me^y an you five.	
[C appeals to Mother for confirmation of brother's age Mother does not respond]		
Exchange 5		
M : Mo'i me and her wouldn't ea-at!		
	[Mother does not respond]	
Exchange 6		
M : Five		
	C : [to S] Her not five.	
		Her not in kindəgarten.
Exchange 7		
	M : Mommy, I go ^{t}schoo'?	
	C : Da man--Mommy sai'--	
	M : No, wha' my mothə say--me an her is	
Exchange 8	fi-ive!	C : Ae-ae you bu'laia!
		M : You cry I put dis ...inside ə you' eye.
Exchange 9		
		M : Blinked you' eye.
		C : You blinked your eye.
Exchange 1		
C : (Momma, how old--) (requests information from Mother)	M : (Five.) (claims age)	
	C : [to S] (She's four.) (contradicts, corrects M)	
	M : (No, I'm five.) (contradicts, repeats claim)	
Exchange 2		
		C : ("I'm the one who is five.") (argues)
	M : ("I'm the one who is five.") (returns argument)	
Exchange 3		
	C : (I'm five [fast].)* (argues, stylistic shift)	
		M : ("Just ask Mommy.") (challenges)
	C : (no reply)	
		M : ("Just ask Mommy!) (repeats with stylistic emphasis)
Exchange 4		
	M : ("My Mommy said that we are both five.") (argues, quotes authority)	
	C : 'm'm [mouth closed] (contradicts, style inversion)	
	M : ("The Mother, Mother said we are both five.") (repeats, stylistic de-emphasis)	

continued

Example 6.8. *continued*

Initiation	Reply	Escalation
	[C appeals to Mother for confirmation of brother's age Mother does not respond]	

Exchange 5

M : ("Ma, she and I are not eating!") (attempts to gain Mother's attention)†	[Mother does not respond]	

Exchange 6

M : (I'm five.) (repeats claim, de-escalates)	C : [to S] (She's not five. (contradicts)	She's not in kinder-garten.) (argues)

Exchange 7

	M : (Mommy, I go to school?) (appeals to Mother for evidence) C : (The man--Mommy said--) (starts to quote authority) M : ("No, what my Mother said is that we are both	

Exchange 8

	fi-ive!") (quotes authority)	C : (Ae-ae, you're a bull-liar') (dismisses, insults) M : (You will cry if I put this in your eye.) (threatens trial by ordeal)

Exchange 9

		M : (You blinked your eye.) (claims victory) C : (You blinked your eye.) (counter-claims)

---

* Note use of "I'm" in text, which is rare.

† For use of reporting to gain attention see Chapter 5.

Among children 10 to 12 years of age, there is a difference: contradiction more often arises from the discourse itself, rather than circumstances outside the discourse. It is used to deny a simple allegation or report where the speaker is making no claim other than the knowledge of what he is talking about, as illustrated in the following episode.

Example 6.9. (Tui, Fiti, and Andrew, 10 yrs. Another adult present.)

Initiation	Reply	Escalation
T : ...den aftʒ that we gon call the policeman. [material deleted] Den he wn go wake up came...sometin-	me: Um hm. [others not paying attention]	
T : Da ahm-- policeman come. An den--um--an den--um da monster-- um-um--den da police-	me: m-m-m-m.	

Example 6.9. *continued*

Initiation	Reply	Escalation
man--come in...an was one dead--an--an de'-- an den whe'--whe'-- when we		
...		F : Hae! You a laia!
T : ... [stammers on]		A : Laia!
	T : Some guys do like dat [low]. [2 turns omitted]	F : Hae, a laia.
	me: You mean call a police-man?	
	T : Yeah.	
	me: The policeman come in?	
	T : Yeah, but--	
		F : Fat lai-ia! He keeps [gibberish].
T : (...then after that we were going to call the policeman.) [material deleted] (Then when he woke up something...came) (narrative clauses)	me: Um hm. [others not paying attention]	
T : (The-- policeman came. And then--the monster--then the policeman--came in ...and one was dead --and then--when-- when we--	me: m-m-m-m.	
...		F : (Hae! You're a liar!) (accuses, insults)
T : ... [stammers on]		A : (Liar!)
	T : (Some guys do that [low].) (argues to defend self) [2 turns omitted]	F : (Hae, a liar.)
	me: (You mean call a policeman?) (request for clari-fication)	
	T : (Yeah.)	
	me: (The policeman came in?) (attempt to return to story)	
	T : (Yeah, but--)	
		F : (Fat liar! He keeps [gibberish].) (accuses, insults T, enacts speaking nonsense)

It could be argued that the narrator, Tui, may be claiming a status because of his association with the event (''we gon call the policeman''), but it seems that his accuser is reacting more to the factual unlikelihood of the alleged event—he is accusing the narrator of telling an untrue story. As reported earlier (Boggs 1978b), these children do not deliberately make unsupportable allegations at any time, unlike White American children (Brenneis and Lein 1977), because to do so would subject the speaker to the kind of ridicule illustrated above. Here is a prime contrast with the use of contradiction by parents, for they do make incredi-ble allegations and threats in playful disputes (see Example 6.3 above). But they were joking, and children are not joking with one another when they are disput-ing. It is serious.

Factual inadequacy is only one issue, however. Closely tied to it is the claim of the speaker to possess knowledge of the fact. Thus, David in the following episode is not so much interested in the facts of the case as he is in Kevin's claim to know them. The two had been feuding for hours before this exchange.

Example 6.10. (Kono, Kevin, and David, 10 yrs)

Initiation	Reply	Escalation
me: ...Kono, what happen' to your <u>foot</u> the other day, huh? Wha' was dat?		
	Ko: Ah gŏt--a kind of--	
[irrelevant material deleted]		
me: Wha'd you--you said --	Ko: Uh-	
Ke: <u>Ya</u>	-ʰh-	
even <u>me</u>! Hit the <u>san'</u>!		
	D : Hae, shut up,	
		you know evyting.
	Ko: Not hit the sae--uh --when I was swimmi' ⁿaet--stʌf--ⁿaet cramp came ahtch... [continues story]	

me: (...Kono, what happened to your <u>foot</u> other day, huh? What was that?) (request repetition of prior story)		
	Ko: (I got--a kind of--) (stalling, note nasalization)	
[irrelevant material deleted]		
me: (What'd you--you said --) (repeat request)	Ko: (Uh-	
Ke: (<u>Yah</u> me too! Hit the sand!) (claims experience referred to)	-h-) (continues stall)	
	D : (Hae, shut up, (interdicts)	you know everything.) (accuses, insults Ke)
	Ko: (Not hit the sand-- when I was swimming that--thing--that cramp "made me go ou-utch."...) (contradicts Ke, improvises different story)	

In Chapter 4, it was argued that children this age are exceedingly sensitive to any sign of assertiveness in peers. That would appear to be borne out by episodes like Example 6.10, in which claims to know are the basis of a dispute.

We have, then, from age 5 to 10 years an increased use of contradiction to contest simple allegations and reports. There is, moreover, a tendency for disputes to begin as contradiction and end in insult, threat, or trial, even in actual blows. Verbal disputing appears to have reached an impasse, failing to resolve the grounds that give rise to it. Moreover, this occurs simultaneously with increased verbal disputing for its own sake. What is the solution to such an impasse?

The resolution of disputes

As argued in Chapter 4, a decline in the frequency of disputing comes about partly as a result of learning to tolerate hazing by older siblings and relatives and to negotiate rules for structuring competition in games and sports, at least for boys. But verbal means also contribute directly to the resolution and prevention of disputes. Humor enters into more disputes as well as the circumstances that give rise to them, and this helps to prevent or resolve disputes. What I have termed "situational joking" (2.2.6 in Appendix 2) begins to displace contradicting past the age of 10 in boys. Situational joking consists of exaggerated threats, interdiction, word play, allegations, sharp rejoinders, and buffoonery intended to cause laughter. Instances in which everyone ended up laughing have been classified as situational joking (to distinguish it from the telling of genre jokes). The same tapes from which the disputes were extracted were examined for episodes of situational joking. All of the latter were found to occur in the same circumstances that frequently led to disputes, such as sharing treats of food and drink, keeping score in a competitive game, giving directions to peers, and discussing one's own skills, injuries, etc. Thus, it was inferred that situational joking might either terminate or prevent disputes. Comparing the number of disputes that did not end in situational joking (i.e., with all laughing) with the number of instances of situational joking on the same tapes, there was a difference in the two age groups, as shown in Table 6.2.

These figures are not definitive, since they do not represent a systematic sampling of events from the children's lives, nor the identical individuals.[18] An actual connection between humor and the resolution or prevention of disputes is illustrated in particular episodes, however. Thus, assertiveness was ridiculed in one classic episode:

Example 6.11. (David, Warren, Kono, and others, 10 yrs)

Initiation	Reply	Escalation/mediation
D : 1 an plus da cop, da FBI came to oua class.		
	W : 2 Not!	
	D : 3 Aes right.	
	W : 4 Aeh, d'+uy neva come to oua class [nasal].	
	K : 5 No, aes fo, ony fo me, Fat, n Cha'lie n de', aes wha'.	
	D : 6 Shut aep.	
		K : 7 You two ddu know. *
	D : 8 Not "you ddu know"--	
	K : 9 Da+p'li-is, da+p'li-is--	
	D : "you don'#know." **	

[10 turns deleted in which I try to determine what happened]

continued

Example 6.11. *continued*

Initiation	Reply	Escalation/mediation
		K: 10 Y'got one broken step, an, o'a dea--on--you come undaneat da-- y'craw' straight. y'come diis one, y' come out [gesturing].
	me:11 Uh huh.	
	D :12 Stop,	
		you know everything, eh?
		K:13 Yeh, an you know everything, eh, dduddu tru yo nose.
	D :14 Ya-ya--[breaks up]	
	[general laughter for several minutes]	

Initiation	Reply	Escalation/mediation
D : 1 (And also the cop, the FBI came to our classroom.) (preposterous allegation)		
	W : 2 (Not!) (contradicts)	
	D : 3 (That's right.) (affirms)	
	W : 4 (Aeh, the guy didn't come to our class- room [nasal].) (contradicts, derisively)	
	K : 5 (No, that was only for me, Fat, and Charlie and those guys, that's what.) (corrects W and D)	
	D : 6 (Shut up.) (interdicts K, sassy)	K : 7 (You two don't know.)* (challenges, accuses D and brother with excited style)
	D : 8 (It's not "you ddu know"--)	
	K : 9 (The police, the police--)	
	D : (It's "you don't know.") ** (corrects K's pronunciation)	

[10 turns deleted in which I try to determine what happened]

Initiation	Reply	Escalation/mediation
		D : 10 (There's one broken step and, over there-- you go underneath the-- you crawl straight. You come to this one and you come out like this [gesturing].) (explicates a disputed fact, mediation)
	me: 11 Uh huh.	
	D : 12 (Stop, (interdicts K)	
		you know everything, eh?) (challenges, accuses K)
		K : 13 (Yeh, and you know everything, eh, dduddu through your nose.) (returns accusation, insults, quoting D's correction)
	D : 14 (Ya-ya-- [breaks up])	
	[general laughter for several minutes]	

---

   * dd is a trill.

   ** # is prolonged juncture. Note that D stresses the uncorrected morpheme.

For a description of mediation see Chapter 7.

Table 6.2. Age and Relative Frequency of Situational Joking vs Disputing

	Age	
	10–11 years	**11–12 years**
	Number of instances	
Disputes without situation joking	20	6
Situational joking	9	8

Source: All occurrences of situational joking (2.2.6) and disputing (2.3 in Appendix 2) which did not end in general laughter.

The principal antagonists in this episode were W and K, who spoke as one team, versus D and his brother (who is referred to but does not speak in the above excerpts). When D accused K of "knowing everything," i.e., of being assertive (line 12), K adroitly returned the accusation, adducing by means of mimicry an earlier instance in which D corrected him (line 13). K's "yeh, an you know everything, eh" can be interpreted to mean, "Yeh, just like you." *Dduddu* tru yo nose" is funny because it connotes a genre of local jokes about runny noses ("hanabata") and also is a pun on "dudu," meaning shit. It is important to note that everyone laughed, including the target of the event—and the dispute ended. While the episode occurred among 10- rather than 12 year olds, it illustrates the point, nonetheless, as Kono was an accomplished stylist and acknowledged verbal leader.

The following episode illustrates how humor prevented serious disputing over the sharing of treats at a drive-in. Fiti put on a begging performance that lasted more than half an hour and frequently left the participants helpless with laughter. A sample of it is presented:

Example 6.12. (Fiti, Wesley, Robert, Donnie, and Cha'lie, 12 yrs)

```
    Initiation                    Reply                         Escalation

[F has been excluded from the sharing]

F : three, fo, five.  ...
    I'm getting five guys.
    ...Ahm bʌs um ʌp in
    a tia's.  [laugh]
                                  W :  Name da five guys.
                                       Name da five guys.

                                  F :  Cannot do.

                                  W :  How many guys?

                                  F :  Five.  [counts]
```

continued

Example 6.12. *continued*

Initiation	Reply	Escalation
R : Da Jackson Five.		
	F : Da Jackson Five	
		an da two popolo niiga.
	[laughter]	
		[later, approaching a boy eating a banana split]
F : Hey, man, buy me s∧metiin. I h∧ngry! ..Bamby I gon smash dat ∧p!		
		[acts out doing it]
	[laughter]	
	C : [breaking up] You makin me <u>laugh</u>!	
? : Ae! Sh∧t ∧p! you guys.		
		? : Shut you' ass.
		? : Shit.
F : One time I get my <u>bazooka</u>. You ⌈guy go right down.		
D : ⌊Piss in dɪ ass.		
[continues]		

[F has been excluded from the sharing]

Initiation	Reply	Escalation
F : (three, four, five. ... I'm getting <u>five</u> guys. I'm going to bust them up in tears.) [laugh] (joking threat)		
	W : (Name the five guys. Name the five guys.) (suggests, encourages)	
	F : (Cannot do it.) (refuses, joking)	
	W : (How many guys?) (encouraging q.)	
	F : (Five.) [counts] (repeats threat)	
R : (The Jackson Five.) (name play, a musical group)		
	F : (The Jackson Five (repeats name play)	
		and the two black niggers.) (joking insult)
	[laughter]	
		[later, approaching a boy eating a banana split]
F : (Hey, man, buy me something. I'm hungry! ...Later I'm going to smash that up!) (begging, fantastic threat)		
		[acts out doing it]
	[laughter]	
	C : ([breaking up] You're making me <u>laugh</u>!)	
? : (Ae! Shut up! you guys.) (invites contradiction, see Example 1 above)		
		? : (Shut your ass.)
		? : (Shit.) (obscene commands)
F : (One time I get my <u>bazooka</u> you ⌈guys will go right down.) (fantastic threat)		
D : ⌊(Piss in the ass.)		

Here Fiti burlesqued the role of beggar willing to go to fantastic lengths to get what he wanted. This could touch memories of disputes over treats going back to early childhood. But while Fiti was skillful, his performance was a collective effort nonetheless. Others encouraged him and contributed such routines as name play ("Da Jackson Five"), interdicting ("Shut up"), obscenities, and a traditional group joke ("Piss in dɪ ass"). The episode was highly successful from the boys' point of view: there were calls for Fiti to repeat it hours, and even days, later.

In the examples of joking (4.11; 6.1, 6.2, 6.11, and 6.12 above), initiation and reply columns follow the general definitions given above. Escalations are the same as they are in contradicting, but there are certain additions. These include mock punching, obscenities, and physical and vocal approaches to targets who are able to perceive them. Mediations, which are attempts to explain or evaluate what is going on (see Chapter 7 for definition) sometimes occur in joking. When this happens, they are separately labelled, but placed in the same column as escalation for convenience.

It is no accident, we believe, that disputing develops into verbal play, for both are appropriate in relations of equality. By 15 to 16 years of age, serious disputing is rare, as stated in Chapter 4. Outright contradiction, such as the use of "Not!", is most likely to be interpreted, when it occurs, as a joke, because no adolescent would believe that a peer would be so assertive, unless he had lost his cool. By adolescence, individuals respect one another's equality. Humor appears to be one of the factors that helps to make the achievement of equality possible. If contradicting is the rhetoric of conflict, then verbal play and talking story are the rhetoric of solidarity among equals. We turn next to an examination of how they develop.

CHAPTER 7

Verbal Play and Talking Story: The Rhetoric of Solidarity

Stephen T. Boggs and Karen Watson-Gegeo

The rhetoric of solidarity consists of a variety of routines. Some are in the category termed verbal play. Included also are teasing/joking, jingles, riddles, and story-telling. Many of these routines are reminiscent of traditional Hawaiian oral arts, as mentioned in Chapter 2, and it may be that they tend to co-occur because of a traditional association with one another. In any case, talking story today includes all of them. As mentioned in Chapter 1, local people today celebrate solidarity and equality by talking story. Hence the label: rhetoric of solidarity.

The routines just cited are described in this chapter and their use by children illustrated. The functional relationship between story-telling and the other routines is then analyzed. This allows us to suggest how narrative may emerge developmentally from the other routines. The structure of talk-story narrative performances is then defined, following Watson (1975). The role of an adult in promoting narrative performances in groups of children is then discussed. Together, these last two analyses provide the basis for understanding the children's participation in the reading lessons at KEEP, which are discussed in Chapter 10.

The concept of story-telling underwent a profound change in the course of this research. It began with the notion that stories would be told by individuals and responded to by audiences. Instead, we encountered a great variety of verbal and nonverbal routines in groups of children, so that stories were frequently interrupted, told by several children, or disrupted altogether. A turning point in our thinking came as a result of Watson-Gegeo's study of a group of 5- to 7-year-old children in another part-Hawaiian community (Watson 1972, 1975; Watson-Gegeo and Boggs 1977; Boggs and Watson-Gegeo 1978). In 10 months she recorded more stories (155) from Nāpua Team, a group of approximately 55 children, than I had recorded individually from 32 children aged 6 to 8 years over an 18-month period in Aina Pumehana (76). When we compared these data with the recordings made at home, three findings emerged. First, the sessions of

Nāpua Team were full of the same kinds of verbal play routines that had discouraged me. Second, these same routines, but very few narratives, were found in the recordings made at home. Third, upon close analysis it appeared that these routines helped to set the stage for narration and contributed dynamically to a collective, rather than an individual, narrative performance. Instead of such routines preventing the emergence of complex narratives, as had first seemed to be the case, the reverse was true, at least in the circumstances of Nāpua Team. The first and second findings taken together suggested that children did not practice narration much before the age of 5 years at home, but did learn how to relate to one another with a rich variety of verbal routines. The hypothesis that we subsequently reached was that they constructed narrative performances collectively by using these routines to relate to one another in the process of interacting (Boggs and Watson-Gegeo 1978).

Many forms of verbal play are originally experienced as part of the joy and aloha surrounding infants, and they continue to generate humor throughout life. Through a process of development detailed in Chapters 4 and 6, such humor comes to resolve conflict among age peers and to mark the growing acceptance of equality as children grow to adolescence. It is thus natural that persons seeking to relate to each other as equals would use verbal play and other forms of humor to do so. Telling stories is another way of sharing feeling and identifying with one another. So, in this way, verbal play and story-telling both create and symbolize solidarity.

Verbal play and talking to baby

Under this heading are included the routines labelled "free and entertaining" (1.1) in Appendix 2. Several of these, "laughing it up with the kids" (1.1.2) and "teasing contradicting" (1.1.3), have already been defined and illustrated in Chapters 3 and 6. "Word play" (1.1.4) includes various forms of deliberate distortion of speech, such as punning, alliteration, rhyming, and cospeaking, the first three of which are practiced upon one's own speech or another's. Distortion of another's speech functions as a form of teasing, derision, or mockery. A special form of distortion applies to personal names and names made up upon the spot. This is referred to as "name play" (1.1.5).

The child first experiences forms of verbal play in the speech addressed to her or him as an infant (1.1.1 in Appendix 2), and then practices such speech in addressing infants as a young child. As noted in Chapter 2, talking and playing with babies is marked by great aloha and joy—'a'a. Verbal play is part of this, appearing in the form of word and name play, chant-like verbalizations and singing, exclamations of greeting, and suggested dialogue. The six episodes of talking to baby in the recordings contain the following utterances:

Example 7.1. (Adult, Child. Number of episodes shown in parentheses).

C:	ooh, oh, ho, ə, ' ɔh, oh' (repeated or prolonged)(4)
A,C:	ah,aw [repeated or prolonged, with sighing or irony](3)
A,C:	ae, hae, ᵘhae [repeated or prolonged](2)
C:	boo! [with gleeful laugh](2)
C:	bə, bae [prolonged](1)
C:	hello! [nasalized] hel lo (2)
A:	toot! [repeated](1)
C:	umbah [murmured](1)
?:	ṇaṇ [repeated](1)

Chantlike distortions included:

Example 7.2. (Adult, Child)

?:	ho, dow dow!
C:	hel lo, aiy yo
C:	Ca rnəbu', carn bəw, carnə bul. Carn əbul.
?:	bah lah
C:	aw-wah
C:	Dɛz zi zaw [there she saw] Oh yöi yöi yolo. Dəvəlolo [sleepy head-Hawn] oh' oh' lovo lolo Oh' oh' lolo lola. Oh' oh-h. Lolo lolo la [chortle].
C:	Lika doesn't mother's boy! [chanting] Dədə-ə, Lika dədənt mother's wae? [rising intonation]

Active participation of infants is indicated in two of the episodes by cooing or babbling in response. Note that there are few instances of simplification in the above. Rather, the utterances appear to be aimed at playful variation of sound patterning.

Exclamations of greeting and name play occur in one episode in which a new grandchild is brought to visit. It illustrates particularly well how the mood of the occasion is created and reflected by these routines:

Example 7.3. (Andrew, 4 yrs; Eva, sister, 13 yrs; Ellen, cousin, 8 yrs; Kennet, 4 yrs, her brother; Lupe, 5 yrs, cousin; Jim, 2 mos, Father of Andrew and Eva; Aunt)

Aunt:	Hiy's the baby!
El:	Aw-w, I like . . . [fondly]
?:	[laugh] ⌈Hi-i, baby [fondly]
Fa:	⌊Hey-y!
Aunt:	De's da baby!
El:	⌈ Hi, Jim!
L:	⌊ Hi, Jim!
El:	Hi, Jim Jim.

Example 7.3. *continued*

A: Hey! Jim!

Aunt: Come feel a bɛbɛ! C'mon!

L: Hi, Jim Jim-m.

K: Hi, Jim Jim.

sev: [cooing]

L: Jimmy Jim.

El: Didju have good time when I carried you? [rising] When I came d'you' hahs? [rising] Hmm? [rising]

L: [to baby] Know how da tape recʌdʌ stay on, eh? [nervous chortle]

El: Hi, Jim Jim.

Fa: ae-ae-, hae-ae!
      [material deleted]

L: Hi baby, Jim Jim.

El: He name is Jimmy!

L: Jim Jim! Yah? . . . Jimmy and Jim Jim.

Ev: Oh, look at him! He smiling, Ma!
      [continues with Example 6.1]

Ev: Hi, big eye boy!

L: Hi big w——, eye bo-oy-y [laughing].

Like the mainland Americans studied by Ervin-Tripp (1978), Hawaiian adults and children attempt to carry on conversation with infants by suggesting things for them to say, or supplying responses. An example of the former is:

Example 7.4. (Charlene, 5 yrs, and Molly, 4 yrs)

M: Bə-bye Charli-in [to baby].
      (''Say bye bye Charlene.'')

C: [to baby also] Say ''Bye''.

M: Bye a da dzu-dzu [Bye to the sister].

But unlike the adults quoted by Ervin-Tripp, Hawaiians do not address a lot of conversational questions to the infant, nor attempt to repair the infant's utterances so that they make sense. The only speaker to request information from an infant was Ellen in Example 7.3 above. Her mother was a mainland Caucasian. Rather than ask such questions, part-Hawaiians appear to concentrate upon playing with speech sounds, perhaps imagining the infant talking in such a manner. The net effect of such speech to infants may be to encourage children to explore sounds and words. The absence of requests for information in speech to infants once again associates such questions with the rhetoric of correction and punishment (see Chapter 5), rather than the rhetoric of equality, in the child's experience. This constrasts with the overwhelming use of questions by middle-class teachers in conversation with their children (Heath 1982).

Name play

One of the forms of verbal play which continues throughout childhood and beyond is name play. In the following episode, a mother deliberately instructs her young children in this routine (1.3.3 in Appendix 2).

Example 7.5. (<u>B</u>oy, 5 yrs; <u>L</u>ika, 4 yrs; <u>H</u>oward, 3 yrs; and <u>M</u>other)

L:	. . . Tony, Tony, Tony. [a passer-by]
M:	[singing] Tony, Tony Baloney [grinning].
L:	ah-ah ⌐na-at!⌐
B:	⌊Tony⌋ dudu [shit]
	[someone laughs]
H:	<u>Look</u>!
M:	Evyting going Tony dudu evyting dudu. ("Always saying dudu, always dudu.") [irrelevant noise]
M:	[singing] Tony, Tony Baloney. Fi Fai More Onei ('ono means tasty in Hawn.)
B:	[laughs] Tony Tony dey dudu.

Note that the 4 year old responds with the contradicting routine (1.1.3 in Appendix 2), which was frequently part of the verbal play between these children and their mother.

Some good examples of children's name play come from Watson-Gegeo's recordings of Nāpua Team:

Example 7.6. (Numbers at left indicate separate routines)

(1)	1:	. . . had about t'ree auntie—Lori (a participant)—o.k., not Lori [as Lori hits her].
	2:	[singing Battle Hymn] Lori, Lori, Halleluyah.
(2)		And one dat girl one was walking. An her name's Butubutubutu. (Her name was Pua.)
(3)		[Said of Kila] Kila Bila Ila. Kila Bila Ila. Make dudu in his pants.
(4)		[Said of Ty Kahale] Not Ty Kahale Babale.

In (2), connotations include *botoboto* [sex organ] and *utu-utu* [intercourse]. In (3), a derogatory reference is added to the name play. (1) may be a taunt, connoting pompousness. Other examples of name play are provided in the section on narrative below.

Children in two communities played a game the purpose of which was to tease others by sharing with some, and keeping secret from others, the given names of their parents (2.2.3 in Appendix 2).

According to Richard Day and Charlene Sato children at KEEP used name play to create a collective response when asked in a group to tell a story. It would appear to be hard to avoid responding when someone uses a personal name of someone present with teasing connotations. This use of name play illustrates very well children's tendency to relate to adults as a group when "put on the spot."

Word play and mimicry

Illustrations of rhyming and alliteration have been given in Examples 7.2, 7.4, 7.5, and 7.6 above. Punning, along with alliteration, appeared in the following episode from Nāpua Team, in which mimicry is used to mock another speaker:

Example 7.7. (Kapua, Kaleo, and Kona, girls, 6 yrs)

[Kap is telling a sex story aimed at Kal]

Kap: . . . dey make hʌg-hʌg [love].

Kal: What's hug-how? [defiantly]

Kap: Hug-hug! D'you know what is hug-hug? [with irritation]
(challenges Kal's knowledge)

Kal: What's hug-how?
(insists)

Kap: I neva say "kau-kau" [food].
[laughter]

Kal: I say how-how. What's how-how?

Kap: I neva say—

 Ko: Hug-hug.
[Ko urges both to end dispute]

Kal: Talk, talk [to Kap, thrusting microphone into her face].

The close resemblance between this punning and alliteration and forms used in traditional competitive riddling, as described by Beckwith, is striking (see reference in Chapter 2).

Distortion appears frequently in different speech events. It is used to tease, for instance:

Example 7.8. (Boy, 5 yrs; Lika, 4 yrs; and Mother)

 B: Li-ita's [Lika] going!
(Reporting, teasing M.)

M: Haw?

 B: Lita's going downdɛi-iz.
[Lika's going downstairs.]

M: Lika going whea?

continued

Example 7.8. *continued*

B: [pause] Tem pla-ace.
     [Some place.]

M: Down ste-eas?
     [Downstairs?] (Not a distortion)

Counting the above, there are nine examples which contain deliberate distortions on the part of children (as opposed to mistaken pronunciation). Two involve teasing. In two more, both in Chapter 6, distortion is used to provoke contradiction.

It is fair to conclude, then, that deliberate distortion is used to tease. But an additional insight comes from a consideration of five cases of distortion occurring in hierarchical speech, all in Chapter 5. In Example 5.9, warily answering M's trick question, Howard says, "Not 'idahnjahn" (for "Daddy's not downstairs"—M's gloss), while Boy asks suspiciously, "Dad+go' zdezdez?" (for "Is Daddy downstairs?").

The message conveyed by distortion in all five instances appears to be: "Don't take this seriously—it is not what it seems to be." This is quite consistent wth the use of distortion in teasing, contradicting, and making requests that have already been rebuffed. Distortion is thus used like joking, according to Radcliffe-Brown's well-known formula: to bridge social distance (see Bernstein 1969). In this case, it is used to set aside hierarchy, which is similar. Word play, one form of distortion, can even be seen as symbolizing the subversion of hierarchy. It is no accident therefore that it served as a means of competition in ancient Hawaii, when challenging hierarchy was a matter of life and death (see Chapter 2).

Obscenities, jingles, and sexual teasing

One of the children in first grade at Aina Pumehana school reported with great glee, "My sista teach my baby to swea' for ri̠u!" Just what he meant by this was unclear, but there is evidence that young children learn to use obscenities. The most common obscenities are "dudu" and *kākā* [shit]. Other popular ones include:

> *okole* [butt]
> fut [fart]
> fuck, synonyms: *utu-utu,* kiss-kiss, hug-hug, and *honi-honi*
> *puka* [vagina] (see Bernstein 1969)
> skinny [penis], synonyms: head, *boto-boto.*
> As elsewhere, children learn jingles and counting-out rhymes (2.2.4 in
>   Appendix 2). Typical were:

Example 7.9. (Numbers at left indicate different instances, speaker's age in parentheses follows)

(1) Brown, brown, kiss your honey upside down. (11 yrs)

(2) Green, green, gasoline
     Don' fo'get to dingaling. (10 yrs)

Sexual teasing (2.2.5 in Appendix 2) is ubiquitous at all ages in Hawaiian culture. Adults frequently engage in it, and Bernstein has pointed out its central importance in organizing relationships among a group of Hawaiian adolescents. We have seen in Example 6.3 how parents engage their children in such teasing. It consists of allegations of sexual attributes, acts, or relationships made by a speaker against a target individual. Typically, such allegations are then exchanged, as in the following instances from KEEP kindergarten.

Example 7.10. (Speaker indicated by letter)

(1)a: You get peepee.

   b: Kulei like you' skinny, ae?

(2)a: Press yo' *okole*. Poosh!

   b: Come ova hi' and pus' [push] dis <u>head</u>!

Usually, targets take such allegations as insults, but in the following example from Nāpua Team there is a friendly exchange. The boys started out talking about others, then about one another:

Example 7.11. (<u>Moku</u>, 7 yrs, and <u>Malo</u>, 6 yrs, boys)

Mo: 'keh—um. You know Nakau, an dey—an dey wen kiss.

Ma: You know Maile, hah? M-Mai—uh Kehi love Maile. Kehi love Maile.
     [more of this, then:]

Ma: You know Moku, hah? He talk to someone.

Mo: You know Malo, hah? Malo—Malo—Malo going make Kaipo, yeah? Yeah, you knoa Malo, Malo going kiss Kaipo.
     [laughter and more friendly talk, then:]

Ma: You know what? Moku love—and get plenny girl+<u>friend,</u> you know.
     [laughs]

Mo: Malo you know, Malo, Malo—Malo—Malo going wit his sista. His sista [love] Malo.
     [laughs]

Ma: You know—you know me, hah? Everytime I saw um Moku went inna movie. Moku went inna movie.

This set of exchanges includes sexual connotations that go beyond the literal meaning of the words used, some of whose meaning is given by the routine itself. "He talk to someone" would not be given a sexual connotation outside this routine. "Went inna movie" on the other hand carries sexual connotations by itself, since "go show" is an idiom for having intercourse. "Get plenny girl friend" is an allusion to being profligate, which is a major theme in many of the sex stories (see Example 7.16 below).

Genre jokes and riddles

If a boy says, "I teu you guys one joke," one can expect to hear either a narrative or a riddle. Either will be told "just for fun," meaning that it is not to be believed, or that there is some trick to it. Jokes, so defined, contrast with local folktales and personally attested anecdotes or stories, which are to be taken seriously, as we shall see in the next chapter. Because these standardized jokes are also found in substantially the same form in American culture, we term them "genre jokes" here, to distinguish them from situational joking (see Chapter 6). Jokes share with traditional Hawaiian riddles the battle of wits which was central to *ho'opāpā* (see Chapter 2). The liking for such jokes continues in contemporary Hawaiian culture. Adolescents especially enjoy them, and telling such jokes signifies solidarity in talk-story sessions.

Riddles involve tricking the target into saying something that can be ridiculed. Punning or rhyming is often involved. For instance:

Example 7.12. (Speaker indicated by letter)

(1)a:	What come afta twenty-nine?
b:	Thirty.
a:	Your ass is dirty.
(2)a:	What's the firs' letter on "yellow"?
b:	"Y."
a:	Cause I wanna <u>know,</u> thas why.

The relationship between verbal play and narrative performance

Name play, mimicry, word play, and verbal games are ways to relate in a situation where unequals are striving to be equal (see Chapter 6). So it is natural that children turn to the routines of verbal play when they attempt to tell their own stories in groups. Some of the uses to which they put these routines when telling stories are examined in this section. It should be noted also that children are undoubtedly influenced by the model of talk-story provided by adolescents and adults, which likewise involves the interweaving of verbal play, situational joking, and narration.

Faced with the task of starting a report before the siblings of a friend, who ranged in age from 6 to 13 years, Malia indicated by her pauses, as well as name play, that she was inviting members of the audience to heckle her:

Example 7.13. (Malia; Ruby, her friend, 11 yrs; Laura, 13 yrs; Nick, 12 yrs; and Elizabeth, 6 yrs; siblings of R)

M: [giving a list of those at the party]
    Bryon, Gorilla, an Geo'gie. [Pause]
    ("Gorilla" is really "Kawila")

R: Gorilla! [laughter]

M: Kawila [laughs]   ⎡ Ka—[laughs]
E: ⎣ Okay,
    my tu_r-rn.

M: Wait, wait, wait. I not fin-ish.

E: I'm not finaeth [falsetto]
    (mimicry, note distortion)
    By yo go!
    (chant, alliteration)

N: Bahin (rhymes with "kine") yin yo.
    (variation on E's chant)

M: Yeah, A-an', a-an'—ah—
    (stalling)

E: You said   ⎡ "gorilla" already.
               ⎢ ("Get on with it.")
M: ⎣ My cousin—
    my cousi—I sai' "Kawiila-a."
    (continues, then corrects E)

L: I go tell, Elizabeth. You say, "Oh, 'Kawila," I though' was 'Gorilla'" [laughs]
    (feeds line to E)

M: My cousin [resumes report]

The target of a sex story can use word- or name play to retaliate against the speaker. In the following instance, Kaleo, a girl from Nāpua Team, retaliates with word play, but the speaker turns the phrase against her detractor and is thus able to proceed with her story:

Example 7.14. (Kapua is telling a sex story aimed at Kaleo, 6 yrs old)

Kal: Kapua honey-honey bun.
       ("honey-honey" = make love.)

Kekoa: And Kaleo love—

Kap: And da honey-honey bun (imitating and thus referring to Kal) [laughs] [Story continues]

Nonnarrative routines under appropriate circumstances contributed to narrative performance. In the following instance, the interjection by a member of the audience of a counting-out-rhyme, which was directed against the target of the ongoing sex story, was incorporated by the speaker:

Example 7.15. (Keaka, Kekoa, and Kapua, girls, 6–7 yrs)

(Kea has been telling a sex story at Kek's expense. In retaliation Kek has just shouted at Kea to give up her turn. At this point Kap, who has also been trying to narrate, breaks in:)

Kap: "one, two, t'ree," she say [referring to Kek].

Kea: She ya, she said, she said, "Pink, pink, I choose pink." An den she says—
         [Kek hits Kea, who screams]

The next line of this jingle is, "Pink, pink, you stink." We think that Kekoa took it to refer to herself. The story then resumed, with Kapua contributing further ideas, some of which were incorporated by Keaka. The incorporation of verbal play was thus one way in which conarration came about.

Nonnarrative routines provide means for audience members to speak without waiting for the story to end, while would-be narrators can use them to heckle, and thus attempt to limit the length of the narrative performance. The target of a sex story can use them to retaliate against the accuser. Skilled narrators, however, can use the same routines to retaliate against detractors, coopt them as conarrators, or enlist the attention of a potential audience. The outcome of all of this is a volatile speech event. In some ways, it seems incredible that structured narratives are possible at all. Indeed, these moves are not sufficient to produce a speech event in which narratives are predictable. For that to happen, something else is needed. That occurred as a result of particular circumstances in Nāpua Team for awhile.

Evolution of a context for narration

Nāpua Team, the 5- to 7-year-old group studied by Watson-Gegeo, was unusual in that it produced more narratives than any group or setting studied in Aina Pumehana over a comparable period, even among children considerably older (see Table 7.1). The narratives collected in Nāpua Team were extraordinary, moreover, in complexity and structure for children so young. One of the stories told by Keaka, which is discussed below, lasted for almost 40 minutes, and drew an audience of 12 enthusiastic listeners. The 102 stories referred to in Table 7.1 everaged 148 words (mean, which compares favorably with stories told by 5 year olds of superior intelligence from professional families in New Haven recorded by Ames. The mean of the latter was 93, 63 for boys and 124 for girls (Ames 1966; Watson 1972). All but one of the Nāpua Team stories was "extended," i.e., contained clauses in addition to those reporting the essential action (Labov and Waletzky 1967). They averaged 10.8 narrative clauses and 12.4 nonnarrative clauses per story. Two-thirds or more of a sample of 30 stories contained initial orientation, later description, summarizing, and formal closings, while half contained interpretation (Watson 1972). Such a performance not only dispells any question about these children's verbal and cognitive abilities, it also has important implications pertaining to the kind of circumstances that enable such

Table 7.1. Number and Type of Narratives

Type of Narrative	Nāpua Team, 5–7 yrs, %	Aina Pumehana	
		6–8 yrs, %	10–12 yrs, %
Personal experience	24%	92%	53%
Local folklore	11	3	20
Movie, TV, books	20	4	8
Sex stories	45	1	7
"Jokes"	—	—	12
Total	100%	100%	100%
Number of narratives	102*	76	60
Time in months	5	18	18

*This is a sub-set of 155 stories collected over 10 months.

abilities to be demonstrated. Developmentally, these data suggest that children possess narrative skills many years before they normally have opportunity to demonstrate them.

There must have been something special, therefore, about the circumstances that enabled the children of Nāpua Team to produce so many long and complex narratives. What was it? It had something to do with telling sex stories, since Table 7.1, indicates that Nāpua Team exceeded by far both other groups in the proportion of sex stories produced. Sexual teasing has a potential for being elaborated into narrative. There are a number of reasons for this. For one thing, sexual teasing refers to acts which can be expanded by use of the imagination into narratives. As we shall see below, this is just what happened in Nāpua Team. Another reason why sexual teasing may have led to narrative development is that it generated great interest and excitement—so great that serious arguments and fights followed serious teasing (Watson 1972). It was thus good material for attracting and holding audience attention under conditions of severe competition for speaking rights.

But story-telling in turn has an advantage over teasing. The "as if" or make-believe aspect of story-telling provides the narrator with certain protections. The make-believe aura, as well as its stance of merely reporting, remove some of the directness of allegations, since the narrator claims that he or she is not responsible for them. By their tone of voice, narrators of Nāpua Team clearly took this stance both in sex stories and in the more fantastical events of folktales (for evidence of the latter, see Watson 1975).

In addition to all of this, it seemed clear from the start that the emergence of a norm in Nāpua Team, allocating speaking rights to a series of narrators over a number of occasions, was crucial in explaining the superior performance of this group, for such a norm was not present in any group or setting in Aina Pumehana (Watson-Gegeo and Boggs 1977). Examination revealed that this norm evolved under particular circumstances as a means of retaliating for sexual teasing (Boggs and Watson-Gegeo 1978). Other kinds of narratives were told, but their telling was later facilitated by the establishment of a context for narration, and this was negotiated initially in the context of sexual teasing. This negotiation is described in the remainder of this section.

For two months prior to the first occurrence of sex stories, the children of Nāpua Team had been accustomed to Watson showing them hand-drawn pictures based upon Hawaiian mythology (which they took to be pictures of American Indians!) and asking them to tell stories about the pictures. Most of these stories were in fact simply descriptions of the pictures. On the first day of school after the Christmas recess, however, Watson decided to switch tactics and arrived without the pictures, which was immediately noted. In fact, months later they would still occasionally ask where the pictures were. Watson explained to Kekoa, who was the first to request to record that morning, that Watson wanted her to make up a story. Kekoa wanted to sing instead, however, and proceeded to tape several songs. Again an attempt was made to elicit a story, and Kekoa, still alone with Watson at this time, obliged by telling a version of the Three Bears. But her tone was task-oriented and she was not interested in the story. More conversation followed between the two. Then Keaka appeared on the scene, and the situation changed. Kekoa launched into another story when prompted, as follows:

Example 7.16. (Kekoa, 7 yrs; Keaka, 6½ yrs; and Watson)

W: I like to hear stories. You make me up a story, okay?

Kek: Uh-h-h.

W: Just make up one.

Kea: [says something unclear about ''story'']

Kek: Once upon a time dey was a girl name—Keaka [laughs].
       [Kea and W laugh]

As it turned out, Kekoa was about to tell a sex story about Keaka, the first one ever told in Nāpua Team. But Keaka had no idea that it was coming, since she was expecting stories about pictures. Hence her laugh, instead of a instant defense—as would have happened in the case of a sexual taunt.

W: Funny [very low]. What's she do?

Kek: Sh-she w-w-w-a-s- [laughs]
       (teasing)

Kea: Don' talk about me [very softly, only slightly protesting].

Kek: I going [matter of factly].

Kea: ⎡ No.
Kek: ⎣ You
        kin talk about me, I talk about you. [laughs]
        [Kea laughs also]

In the foregoing, a mild dispute breaks out in which the girls make explicit comments about what they are going to talk about. The quid pro quo—I'll talk about you then you can talk about me—in fact was the norm that eventually emerged. Neither participant could have envisioned the outcome when Kekoa struck her bargain with Keaka, however. Continuing:

Kek: She was married to Aggi [a boy] [laughs]. And [laughing]—[silently, Kea swings at Kek]
Kek: You goin get it!

There follows a 6½ second break in the recording as Keaka complains, demanding the right to talk so as to retaliate against Kekoa. Note that once the storyteller gets into Hawaiian territory—pregnancy and childbirth with their close links to sexual teasing—her intentions are clear and Keaka reacts typically. This sets the stage for acting out the quid pro quo suggested by her detractor.

More exchanges occurred before the context was fully established, however. Trading of insults was nothing new in the group. By suggesting narrative as a way of insulting, though, Watson had started something new. Her further questioning provoked Kekoa to elaborate: "She (Keaka) was big (pregnant)." "She had a baby." To each, Keaka replied with a contradiction. But instead of switching into the contradicting routine, the three proceeded to discuss details for Kekoa's story! This is something that never happens in contradicting. Suggestions do occur in story-telling, however. By this criterion, therefore, one can judge that a context for story-telling has been created at this point, however temporarily.

Subsequently, Keaka started to converse directly with Watson, having gotten her attention, and appeared to ignore Kekoa. Thus provoked, Kekoa enlarged upon her story:

Kek: Then Keaka—then Keaka [rising intonation]—
Kea: Den Kekoa [voice imitating Kek].
        (imitating, mocking)
Kek: —got ba—five baby sitters, [meaning unclear]
        ⎡ . . . (unintelligible)
Kea: ⎣ Kekoa got—
Kek: ⎡ den the nex two babies
Kea: ⎣ a—seven.
        (competing narration)

continued

Kek: was Pono and Keaka agɛn.

W: [laughs]

Kea: Da next baby was _You! [cut off as Kek pushes Kea]
       (_Y is fricative, excited style)

Stung, Keaka sought retaliation by telling a competing narrative directed at her detractor:

Kea: [from a distance] Kekoa has t'ree t'ousand babies in 'er stomach. Dats why she climb aw' da
       way ʌp to sky.

Kek: Ah shɛt ʌp! [angry]

Kea: [laughs]

Kek: Den wen—

Kea: [gives a whoop]

Kek: Da three [high pitch] boy babies—

Kea: ⌈ How you—?

Kek: ⌊ Then then f-w-a-ai-v babies came—

Kea: An punch 'er in da nose!

W: [laughs]

Kek: An then she goes a—the mother Keaka counted all her baby. She counted ʌp to ten. One two
       t'ree fowa five siix seven eighd nine ten. She said, "Aw, my gosh!
       [sounds slightly horrified]

W: [laughing] I would too.

Kek: [continuing] "I din know I had ten babies." Heya. Finish now.

Unable to compete successfully by turning details of Kekoa's story against her, Keaka then demanded the right to retaliate by telling a story on Kekoa—as Kekoa had suggested near the beginning. This led into her epic performance—a story that lasted some 36 minutes, a masterpiece of outrage and style that attracted more than a dozen excited spectators before it was over. Midway in this story, Kekoa, ridiculed to an extreme by Keaka's art and unable to wrest the microphone away from her, or to retaliate effectively by interjecting other routines, began compiling a list of persons that she was going to tell stories about (a list she insisted that Watson write down). This list helped to structure several story-telling sessions for a month, and was a concrete expression of the norm that had emerged in Nāpua Team: speaking rights for narrative allocated by quid pro quo retaliation.

Structure and function of talking story

The underlying structure of talk-story narrative, according to Watson-Gegeo, consists of a series of exchange sequences that begin with a "summons or question followed by a response or answer," then "a proposition . . . eliciting a response or corroboration,'' followed in turn by "some form of mediation." Another response or corroboration usually follows this before iteration begins with a new summons/question or proposition (Watson 1975: 60). Several speakers, plus members of the audience, follow this pattern in their utterances: "all co-speakers may offer propositions as well as responses" (ibid.). This is what makes talk-story narrative a joint performance, as we use the concept in this book.[19] Let us examine these features in turn.

The summons or question consists of such utterances as these:

Example 7.17.

You know her?   (Watson 1975)

You kno' we saw him at da zoo. . . . membə da time we aescursion, ae?   (Ex. 4.7)

Hey! I know one.

I teu' you guys one story.

As Watson states, "a story does not proceed until the audience and story-teller have arrived at shared information or identification" of characters (1975: 58), provided it is a personal experience narrative or local folktale, that is. Identification need not be accomplished by an initial question, however. Initial utterances that frame the routine to follow are called "formal openers" when applied to narratives in this book.

The response or answer to the summons/question may be an affirmation, verbal or nonverbal; a request for information; or a signalling of attention. The entire initial exchange may be omitted once iteration of the routine has begun (Watson loc. cit.) to reappear, perhaps, when another speaker claims a turn, or a new routine is introduced.

The proposition may be a new narrative clause (Labov and Waletzky 1967), report or allegation, or an abstract for a report or narrative. The response to the proposition may be an affirmation, other corroboration, contradiction or details contributed to the prior proposition. This point in the routine is particularly important, since it may lead either to disruption of the story, conarration, or development of the narrative or report. Mediations qualify, round out, or assist in interpretation. They include summary, emphasis, emotional expression, repetition (used as emphasis), evaluation, and recapitulation (Watson 1975: 60).

Examples are as follows (the reader is referred to the complete text in Chapter 4):

Texts	Comments

(Example 4.7) (Atta, Bobby, Frank, and Faatau, 10–11 yrs)

B:	Yah,	Response to opener.
	at da zoo he [go tell]	Proposition—new narrative clause.
	"Get da heu' outa	

continued

Texts	Comments

A: ⌈ hiyə, kiids! [gruffly]   Mediation—enactment.
    ⌊ Yeah, he wa' tellin <u>as</u>   Response, corroborates.
    He—we tell um why,
    "Get da hell outa hiyə. . ."   Proposition—new narrative clause
                                   ["We asked him why. . ."].

(Example 4.1) (<u>Ko</u>no and <u>Ke</u>vin, 10 yrs)

Ke: M-ma bike ⌈ da buggah bʌs <u>ahp</u>   Proposition—narrative clause.
Ko: ⌊ M-m-m   Delayed response to opener.
      [the thing go].   Corroborates.

(Example 4.9) (<u>Fa</u>atau, <u>Fr</u>ank, <u>Al</u>an, and <u>At</u>ta, 10–11 yrs)

Fa: Yeah, he ʷgon make trobu
      [with] da haole.   Response to opener, orients.
      Den we stah't fight, n den
      we fight.   Proposition—new narrative clause.
      [later]

Al: I <u>hate</u> Michaels!   Mediation—evaluation.

The narratives presented in Chapter 4 have been shown in columns which are defined as above. "Summons" and "proposition" have been shown there in a single column, likewise "response" and "corroboration," for ease in presentation. Since the members of each pair rarely overlap sequentially, they are not easily confused.

Joint performances are indicated by the fact that different speakers make propositions, corroborate, and mediate. Conarration occurs whenever two speakers alternate to develop the same story. Again, examples are numbers 4.7, 4.8, and 4.9. Conarration contrasts with two speakers attempting to tell competing stories or engaging in competing routines. It also contrasts with the structure of a lecture, where a single speaker moves from proposition to mediation to proposition without contributions from the audience. This was the structure which we had initially anticipated for story-telling.

The underlying structure also enables participants in talk-story narratives to allocate turns with a minimum of overlapping speech, as Watson has likewise pointed out (1975).[20] There is overlapping in Examples 4.1, 4.7, 4.8, and 4.9, including some not shown, but the average number of overlaps in these four, plus another narrative not shown, is slightly less than two per narrative. Moreover, one speaker usually yields to another when overlapping occurs, and also responds to what has been said, rather than ignoring it. In brief, overlapping in talk-story is an aspect of tight sequencing, not of competing performances or routines.[21]

It should be noted that responding in unison does *not* constitute a joint performance as the term is used here, unless there is other evidence that it is the outcome of a joint argument or mediation (for an instance of this see Transcript 10.2). "Chiming in" may be a joint performance when it relates to another's proposition or response, i.e., is not a competing performance. An instance of true joint performance is the first narrative presented in Michaels and Cook-Gumperz (1979), which is discussed on pages 166–167 below. "Topic-chaining," on the other hand, has nothing to do with talk-story narratives (see ibid. for reference). The latter are typically well-formed around a single theme or related themes, while the former are not.

Modes of speaking

The routines discussed in this book, defined and illustrated in Appendix 2, vary along the dimension of hierarchy and equality. Ordering, punishing, and questioning children, as well as responding to children's requests, are hierarchical, that is, one-sided both in participation and control. Thus, when ordering or punishing children, parents initiate much more frequently than children do. Parents also escalate, and issue directives, usually imperatives, over half of the time, whereas children escalate hardly at all, and do not use directives (see Appendix Table 2 for supporting data). To do so, of course, would be interpreted as "talking back," a serious offense. The pattern for questioning children is similar, except that parents do not escalate. They do not have to, since most of their questions are answered at least minimally. When children make requests, parents reply only about 20 percent of the time, thus reflecting their control over both the exchange and the outcome of the request.

Playful contradicting with parents contrasts in every one of these respects. Rates of initiation are more equal and so are escalations. Directives, when they occur here, are nonserious: e.g., "Shut up!"[22] This egalitarian mode of speaking with parents also prevails when children are contradicting and joking among themselves. By these same criteria, narrative is likewise egalitarian when performed by peers: different participants initiate at a high rate, and all attempts to initiate are successful in producing a response, thus creating joint performances.[23]

In previous publications, we have addressed the question of the origin of the underlying structure in talk-story, suggesting that it might originate in contradicting (Watson-Gegeo and Boggs 1977). We can now see that this hypothesis, while relevant, is too simple to account for all of the facts, particularly the fact that various routines share to some extent the underlying structure of narrative, as Watson-Gegeo has pointed out (1975). Accordingly, the following hypothetical development of the structure is proposed. Children's earliest experiences are with verbal play, which is inherently egalitarian, as well as entertaining and full of aloha. They next experience a higher proportion of one-sided, adult-controlled, routines in a context relatively lacking in aloha. Sibling relations are structured to a large extent by these latter routines—which is not to say, however, that sibling relations are lacking aloha. As they gradually interact more with peers, the struggle over assertiveness develops. At this point, there is normally little chance for contributions to story-telling to be accepted by peers, as well as few occasions for engaging in story-telling with anyone. As children grow older, they discover that the assertiveness they perceive can be handled by verbal play and humor, as well as by contradicting. Perhaps the playful teasing by parents has provided a model for this development. At any rate, when this point is reached—and this depends upon other developments in social relationships as well—an egalitarian structure has been established by those routines which offer preferred means of relating. Collective contributions to story-telling are now possible, and thus, when story-telling occurs under favorable conditions, it is fundamentally egalitarian in character. Adolescents have no difficulty narrating, and frequently do in the absence of adults.

The circumstances described above in Nāpua Team may have fortuitously illustrated these links in a brief, observable period of time. The resolution of conflict reached there in a few minutes probably takes years to develop under usual circumstances. It was also unstable, disappearing in a little over a month's time. Although story-telling continued for over a month after the disappearance of the norm described, performances deteriorated gradually to those observed before the norm developed.

The adult's role in children's talk-story sessions

Adults play a crucial role in eliciting narratives among children. Only three narratives were recorded among children 5 years and younger at home and in the KEEP kindergarten when no adults participated. Among 8 to 12 year olds, less than six narratives were told when no adult was around. By contrast, all of the narratives referred to in Table 7.1 were delivered in the presence of an adult: Watson-Gegeo or Boggs.

Why should children so rarely tell stories to one another? Experience suggests that story-telling is considered by children to be an adult's role, since adults tell stories and children normally do not. Children, however, eagerly respond when afforded an opportunity to tell stories to an adult. It may be, therefore, that they take such an invitation as a sign that the adult is willing to act in an egalitarian way.

But adult invitation alone will not produce narratives when recording a group of children. Instead, what repeatedly happens is that the child who is first offered the microphone has nothing to say even though he or she was eager for a chance to record. As soon as another child begins to talk, however, nearly everyone tries to talk at once. The verbal routines that occur in this burst, taken in order of approximate frequency, include greetings, shouts, obscenities, nonsense words, entertainer routines, singing, chant-like alliteration and rhyming, personal insults, threats, the contradicting routine, and questions about the recording machine or the adult. One could infer that the invitation to equality signalled by the adult's invitation to tell a story produces a competition for status in which narratives are impossible because other routines provide more familiar and efficient ways to compete.

It takes a special set of circumstances to produce narratives in a group of children. One of those sets was described above. Crucial to this development was Watson-Gegeo's nondirective role. Except in cases of physical violence, she consciously avoided attempting to control the discourse or the children's interaction with one another in any way. She did not attempt to assign turns or to defend speakers, and was nonjudgmental no matter what the children said (Watson-Gegeo and Boggs 1977: 88). Boggs found that, whenever he acted in a more directive way, competition for attention by means of reports was more likely than developed narratives (reports contain a lot of orientation, but lack a sequence of at least two narrative clauses). In order to produce narratives, a group of peers has to be free to develop its own organization, and this requires a degree of nondirectiveness on the part of the adult.

In a classroom, there are other possibilities for eliciting stories in a group of children. As we shall see in Chapter 10, these share with Nāpua Team the relaxation to some degree of adult control over selection of topic, assignment of speaking turns, and acceptability of responses. This relaxation has the effect of making the teacher–student relationship more egalitarian. As we have argued in this and the preceding chapter, talking story results when relationships are more egalitarian—and vice-versa.

CHAPTER 8

The Roots of Folktale:
Observation and Speculation

The preceding chapter was concerned with the interaction process that produced narrative performances. Next to be considered is the content of the stories told, the motivation for telling them, and the source of this motivation. It is suggested here that stories of a particular kind—those based upon local folktales—are in part speculations, told in an attempt to evaluate alleged dangers. Speculating appears to be general when one is forced to learn by observing without the opportunity to ask questions and have them answered. It is important because, in the reading lessons at KEEP, children frequently respond eagerly by speculating and anticipating. The lessons thus provide them an opportunity to act upon a motivation that is well established.

In labelling certain stories as "local folktale," I am referring to content which refers to extra-ordinary experience.[24] The motivation for telling stories about extra-ordinary experience, we hypothesize, is to comprehend and thus to avoid alleged dangers by speculating about their causes and the effects of certain actions. This was illustrated by Ike, who was then 10 years old, in a walk through his neighborhood. We were accompanied by his long-time friend and neighbor, Pita, also 10. Although the comments and stories cited below were addressed primarily to me, Pita was a quiet listener, and he conversed with Ike in between these excerpts.

Example 8.1 (Ike and Pita, 10 yrs, and me.)

(I had been describing chasing domestic pigs with a stick.)

    I: One—one—one mo'ning ma bradə, ma bradə, ma bradə, ɛh? he work in Job Co'ps now. . . .
           When guys gon go camp one, one on top da mountain—
           (". . . When the guys were going to camp at certain place in the mountains—" (formal opener, orientation for narrative)

    P: [points out his house to me]

    I: Den, den, ae?
           (starts narrative, but repeats opener: "ae?")
           [I still attend to P]

Example 8.1. *continued*

I: Steven!

me: Yeah?

I: Ha' wa'—ha' one <u>pig</u>. Ma bra'ə dem wa' go hitch-hike. One on top da mountain . . . was-ah—look for <u>pig</u>, eh? hunt fo' <u>pig</u>.
     (continues narrative. "There was this pig. My brother and his friends were hitchhiking. At a certain place in the mountains they went hunting for <u>pig</u>.")

me: U-huh.

I: No had. Ba da bushes was—ha' one piig. Piig, eh? An da piig was hidin ba da <u>bush</u>es. An ma—one a—ma b—ma bradə saw <u>dd</u>a pig, da pig wen sees ma bradə, ma bradə wen <u>run</u>. ("They thought that there was no pig, but by the bushes. . ." <u>dd</u> is a trill—excited style.)

me: Oh, I see.

I: Ha' one cliff, huh? an da cliff—da cliff was broke+in an ma bradə awmos fall off.
     ("There was a cliff and the cliff was broken. . .")

me: Wow! [pause] He didn' see um? [pause]
     [Ike was distracted for a moment]

I: Bu' ah'—But I had a good i<u>dea</u>. I took da knife outa my bradə's pɔckit.
     (resumes, puts self into the action)
     [pause] (for dramatic effect.)

me: Uh hm.

I: An, da pig was runnin fo me, eh?
     (mediation, to increase impact)

me: Um hm.

I: I got da knife. Ah slai um. (rhymes with "sly") Rai' (?)in da <u>head</u>.

me: [chuckle] Hump!

I: Da p—da pig wen <u>die</u>

Ike had in all probability many times overheard a story like this one, in which the pig god, *Kamapua'a,* often figures. Ike so identified himself with his brother's plight that he introduced himself at the crucial moment in the story.

A little later, walking through a graveyard (it was daytime), Ike asked Pita if it was all right for him to step on a certain rock, explaining:

Example 8.2. (same as Example 8.1)

I: Sometimes I really gotta aks, you know. Cau' ah do' know what is what—what is what ova <u>dea</u>.
     ("Cause I don't know. . .")
     Cause I gon let you walk das why I gotta <u>aks</u> fo' <u>step on</u>
     ("Even though you walk I have to ask what is safe.")
     [pause] Ah do' wan+to die <u>early</u>, man. stI+lIv. [I stay liv.] ("I want to be alive.")

Ike clearly believed that it might be dangerous for him to step on a rock in a graveyard. This may derive from the widespread belief that stepping on the stones of a *heiau* (temple) or place where people have died is dangerous because of the *mana* which such stones possess. He appears to be using this occasion to present this inference for consideration, even though he fails to get a response from Pita on this occasion. (Interestingly, he did not ask me.) It is worth noting that "Do you want to die early?" is often heard as a warning when someone is tempting danger, while "You don't know what is what" is an accusation heard in similar circumstances.

Observation, inference, and speculation about natural events

I first became aware of the children's tendency to draw inferences from close observation in connection with more mundane events. For instance, boys were likely to pay close attention to the way in which any mechanical device worked in order to try it out on their own. Observing me operate a camp stove, they would wait until a particular act in a sequence was required and then ask for permission to perform it. But they did not stop here. They would typically ask what would happen when the indicated act was performed, or if it were to be omitted. They also asked about possible difficulties: e.g., what happened if the stove flamed out. For another example, one time I introduced a Time Bomb—a wind-up toy that would tick loudly for a time and then make a sharp bang. This became very popular, because the boys learned how to anticipate when the bang would occur and could thus avoid holding it at such times. This became apparent when several were regularly able to count in unison correctly to the "explosion." This development was the basis for the invention of the game mentioned in Chapter 4. Boys as young as 8 years learn by observation how to set and release brakes and make cars roll by turning on ignition keys. It may be in this way that many learn how to drive by age 12 or 13.

The younger children made inferences about natural events, sometimes drawing parallels between analogous events. Shari, for instance, drew the following parallels at age 7 years:

Example 8.3. (S̲hari, 7 yrs)

> S: Chickens fight, right?
>
> me: That's right. [repeated throughout the following]
>
> S: Can lay eggs, right? An hen make chicks. An hen take her chicks to walking, right? Or play aroun'.
>
> me: Where did you see um?
>
> S: . . . we get plenny chicks.
>
> me: At your house? Uh huh. What else does chicks do?
>
> S: Chicks learn. They learn from their mothə, an they learn how to eat.

After learning at a "fun fair" conducted by a group of former Peace Corps Volunteers that the length of the day was affected by the tilting of the earth relative to the sun, 10–11 year old boys deduced next day that Aina Pumehana must be tilted towards the sun because it was sunnier than any other place around, but this provoked an argument about whether the sun went down later there.

Given an observation or alleged fact, there was often a tendency to speculate about it. For instance, one time while camped on the beach we were watching shore birds run through retreating waves as they fed. Kevin speculated that, in case of a tidal wave, they would have to fly up to the mountain, but there they would probably starve in a hurry. Typically, he announced this conclusion, and then asked me for confirmation. Later, he thought of "God's book with all the names in it" and concluded that, if it ever fell onto the earth, "we had it. Because all da names"—i.e., it would be big book. One of the commonest forms of conversation was to speculate about something mentioned, "What if. . . .?"

This tendency to learn by close observation is obviously related to the traditional injunction to learn by observing, not by asking questions (see Chapter 2). It is reinforced today by parents' frequent lack of response to requests for information (see Chapter 5), which leaves the child with little recourse other than speculation, further observation, and reasoning by analogy—or talking story with others. Thus, the entire pattern is rooted in Hawaiian traditional culture.

Encountering the extra-ordinary

Children express the feeling that some things are "spooky." These include dark places in the forest of the *kula* zone, which lies between the *pali* [ridges] and the seashore. Thus Kevin, 11 years old, told me about Blue Valley, a dark place full of wild pigs with sharp tusks. When I took the boys back up in such a valley, they called it "spooky," would not think of camping there, and were anxious to leave. Some things seemed uncanny on the basis of their sensual quality.

Manny, 11 years old, told me that his brother had been scared by a cat one time: "He t'ought i' was awa small kitty . . . bu' wasᵊ'." [He thought that it was our small kitten but it wasn't.] Looking into the cat's eyes as he petted it, something about the eyes made him suddenly scream and sweep the cat away with his hand.

Actual contact with a spooky thing or place causes genuine fear. This was demonstrated vividly to me on a camping excursion which several 4th and 5th grade school classes took together. A girl discovered at about bed-time a sculptured crucifix on her bed in the camp dormitory, placed as if for a blessing. She and two of her friends became quite hysterical. A half-hour later, they were still sobbing occasionally, and one complained that her head hurt, which indeed appeared to be the case. While no one at any time could explain how they thought that it might harm them, the girls involved wanted it removed from the building entirely, and made immediate arrangements to sleep with friends in another building in case it was not removed. One of the boys who was present at the time of discovery was curious enough to touch it, but later became so apprehensive that I had to reassure him by reciting a prayer. My attempts to reassure the girls had no effect. One of the girls later reported to her mother that they had been scared on the trip. Several expressed the wish at the time that they had not come.

A certain cave has a local reputation as the site of extra-ordinary events. Legends associate it with brigands and murder in precontact times. Boys do not visit this cave at night just for fun. My first visit there when I took a group of 10–11 year old boys inside at night was a great mistake. The boys were so frightened afterwards that they could not fall asleep until we said prayers. I never took a group inside again, except in the daytime.

Speculation and inference as motivation for story-telling

Contact with spooky places and things produces speculation. Even quite young children speculate about death. Thus, Leilani at 6 years of age told a complex story about the death of a sister (see Boggs 1978a: 90), following which she was obviously wrestling with the ideas that the dead go to heaven, while the Devil can kill:

Example 8.4. (Leilani, 6 yrs)

L:	And heavens really can kill us. Devils too.
me:	[noncommital comment]
L:	When devils come down they kill us an we die. We go up in heaven and heaven ha' go keep us up thea.
me:	[noncommital comment]
L:	Devils like babies, yeah? They no like naughty boys an girls but they like goo' boys and girls. (Boggs 1978a:91)

The idea that the good go to heaven may have contributed to the speculation that devils like good boys and girls. That conclusion could hardly have been reassuring to Leilani, and may have contributed to her desire to discuss the matter.

The emergence of a story in discussion based upon speculation was illustrated by the following. The transcript indicates that some of the participants were speculating, since they were being exposed to the phenomenon for the first time. The object referred to appears to resemble an amulet, but I have been unable to identify it from the information given.

Example 8.5. (M̲anny, A̲ndrew, F̲iti, others, 10–11 yrs) (Andrew was prevailed upon to tell about a "gohanzel" despite objections. After averring that it was real, he continued:)

Initiation	Reply	Mediation
A : Get da kine necklace, look like da <u>body</u>. Aw <u>brown</u> iinside. An get one <u>body</u> hangin. <u>Smaw</u> one ni' da body.		

Example 8.5. *continued*

Initiation	Reply	Mediation
		In you' <u>cah</u>' when da ting broke+en
		[...]
	F :	If was broken li' diis [noise] --li dat, whatchu ii (?)
	A :	Ma ancu broke in half [solemnly].
	M :	An what if you trow um in da wata, he drown?
	A :	Yeah, he drown. You burn um ma ancu get aw burn.
	[2 turns deleted]	
	F :	If he bring whatchu do?
	A :	If somebody <u>touch</u> em, ɛh? Ma ancu lose his life awredy.
	F :	He gon die?
	A :	Die [softly].
	[everyone was hushed]	

A : ("That necklace looks like a <u>body</u>--all <u>brown</u> inside. And there is a <u>body</u>--a <u>small</u> one--hanging underneath it." (describes object)		("If the thing breaks in your <u>car</u> ... ") (explains how it works)
	F :	(If it was broken like this [noise]--like that, what would you--) (speculates about effect)
	A :	(My uncle would break in half [solemnly].) (announces effect)
	M :	(And what if you threw it in the water, he would drown?) (generalizes)
	A :	(Yeah, he would drown. If you burned it my uncle would get all burned.) (confirms, elaborates)
	[2 turns deleted]	
	F :	(If he brought it [to your house] what would you do?) (asks for directive)
	A :	("If somebody even <u>touches</u> it, my uncle dies immediately.") (explains and warns)
	F :	(He would die?) (wants to make sure)
	A :	(Die [softly].) (confirms)
	[everyone was hushed]	

While the above was not a story, it had the obvious ingredients for one.

When telling a story based upon speculation, the boys interjected themselves into it. This appears clearly in the following:

Example 8.6. (Kevin and Patrick, brothers, 10 and 9 yrs, respectively) (I asked Kevin to repeat in front of Patrick the story he had told me the previous day about the young surfer's death.)

Initiation	Reply	Mediation
		K : Na bugga he--he fo'-get his piu's, da granmadə say, ah?
	me: Yeah.	
K : n--den he came down da beach, down 'a schoo' beach.		
	me: Your granmudder.	
	K : No, hiis!	
	me: Hiis.	
K : Den, uhm, once he ᵂen reach tha' beach,		
		he 'en go tell--as, [inspires] [pause] "Ah-ah no can go swimming! No moª piu's." An he sai'+ da'--to us, huh?
K : Big wave. He we-en go wid um.		
	[more discussion followed]	
		K : (The bugger he--forgot his pills, the grandmother said, ah?)
	me: (Yeah.)	(explains outcome, attributes)
K : (and--then he came down to the beach, the beach at school.) (narrative clause, emphasizes known)		
	me: ("You mean your grandmother?") (attempt to clarify)	
	K : (No, his!) (clarifies)	
	me: (His.) (confirms)	
K : (Then--once he reached that beach, (narrative clause)		
		he told--us, [inspires] [pause] "I cannot go swimming! I never took my pills." And he said that--to us, huh?) (enacts, "brings it home" to audience, dramatic style)
K : ("A big wave came, and he took it.") (narrative clause)		
	[more discussion followed]	

In this story, the narrator put himself and his brother, listening, on the scene, and portrays themselves as having been addressed by the youth just before he went to his death. Kevin had not told me this when recounting the event the previous day. His speculation then about what caused the death is now attributed to the words of the youth himself.

The sources of story content

When I began searching for narratives in 1966, I assumed that children would repeat folktales which they had heard told by adults and elder children, changing them in accordance with their own interests and limitations. In the intervening years, a few occasions have been observed in which children of various ages listened on the fringes to a group of adults telling stories of the extra-ordinary, and a few occasions in which older children told such stories to younger ones. However, children have not been observed asking adults to tell stories. Presumably, in the past, when legends (*mo'olelo*) and chants (*oli*) were recited at public events, children had the opportunity to listen, but whether they had opportunity to discuss and question seems doubtful, for it would violate the exclusive right of adults to initiate interaction (see Chapters 2 and 5). It seems more certain that, today, adults do not attempt to elicit reports and stories from children.

Some of the stories cited above may have been influenced by stories overheard. These include Example 8.1 (pig hunting) and the one about Blue Valley. Others, like Example 8.4 (devils like babies), may have been based in part upon teachings in church; Example 8.6 (the young surfer who did not take his pills) upon overheard conversations; observing that certain objects were treated with great respect, such as Example 8.5 (the "gohanzel"), or the sensual quality of the experience itself: the cat's eyes. All of these have one thing in common: they encourage speculation by not providing any explanation or opportunity to ask questions about something that seems threatening. Story-telling may in some cases be motivated by a desire to explore speculations arising from experiences that were not understood at the time they first occurred.

A similar motivation must exist in children everywhere. It happens, however, to be particularly consistent with two central features of Hawaiian culture that have appeared in earlier chapters. These are learning by observation, rather than by asking questions or having things explained, and obeying *kapu,* which requires doing the right thing to avoid danger without necessarily having to understand the reason for doing so. I would argue that these factors result in speculation and the exploration of inferences by talking story.

Speculation in the KEEP reading lesson

As described in Chapter 10, KEEP teachers invite children to speculate about what happens in the story that they are about to read, and they respond eagerly, even to the point of reading ahead when told not to do so. They also offer personal stories based upon speculation, which are not responses to the teacher's questions (see Example 10.14 and line 1-148B in McMillen et al. 1979). Finally, it is argued in Chapter 10 that the children tend to recapitulate the story which is read during the lesson without waiting for the teacher's questions. All of these observations are consistent with the analysis presented in this chapter that part-Hawaiian children have a well-developed motivation to speculate.

CHAPTER 9

Adaptation to the Classroom: First Grade, Aina Pumehana

When children enter school, they are prepared to interact in ways that are familiar to them. But circumstances in school and cues for appropriate behavior are often different. Routines that resemble those used by adults at home often do not call for the same kind of response in school. And teachers often do not respond as parents would when children act as they do at home. It is the thesis of this book that the lack of fit between routines and participation structures learned at home and those encountered in school is the principal cause for the poor performance of part-Hawaiian children from low income families in school. This chapter presents evidence for this thesis which was obtained by participant observation and recording in one first and second grade class in the community of Aina Pumehana during 1966–68.

The chapter examines the children's experience in this class as it relates to the verbal routines described earlier. We find them engaged in name play, for instance, and avidly learning to write names. But aside from this, the routines of verbal play find no role in the development of academic skills. Rather, when used, they contribute to the struggle for control that goes on almost continually between teacher and children. Talking story occurs readily, but it is not made part of instruction. Instead, it is frequently seen by the teacher as disrupting her efforts to gain the children's attention. The children attend overwhelmingly to one another, rather than to the teacher, as Jordan has described in another setting (1977). But roles that suited the strict sibling hierarchy at home do not fit classmates, who are the same in age. This circumstance provokes the struggle over assertiveness which was described in Chapter 4. Efforts to help one another, moreover, are reproved by the teacher.

The most important cause of the struggle for control can be traced to miscommunication centered on discipline. There is a major mismatch here in contextualizing cues between the culture of the classroom and that of the children. Teachers typically insist upon supervising and directing activities in detail, while the children are accustomed to occupying themselves, initiating and carrying out tasks without attracting adult attention. The more the teacher attempts to gain their attention and control their activities, the harder they try to avoid her. In the resulting confusion, directives by the teacher occupy an inordinate amount of instructional time, so that children receive relatively little direct and meaningful instruction. Attempts at recitation become instead a stream of directives, which heightens the struggle for control already underway.

The chapter concludes with an analysis of reading instruction in this classroom. The content of these lessons was "decontextualized," as the Scollons (1980) and Heath (1980, 1982) use the term. Moreover, elicitation occurred in a context that was devoid of social meaning. For these and other reasons, we believe, reading instruction was ineffectual, despite the fact that teacher, and often students, worked hard. When appropriate social contexts appeared in the classroom, on the other hand, the contrast in learning was observable. The contexts that produced this result closely resemble that provided by the KEEP reading lesson, which is analyzed in Chapter 10.

The first grade was chosen for study because it appeared to be an average class and the teacher was enthusiastic about having the observer present. Although an experienced elementary teacher, she had not taught long in Hawaii and was teaching the first grade for the first time. At the end of the school year, she left the school, as was typical at the school. During those years teacher turn-over was about 60 percent per year.[25]

While known as a school attended mostly by "Hawaiians," the children were of mixed origins. Of a total of 27 students in the classroom who were enrolled through most of the year, 14 were part-Hawaiian (none were pure Hawaiian). One half of the part-Hawaiians lived on the homestead. The remaining half of the students were about equally divided among Portuguese, Samoans, Filipinos, and those of unknown origin. While examples and generalizations in the following account are based upon the part-Hawaiians, except as noted, few differences in behavior were noted between them and the other children. Whether this was due to the preponderance of the part-Hawaiians in the class, or to similarity in general cultural backgrounds, is impossible to say. Many if not most of the non-Hawaiians had grown up in communities which were mostly Hawaiian.[26]

Getting acquainted and recording

Recording their stories became a part of a relationship with the children that evolved naturally out of their preoccupation with names. My notes for the first day state:

Met Helen B., first grade teacher, a few minutes before the end of the morning recess and told her briefly why I wanted to observe and record children's speech. [We had a brief conversation after which] she stepped out for a minute. Before she came back into the room a girl looked over from her seat and, grinning, asked my name. I told her, "Steve." She repeated it, and another one or two repeated the question and my name. Miss B. came back and started to introduce me, whereupon the first girl volunteered that she knew my name, giving it. Miss B., surprised, asked how she learned that.

[Later, several came over where I was to play educational games with them, according to the teacher's announcement.] Leo immediately introduced himself and repeated my name. Another said simultaneously that my name was "Stephen"— i.e., the full name—that she had a brother by that name. . . . Shortly after his first question Leo asked, "What's your real name?" and I told him "Boggs." He couldn't get that, and the others could not, later on. Then, during story time, one referred to me as "Mister Steve" and Miss B. followed suit.

Throughout the day children would say to me, "I know your name, it's Steve," and then tell me their names, or challenge me to give their names. Late in the day, when I began to respond accurately to their names, they tried to mix me up. There was more preoccupation with names than with any other subject [on this first day].

This preoccupation with names is part of the name play described in Chapter 7, although at the time I had no idea that such a routine existed. Claiming or alleging the wrong name is one form of such play. Over subsequent weeks, I noted a strong motivation to write and and to copy names: Thus:

Oct. Shari comes over to me and says that she can write my name. She picks up a piece of chalk and asks me what my name begins with. There follows about five minutes or more in which she picks out the letters of my name [by] looking up on the walls where the letters are posted. She writes it on the board two times. John has come over to write my name also. Ruby also comes over and when space is available, copies my name.

These three became special friends of mine throughout subsequent visits to the community.

Children copied one another's names as eagerly as they did mine:

Oct. Ernest says to Kele who had leaned over the paper on which he is practicing, "This is the way you spell your name," pointing to the "K's" which he is practicing. Kele turns Ernest's paper over then and starts to write his [own] name on the back side. He writes "K e" and then leaves. Ernest finishes it and then goes over to Kele's desk to check the way his name is spelled.

This care to spell names correctly is matched by care in pronouncing names. It is striking that intervocalic /r/, which is often not pronounced, is invariably pronounced by the children in one another's names. (As this was being written, I had a chance conversation with a college student from Aina Pumehana. Referring to learning to read, he volunteered: "When we went to school us guys jus' wen go get ou' letters—the alphabet, you know—an learn how write ou' name, an then play ukulele all day.")

Taking advantage of this interest in names, I started having them record their names and playing the tape back:

> 11/3 It was tremendously popular, the kids competing to be next to hold the microphone and continuing as long as allowed. Sometimes a kid would ask for another turn as soon as he finished and deny that he had one.

Again there was some play, as when a child would claim to be someone else, and then correct himself.

Frequently after this children would ask to record their voices. I did not always allow it, keeping it as a reward.

> 3/9 After he had talked on the tape at my request, Kala had asked for another chance to talk. I promised him one later on and subsequently four times he asked me for the opportunity. He finally did get a chance.

Even children who declined to talk when I invited them subsequently joined in when others were recording, or asked to talk later on.

The motivation to talk developed in the context of an unmistakable effort to incorporate me into their families. This started on the first day and continued throughout my stay. Thus:

> 10/27 After a few minutes one child, and then another, touched me with their hands on my knee. After lunch Ruby hung back at the door grinning at me. I recognized and greeted her. When the children sat for the singing, she sat next to me, began to lean on me and continued to do so. . Soon after Kapono did so, and finally [a Caucasian girl who subsequently left the school]. As each did so, they would look and grin, and often converse. When I said that I would be back next week they passed this news along.

I also played with them during recess, as I had observed their fathers play with them. Subsequently:

> 11/3 While sitting in my lap Ernest asked, "why you come some time and don't come some time." I said that I had other classes to go to. He said I should come every day and be their daddy.

Attempts to incorporate me continued for several months:

> 3/9 Foa says out of the clear sky that he hopes I will take him home with him. Later Ruby leans on me and says, "You're my daddy," grinning. I said nothing. She repeats and several talk about whether I am a daddy. John asks if I have any boys. Foa then suggests that the teacher is the mother and I am the father.

Such behavior exemplifies the strong tendency towards incorporation and fosterage discussed in Chapter 2. While children of all ethnic backgrounds act this way, in this class the Hawaiian children were the most persistent and confident about these attempts.

Initiating conversation was part of this relationship with me. Children would approach me unexpectedly to report such things as birthdays, babies at home, where they lived, and events that had occurred. When the tape recorder was set up, I recorded these accounts, and from them came most of the stories which were presented in Chapter 3 and elsewhere. While I knowingly initiated conversation at times, at other times simply my observing, being friendly, and not critical or directive, led them to assume that I would welcome an approach. As mentioned in Chapter 2, these are cues that adults are receptive to being approached, which contrast with the behavior of parents who are busy or issuing directives. Children monitor adults for cues of receptivity (see Gallimore et al. 1974: 224, and Ch. 11). Without knowing it, I was giving cues of being receptive, but, not knowing this at the time, I was often startled when one would come up and initiate a conversation, recite a jingle, poke at my notebook, or comment on something I had written there.

This desire to converse with an adult turned out to be of great importance for this entire inquiry. I realized, however, that conversation was important on the very first day, my note prophetically recording:

> The mood which Miss B. sought to maintain was one of [individual] intellectual concentration and interested participation in intellectual tasks. The children seemed constantly to prefer socializing.

Later on, the thought kept recurring—what if the two could be combined in the form of conversation? It was to be 12 years, however, before a concrete method for accomplishing this and relating it to reading instruction emerged, and then only from others' efforts. Looking back, it is tantalizing to note evidence of the strong motivation to read and write in these early notes, when reading and writing served the purpose of communicating and incorporating me. The writing of names provides one example. Another:

> 4/27 During the recording session Rachel (who had hardly talked all year) came up and presented me with a paper on which she had written some words. Kala immediately showed a great deal of interest and asked me what I was going to do with the paper. When I told him that I was going to take it home with me, he asked if he could give me one too. When I said that I would like to have one, he immediately started preparations to write one and then made detailed inquiries about how much time I was going to be there and what the time was at that moment. He checked up again later and each time added another sentence to the paper which he eventually gave me. Several more then gave me papers to carry home and Rachel gave me at least three others. Shari had read all of the words on a picture puzzle to me and afterwards I suggested that she write them out. She did so and then brought the paper to me saying. "My head hurts" (meaning from all that work).

This episode shared with the KEEP reading lesson described in Chapter 10 one crucial feature: reading for the sake of communicating something important to an adult. In this case, the importance was derived from conversations and attempts to incorporate me in their classroom and family *'ohana*. But, at the time, the significance of this was missed. Instead, I classified the episode as one more seat-work assignment, such as I had not been able to get them to do. But, then, I hadn't taken those home with me. Rather, most of them were erased by the children once they had been checked! This is a good example of what it means to "de-contextualize" the use of language. This is discussed again in connection with reading instruction below.

Familiar routines in the classroom

Children were constantly conversing and incorporating one another in activities. Routines comprising the rhetoric of solidarity described in Chapter 7 were in evidence. None of them, however, had a positive role to play in instruction. The consequences of these routines upon classroom behavior are described in this section.

Sex joking occurred, although not as frequently as it did in the recordings made in the KEEP kindergarten. Teachers who overhear sex teasing and the obscenities that accompany it are often shocked, and complain about "gutter language." The use of such language as an invitation to solidarity went entirely unrecognized. Some teachers, on the other hand, never even hear it, and when told about it refuse to believe that children so young talk that way.

The children's interest in oral arts was obvious. Both teacher and children made use of singing and reciting in unison. The latter somewhat resembled simple chanting. For instance:

Oct. The directions for making the numeral five were repeated in unison several times at the teacher's direction. Then while practicing the numeral at their desks Malia sang the instructions several times with her own tune, without being bidden.

They showed very close attention to the exact pronunciation of lyrics and rhythm when learning new songs. Later on I observed children in the third and fourth grades pronounce the lyrics of songs in Tahitian, Samoan, Maori—and even in Standard English! Particular Standard English phonemes not pronounced in everyday speech would be pronounced in songs, as in names (see above). This again shows the close relationship between verbal learning and socially valued communication. Singing is a highly valued social activity.

The children also frequently engaged in mimicry. For example:

11/3 While lying down before falling asleep [a Samoan girl] was repeating the way others had said their names on the tape with exact mimicry of intonation and voice quality. She also recited many jump-rope rhymes, singing them with marked expression. Other kids, too, were mimicking the speaking of names on tape.

Mimicking is one form of the verbal play described in Chapter 7. No use of mimicry was made in instructing them, except for reciting in unison, the effectiveness of which is discussed in the section on reading below.

Verbal disputing

The disputing described in Chapters 4 and 5 was observed so frequently in the classroom that I began to pay attention to it in subsequent research. It occurred most often when children attempted to give directions to one another or to share possessions. An example:

> 1/24 [A Hawaiian boy] and [a Portuguese boy] are putting the puzzles together on the window still shelf (straightening up). They work together disputing over what pieces go where. The former gives the latter a good blow but they continue working together.

Disputes over possessions often erupted into intense, heartfelt skirmishes which produced moodiness that lasted for a number of minutes, disrupting the work of one or both participants. Thus:

> 4/27 I asked Kala to find a word (written on cards in a stack that he had) which I wanted him to copy into the sentence he was composing. As he was looking through his stack Dano spotted the word first, pulled it out, and said it with glee. This apparently made Kala so angry that he immediately threw all of his cards on the floor and stared down glumly. He made some cracks at Dano. After a heated exchange Dano got angry and threw his cards at Kala, just missing his head. I told Dano to go pick them up, which he promptly started to do. I talked firmly to Kala, but he refused to acknowledge my presence. Dano then started to pick up some of his own cards, which were on the floor mixed with Kala's. At this point Kala rushed over and punched him hard. (The two were friendly again after lunch.)

Despite all of the disputing, there was also a lot of helping. Thus:

> 12/2 I noticed a girl in the next room go to another who was sitting all alone on the playground and crying, comfort her with arm around her, and lead her back into the room.

Help from peers became crucial when the children could not obtain the information from the teacher that would enable them to continue with the assigned work, which happened often, as we shall see below. By far the commonest way to carry out assignments was by copying.

3/9 After about the third line of our exercise (at the reading station) Malia said, "Let's start over," indicating that she had gotten behind. Immediately Ruby looked over on her paper and marked the answer for her.

4/6 Dano said to me with a smile that he did not want to color his assigned paper. Someone else said immediately, "I'll do yours for you."

This pattern was transferred from home, where helping one another as soon as the need is obvious is traditional (Chapters 2 and 3). In school, however, it led to continual reproof, as teachers tried to make each one ashamed to copy. Nor was copying an effective way to learn, since the children not only copied one another's mistakes, but also failed to explain to one another the reasons for their answers.

The struggle for control

The children very noticeably transferred from home to classroom their strong preference for initiating and completing activities without involving an adult. As we have seen in Chapters 2 and 5, Hawaiian children are expected to carry out their activities without being commanded to do them or calling an adult's attention. The teacher, however, unlike parents, desires to supervise activities close-ly—to initiate and terminate them on a schedule that in this case was unknown to the children. Activities were not repeated daily in such a way that the children could anticipate and initiate them on their own, as they could at home. They responded by attempting, continuously and strenuously, to do things on their own schedule. This conflict was the first thing to impress me, and it continued to occupy about three-quarters of my observation time. The conflict and its conse-quences are analyzed in this section.

Chores in the classroom were typically begun unbidden, upon seeing a need:

Oct. Crawford worked like a Trojan putting away the headsets and straightening out their cords at the listening station. We had just finished using them. Simul-taneously, several other children worked diligently without any comment from me erasing the marks on the covers to their exercise booklets. They showed a strong desire to finish these self-imposed tasks, even after the teacher announced that it was time to line up for lunch.

10/27 Several times children picked up minute bits of paper or lint off the floor, unbidden, balled them up and handed them to the teacher, who thanked them. Later in the day she made a point of getting the children to say that they would not like to have a room in their houses which was all messy.

In this last example, the teacher was making good use of the children's readiness to undertake such a task and to continue it on their own. Since it was early in the year, she was concentrating on housekeeping tasks. Later on in the year, however, when the children continued straightening up, they were often corrected. They would be told, ''You are not the room monitor today'' (note the desire to control who does what) or ''No one asked you to pick up.''

Children would not wait for a directive to begin their assignments, but began them as soon as they could guess what was required. This continued unabated throughout the year, despite rebukes. One example:

> 11/3 During the time the teacher was trying to get everyone ready to paint she said to one, ''Let me have your paper. You don't want to paint,'' (a favorite activity) meaning that the child had started after being warned not to do so until told.

Similarly, once involved in a task, even one that they had not wanted to begin, they often resisted strong attempts to make them quit before it was completed. Thus:

> 12/8 When the teacher's assistant came in to supervise their naps, she makes (three children) quit writing and put their assigned work away in their desks. At the end of nap time I noticed two of them have their work out and are continuing it. They are keeping an eye out for the teacher's assistant, who is a Hawaiian parent. (Had it been the teacher they would not have bothered.)

> 1/24 The teacher tries to make Moki stop his work in order to join the group. He opposes her. She finally has to threaten to tear up what he has just spent 35 to 40 minutes working on before he will agree to quit.

There are numerous entries which describe children engaged in some other activity when they were supposed to be doing assigned work. Typically, these other activities were valuable and appropriate to school. I cite here only instances involving Hawaiian children.

> 1/5 At the start of this activity involving the whole class John opted out and worked steadily at his desk while the rest of the class attended to the discussion of the children's pictures.

> 2/2 Kapono told me about the location of fish's gills, pointing to where they would be on his own face. He had spent some time watching them closely earlier when he was supposed to be doing an assignment.

Some days, the teacher reported, she ''did not even try to get them to do anything except what they were in the mood for.'' Such a strategy was the norm in several second through fifth grade classrooms that I observed later. In fact, it was not a bad strategy, provided the children had been given tasks that interested them. For instance:

> 4/27 While supposedly doing arithmetic at their desks the kids were copying words from the board and elsewhere, writing sentences of their own, and dictating sen-

tences to me describing pictures that they had drawn. There was a lot of practice of academic work going on without any effort by the teacher to direct it.

At such times as this, the children were acting upon their tendency to initiate and carry out their own amusements, which they learned at home. Had the teacher consistently taken advantage of this, she would have had an easier time managing her classroom. In fact, KEEP classrooms are run much more along these lines, as described in the next chapter.

The teacher, however, appeared to feel that she had to direct the children's activities most of the time. The result was a constant struggle between the teacher and children for control of their activities and attention. A description and analysis of this follows. It vividly illustrates, in the teacher's use of directives and the children's responses to them, the clash of cultures in classroom routines. Behavior like that described below is a product of the culture of teachers confronting the culture of the children in an area where both have deep, unconscious perceptions, values, and behavior patterns. This particular teacher's behavior was not basically different from that I observed in other classrooms. Unavoidably, the description will be embarrassing, but I want to assure teachers that I have shared the same mistakes and frustrations in this classroom. The welfare of the children demands, however, that we try to understand and prevent struggles such as those detailed below.

Teachers almost universally follow a strategy of "decontextualizing" in getting children to attend to them. That is, they attempt to train children to pay attention to them on demand, before an activity is underway (Scollon and Scollon 1980). This contrasts with the situation at home where attention arises in an on going activity. In addition, disciplinary routines are unwittingly reversed by the teacher, so that her scoldings resemble an invitation to conversation, while they ignore or try to avoid her when she threatens or commands, which most resemble a parent's "grumbling" (see Chapter 5). The overall consequences of this mismatch are that the children, not the teacher, end up in effective control of their activities, and this enables them to accomplish whatever assignments they do on their own initiative, as they do at home. Put simply, the children effectively subvert the discipline of the school.[27]

There were numerous occasions on which Ms. B. wanted the attention of all of the children at the same time. These included starting a new activity, moving a group from one place to another, quieting the class when so many were making noise or misbehaving that she could not continue what she was doing, or making an announcement. At these times, she would invariably use directives to attempt to gain the attention of all at one time. She used the following types of directives.[28]

Imperatives:
Give me your eyes.

Now don't make [me] [Ms. B.] [angry] [use /a/my/ /loud/out-
side/voice]   [send you back to your desks] [have you put down your
heads].
Let's help them get ready

Imbedded Imperatives:
Please don't make me use my outside voice.
Threatened insult: [counts to ten] [. . .] is a rotten egg. (Said by the
class.)

Question directives or hints:
Do you know why Ms. B. used her outside voice?
Do you know what it means, "a last chance"?
Do you have your thinking caps on?

Sarcastic courtesies:
Thank *you!*
Excuse *me!*

Hints or warnings:
You don't want [me] [Ms. B.] to get [very] angry.
You don't want to make [me] [Ms. B.] use [my] [her] outside voice.
I am getting very angry.
Now class this is your last chance.
You have no more chances.
Table [. . .] is not ready.
I think [. . .] [is] [are] going to have to [throw his away]   [get his wings
trimmed] [come up and love each other (i.e., stand in front of the class
holding hands)]/
[. . .] want to love each other (said because they would not sit apart).
I will write your name down so you will [have to work by me tomorrow]
[get no recess].

The routine would usually start with one of the directives at the top of this
list—an imperative—and progress, because of the children's noncompliance, to
the bottom of the list—hints or warnings. The constant need for these hints
accounts, I believe, for their richness and variety.

As a result of widespread noncompliance and inattention (the two were often
one and the same) the teacher would from time to time attempt to bring everything to a halt for a scolding. While this is my term, older children frequently
referred to "scoldings" by teachers, referring to similar types of behavior. This
teacher's scoldings consisted of the following.

Is it fair to the good people to make them all go back to their desks, too?
I have been trying for [half an hour] to [. . .] so now we won't be able to
    [. . .].
Do you like to see people get mad?
Do you know why I am angry with [. . .]? Because he did not [. . .].
He is making us unhappy.
Put your fingers in your ears. Is there anything there that would keep you
    from being able to listen?
I tried to be nice, but that is it!
Put your heads down on your desks.

One can infer from these statements that the teacher perceived the situation as a violation by the children of some rule of fair play: "I tried to be nice, but you. . . ." They imply a contract in which the children pay attention when told to do so, and carry out instructions when ordered, in return for which she maintains an even temper and goes on with her planned lessons. Scoldings are, to her, a legitimate response to the breaking of this contract.

This entire sequence contrasts with the sequence of disciplinary routines that the children are familiar with at home. As described in Chapter 5, parents typically issue a series of imperatives, escalated only by routine threats, i.e., without signs of immanent anger, which children blithely ignore. Before punishment occurs, the parent shows clear signs of anger, and specifies explicitly the circumstances in which punishment will be meted out if compliance is not forthcoming. At the confrontation, the child is forced to incriminate him or herself, judgment is announced, and physical punishment (or a dramatic enactment of it) is immediate. This scenario contrasts fundamentally with the disciplinary routines that the teacher used as described above. First, at home the child's attention is directed to the parent by implicit contextual cues: rising anger in the parent. Second, the teacher does not explicitly state the circumstances and the behavior that will result in punishment, as the parent does. Instead, from the child's point of view, punishment is contextual, implicit in the teacher's mood. Anger does not precede and frame a statement of the exact circumstances of punishment. Hence, it is reasonable to surmise that the children take the teacher's threats as they do routine threats at home—i.e., they ignore them. When she became angry, however, they would try to mollify her, often by engaging in housekeeping tasks—because this is a good way to put parents in a good mood.[29] Finally, instead of escalating by dramatic charges, followed by judgment and punishment, with increasing emotional intensity, the teacher often becomes almost chatty with hints about her state of mind. Her questions clearly invite conversation. Such an outcome, instead of a fierce confrontation, is something new for the children, to judge by their home experience. As we shall see below, conversations with the teacher were often initiated in just this way.

Summarizing, it appears that the teacher and Hawaiian parents are almost completely opposite in the cues that they provide leading up to and administering punishment. Hawaiian children attend to implicit contextual cues about when to pay attention to an activity, whereas the teacher explicitly demands attention in the absence of contextual cues. Hawaiian parents are explicit, on the other hand, in stating contingencies and administering punishment. The teacher, by contrast, is implicit and contextual. The result, we hypothesize, is that children miss the cues. Hard as it may be to believe, they are actually surprised many times when the teacher's punishments occur. Finally, parents administer unmistakable, dramatic confrontations, whether or not they give physical punishment. The teacher, by contrast, administers nothing that the children would recognize as punishment. Instead, she appears to be inviting talk-story. The result can hardly be a deterrent.

The teacher also would often refuse to provide information, with the argument that the children should have listened at the start. This did not serve to reinforce attending, as she intended. Rather, it only made obtaining assistance unpredictable, and thus reinforced imitation of one another, and self-reliance.

Talking with the teacher vs. reciting

The children liked to talk to the teacher. But they resisted her attempts to question them individually in class, turning recitations into a collective response which resembles the structure of talking story. The reluctance to say much in reply to direct questions also appeared in dyadic relationships with the observer, even in the midst of friendly conversation. The consequences for classroom control are examined in this section.

Children were as eager to seize upon an occasion for starting conversation with the teacher as they were with me.

1/27 After class Malia and another girl were standing around talking with the teacher and Malia said to her in an ebullient tone, "You gettin married!" Ms. B., pleased, replied that she was. The talk continued.

Once underway, they prolonged a conversation as long as possible:

6/1 While we were recording Mrs. H. sitting near us leaned over suddenly and was about to faint. After Ms. B. had helped her from the room the kids crowded around the doorway to look and would not go back into the room despite my urging. When the teacher returned there was a great desire on the part of the kids to talk about what had happened. The teacher called upon them in turn, and they waited to be recognized, which was unusual. Shari told about a woman fainting someplace. [A Samoan girl] told about her mother dying. The teacher explained that Mrs. H did not die, and then described what it was like to faint. Malia told a story, and then Leona described how Mrs. H. had started to fall over. Foa told about seeing his mother leaning on a fence one night. After the teacher tried to go on with an art lesson, April put up her hand and when called upon said that her Aunty had fainted one time.

> At the end of the count of ten when the whole class is supposed to be sitting on the floor, D. is not there. Instead he goes out the door of the class. One of the children calls the teacher's attention to this and she says, "D. is being stubborn." She then engages the class in a conversation about being stubborn, asking them if they know what it means to be stubborn. Someone suggests that it means to be sad. Someone else says it means bad. The teacher says that you are stubborn if someone asks you to do something and you say [demonstrating], "No, I won't do it!" At this point one of the children says, "Yes. They ask you and you no like." (Boggs 1972: 304)

I noted conversations three other times when the teacher or myself was ready to scold and asked a question similar to that above. This is puzzling, given the reluctance to answer questions, particularly when scolding was threatened (see Chapter 5). But questions like that illustrated would not incriminate the child who answered (at least in his or her mind), nor was any one individual required to reply. Thus it can be inferred that questions which do not "put an individual on the spot" can be interpreted as an invitation to converse. This inference is confirmed by children's responses to questions during the reading lesson, as described in Chapter 10.

Given their general eagerness to talk, their behavior when called upon to recite individually was puzzling at the time. In fact, the behavior of the whole class during attempted recitations was puzzling. As reported earlier:

> When the teacher asked a question at least a dozen hands would usually shoot up and then, before anyone could be recognized . . . , several would blurt out the answer. . . . When called upon to answer a question . . . a child was likely to answer minimally, if he answered at all. When the question was addressed to another child or to the whole group, however, children who volunteered were more voluble. . . . It sometimes happened that a child would wave his hand in response to a question asked before the whole class, blurt out an answer, and then not deliver the answer he had just uttered when called upon. (Boggs 1972: 301, 304)

I became even more puzzled when I observed that, even in a single conversation with me, the same child would talk at greater length when I simply indicated interest than when I asked a question. Unlike the recitation situation, my questions were almost always answered, but the answers were briefer than the remarks which were volunteered when I did not question. Subsequently, I checked this with a statistical analysis based upon the number of words uttered by the child following a question or some other remark on my part. The differences were significant at the .001 level. It seemed at the time as if "it is basically unpleasant for a Hawaiian child to have a question directed to him by an adult"

(op. cit.: 307). The reason for this was unknown at the time. When the recordings were obtained of parents scolding their children it became clear that parents
use questions directed at an individual child for the purpose of obtaining a
confession of wrong-doing that will lead immediately to punishment. In this
circumstance, the child is expected to say very little beyond what is directly
requested, or to remain silent before his accuser (see Examples 5.8 and 5.10).
Moreover, evidence mentioned in Chapter 5 indicates that parents rarely use
direct questions in any other context, and that when they do children spoke
minimally (see Example 5.9). All of this relates to the behavior described in this
section. Individual answers during recitation carry the risk of being wrong before
the whole class, just as any inquiry into one's actions, e.g., "Where were you?"
put an individual on the spot if only that person is required to respond. By
contrast, a question like "Do you know what it means to be stubborn?" asked
when a scolding may be expected, has the effect of stimulating conversation,
because it is so clearly nonincriminating under the circumstances.

The reaction of the class to attempts at recitation had a drastic effect upon
control of the classroom. The response of several children talking at once shifted
the dyadic relationship to one in which the teacher was forced to treat the entire
class as a whole, rather than one child at a time. Several commentators have
interpreted this, correctly I think, as a defensive maneuver by the children
(Howard 1973; Hymes 1972: xvii, lii). Bernstein has pointed out how older
children collectively defend themselves against teachers by verbal play and joking (1969).

It is of interest to consider by what means such a strategy evolves. I would
trace it to the verbal play which children engage in with parents. Verbal play, as
analyzed in Chapter 7, is collective and occurs in an egalitarian relationship. This
suggests the possibility that children, when threatened by individually-directed
questions in an hierarchical relationship, might seek to escape by engaging the
adult in verbal play. In fact, during the response to recitation they contradict,
mimic one another, play with words, insult, and laugh.

In summary, the response to the teacher's persistent attempts to make the
children answer questions individually and only when called upon had the effect
of turning recitations into struggles for the control of the classroom. This outcome was the same when she attempted to gain their attention and make them
initiate official activity only when ordered to do so. Indeed, both were skirmishes
in one ongoing battle. The consequences for learning were disastrous,
understandably.

Learning to read

This entire investigation was undertaken to determine why Hawaiian children
generally performed so poorly in school, and particularly why they failed to learn
to read. When the above analysis is considered from the standpoint of its effects

upon reading, it is obvious that most of the activity in the classroom was either irrelevant to reading, or positively interfered with carrying out the activities that were intended to develop reading skills. The teaching scheme required them to follow directives for individual exercises which were intended to teach them the meanings of certain words and concepts and to recognize particular shapes, sizes, sounds, letters, and written words. Practice was to occur by silent rehearsal or writing. The assumption appeared to be that, properly motivated, the children would transfer the meanings so obtained to similar stimuli in different contexts.

For example, I spent much of the year supervising groups of four to ten children in carrying out Reading Readiness Exercises. In these lessons, the teacher gave the instructions to mark the picture, one of several, corresponding to a word which she spoke on the tape, e.g., "mark the towel not the tower," or the first of two events in a presumed sequence, e.g., a small child and a larger one, or the object with wheels, etc. The children had individual copies of the page in front of them, enclosed in plastic on which they were to mark their answers.

The scheme appears to be flawed in at least three fundamental ways. First, in execution. The foregoing analysis has indicated the many ways in which attention and instruction failed to occur as the scheme demanded. For instance, the teacher's strategy of telling them only once meant that they often missed information that was essential for carrying out the instructions. Second, and more fundamentally, no attention was given to the contexts in which the concepts learned were to be transferred. As Cole and Scribner (1974) have demonstrated, the context of elicitation plays a crucial role in promoting transfer of training in cross-cultural learning experiments. Day has demonstrated rigorously the nonoccurrence of transfer in the learning of Standard English plurals, except under the most exact similarity of training and test conditions (1974). More particularly, no attention is given in the scheme to the social context in which the symbols to be learned are to be used. This is what we have referred to following Scollon and Scollon (1980) as "decontextualization." Most of the time, the social context was assumed to be nonexistent, since the children were supposed to do the exercises alone, and to transfer what they learned alone. The outcome of this strategy will be illustrated in this section. Evidence will then be presented to indicate that, when appropriate social contexts were provided, the children showed definite evidence of learning to read.

The effect of a social context upon the use of language is illustrated by the following observations:

10/27 During the arithmetic lesson Ms. B. heard the children say "tree" for "three" and had them repeat "three" several times, "putting our tongue between our teeth." Later I noticed children always using "tree" for the numeral. (Note: the actual pronunciation is an affricate *tr* in pidgin.)

12/8 One of the assignments was to count the number of particular objects on a worksheet and underline the numeral corresponding to the number of those objects. I was checking one paper with a boy. On it there happened to be three pictured trees and two numeral threes. Since the boy had it wrong, I asked him how many "trees." He said two, meaning the numeral threes. A girl watching said to him with scorn, "No, it's '*th*ree,' not 'tchree'." This is the first time I have heard one child correct another's use of this phoneme.

I interpret the use of the pidgin form in the first observation, and the use of the Standard English form in the second by the girl, as follows: In the first instance, "three" was something you said when the teacher had everyone practice putting their tongues between their teeth, the whole class performing together. When you spoke your own dialect, you used the appropriate form, "tchree." The resulting homonym created difficulties for the boy in the second observation. The girl, who had somehow realized that a homonym was involved, made use of her knowledge and produced a minimal pair, contrasting "tchree" and "three." Her act was socially meaningful, since children commonly correct one another's speech (for instance, see Examples 6.11 and 7.7.). The teaching in the first instance was intended to be decontextualized, and appeared to be ineffective. In the second instance, learning which had already occurred was demonstrated because of the social context of use. The conclusion is that, in order to be demonstrated, a learned behavior has to occur in a socially appropriate context. It will not generalize without regard to context.

Appropriate social contexts appeared occasionally in the instruction observed in this classroom, usually accidentally. However, striking instances of past learning were then demonstrated. One example already cited was the reading and writing of one another's names. The children were equally interested in reading the notes I jotted down on a small piece of paper that I carried in my pocket.

Nov. A girl comes over and looks at the paper on which I am writing, says, "My name." Again she comes back, turns the paper over with her finger, and says immediately, "There it is. That's where I lived," pointing to "Maui" on my notes.

It took skill to read this word in my script, written small. And yet this girl could do it in the second month of the first grade because it was an important word to her and served to help her relate to me in conversation. When tested, however, she read at about the 20th percentile.

Such words resemble the "key words" described by Sylvia Ashton-Warner in her classic description of Maori education, *Teacher* (1963). Words may be important and thus remembered because they are associated with significant past experience, as she indicates, or because they grow out of, or contribute to, conversation with an adult whom the child wishes to incorporate (see above). Such conversation was part of the procedure used for selecting the key words, as described by Ashton-Warner. Thus we see an important convergence between her findings and those of the present book.[30]

Another example was furnished by the Language Experience Method. A locally developed version of this was used early in the school year:

> 11/3 The teacher had each child, four to five at a time, bring up their paintings and tell the class what they were. She wrote what they said on the back, and commented on them. Later she explained to me that the kids could almost read these sentences, even though "they don't know their words."

By February, a language arts teacher was working with the highest ability group in the classroom, helping them write their own "stories," usually one or two sentences—sometimes longer. The children would ask her how to spell the words or look them up in books which she supplied. The stories were based upon pictures which they drew and colored first. Results of this procedure have been given in several of the examples earlier in this chapter. Contrary to their reactions at the listening station with the Reading Readiness Exercises, it was not hard to get the children to make up and read their own sentences.

Examining a number of these sentences, both the teacher and I were impressed by the length and complexity of the sentences which the children wrote when compared with those written by a group with comparable ability who had only been exposed to the regular readers. The former, for instance, used more prepositions. It would be nice to report that the method produced a marked improvement in reading scores by the end of the year. But no overall significant differences were found. Nevertheless, the observations indicate that the method had potential for producing self-initiated practice. I believe that it was effective because reading and writing were seen by the children as part of a meaningful conversation with an adult. Recall their attempts to incorporate me by writing and conversation, as described at the beginning of the chapter.

There was also a noticeable motivation to discuss with me stories that the children had heard or read. The reading incident that impressed me the most was the following:

> 6/1 A number of children had recorded for me the story of Caspar the Friendly Ghost, looking at the pictures in the book, but not attempting to read the words. Leo had looked closely at several pages while waiting his turn and when it came he literally tried to read every word, even though he knew at most only three or four words on each page. He was tireless in his attempt. He gazed raptly at each word and then at me as if in some fashion he could absorb or imagine what the word was by looking hard enough at it or at me. The teacher came by while we were thus engaged and smiled when I told her that Leo could almost read it. As soon as he finished with some help from me, he wanted to repeat the whole story. By the time we had been through it twice everyone had left for the day, and I finally had to call an end. Leo was still eager to continue.

In this instance, reading was integral to a socially appropriate and meaningful conversation: a part of talking story with me, which we had been doing all year. What if such conversations became an integral part of reading instruction? The first problem that would have to be solved would be to keep the group small, to prevent too much talking at once, and above all to avoid anything resembling recitation in reply to individually directed questions. In the next chapter, one set of solutions to these problems is described. The results, in terms of the development of reading skills, turned out to be unprecedented, because for once the children's patterns and style of communication have been utilized, rather than combatted.

The informal experiments just described are a good illustration of the correctness of the argument advanced by Erickson (1977; Erickson and Mohatt 1982) and Jordan and Tharp (1979) that a relatively small change in patterns found in most schools can effect major changes in performance if the changes are congruent with the culture of the children. It is crucial, however, that this congruence be recognized when it occurs, so that it can be integrated into an overall instructional strategy. That did not happen in my classroom at Aina Pumehana. It has happened at KEEP.

CHAPTER 10

The Kamehameha Early Education Program: Talking Story with a Book

Stephen T. Boggs and Georgia McMillen

Anyone observing a classroom at the Kamehameha Early Education Program, kindergarten through third grade, would note some striking differences from the classroom described in the previous chapter. At KEEP there is much more praise by the teachers and much less scolding. The children are doing what they are supposed to be doing a significantly larger proportion of the time (Tharp 1977; Jordan and Tharp 1979). The struggle for control, so prominent at Aina Pumehana public school, has diminished greatly at KEEP, although it has not disappeared entirely, as we shall see. But in spite of these significant differences, one would still recognize the culture of the children. The verbal routines and patterns of relating that have been described throughout this book are still quite evident in the KEEP children. The classroom, however, has been organized in such a way that these patterns are utilized, or rendered neutral, rather than combatted, as they were in the Aina Pumehana classroom just described.

While these innovations in classroom management may have had some effect upon the development of reading skills, it was not until a new curriculum and method of teaching reading comprehension was introduced at KEEP that reading scores showed marked improvement. This is revealed by the history of the reading test scores, which increased from a dismal 13th percentile nationally the first year to the 23rd percentile by the third year (Tharp 1980: Fig. 2). By that time, most of the classroom management system had been implemented by teachers who had been trained in its use. Despite this, children were reading no better than groups of comparable children in the public schools of the immediate community (Tharp op. cit.). From these results, one must draw the conclusion that proper classroom management, no matter how essential it may be, is not sufficient for teaching children to read well. Something else is needed. That turned out to be a method for direct instruction in reading to comprehend. This teaching method has been described by Au (1979, 1980a). The results were startling: an increase in reading test scores to the 67th percentile in the first year, which have stabilized at around the 50th percentile through 1979 (Tharp op. cit.).

In this chapter we will argue that this method of instruction is effective because it introduced a rich context for the act of reading—a context that integrated immediate, social functions of speech with referential uses of language, both oral and printed. By comparing what happens in a typical reading lesson at KEEP with the verbal routines involved in talking story outside of school, it is concluded further that these reading sessions represent a cultural synthesis of familiar and novel verbal routines and participation structures which enable Hawaiian children to use their sociolinguistic skills in learning to read.

First, however, the organization of the KEEP classroom will be described, drawing upon the work of Jordan and Tharp (1979) and O'Neal and Bogert (1977). As we shall then see, this has not resulted in drastic changes in the children's culture, but rather has accommodated the culture of the children and that of the school to one another (Jodan and Tharp 1979). One consequence of the classroom organization at KEEP, it is suggested, may be the enhancement of cooperation among same age peers, thus mitigating the disputing described in earlier chapters.

The major portion of the chapter describes a typical KEEP reading lesson. The accompanying analysis specifies the ways in which it resembles joint narrative performances in talk-story sessions outside of school, comparing the results obtained here with Au's analyses (1980a, 1980b). The question is then raised of whether such lessons are successful because of a congruence with Hawaiian culture, or because they represent good teaching such as would be found anywhere. The chapter concludes with a brief consideration of other factors which may contribute to the effectiveness of the innovations at KEEP.

The data in this chapter are based upon a total of approximately 2 hours of video-tapes. It is not as comprehensive as that contained in the previous chapter, which was based upon many full days of participation. To offset this, I have made reference to systematic observations by KEEP researchers on key points and supplemented the tapes with impressions drawn from my own participation in the first kindergarten class, a number of visits to the observation deck over the years, and numerous conversations with the research and teaching staff. I have tried to be careful about drawing any inferences based upon what does *not* happen at KEEP, since the data will not support such inferences. Hence, comparisons are limited to features that are evident in both places, or present at KEEP, but lacking in Aina Pumehana.[31]

Organization of the KEEP classroom

Very little time is spent in a KEEP classroom with a teacher directing or instructing the class as a single group. Instead, the children spend most of their time in groups at "centers" in each of which a particular activity is performed (Jordan and Tharp 1979; O'Neil and Bogert 1977). Each child has an individualized schedule of tasks for the day, which is based upon careful assessment of her or his previous work. Since individual programs vary, group composition shifts over a day, but everyone changes centers at the same time, and reading groups stay the same over long periods.[32] Mention has already been made of the fact that praise is frequent and "desists" and/or punishment are infrequent, compared with local public school classrooms (Tharp and Gallimore 1976).

The children react to this organization by spending around 90 percent of their time doing what they are supposed to be doing (Tharp 1977; Jordan and Tharp 1979). But, despite this, they appear to engage frequently in name play, writing of names, teasing by correcting speech and mimicry, and disputing—all routines encountered outside of school and in the Aina Pumehana classroom described in Chapter 9 (field notes, including three 20-minute video-tapes of typical center activity made in 1975). The children's culture is obviously alive and well at KEEP. The following is a typical dispute observed between two first-graders who had been assigned to tutor each other. They were in the first KEEP cohort:

Example 10.1. (Mapuana, a "lieutenant" to the class leader; Anna; and teacher)

Text	Comments
M: Make it in a straight line.	Command, instructs.
. . . a smaw . . .	
A: . . . going down like dis?	
. . . about dat size?	Attempts to comply, requests confirmation.
M: No, 'bout . . . [leans over to do it]	Contradicts, corrects.
Le' me do it for you.	
A: No!	
[A works with M monitoring for about 3 minutes]	
M: 'Uh 'uh. No-ot, no-ot, no-ot. Not. Miss Howe she made um wrong!	Contradicts, complains to t.
[Teacher comes up]	
M: Look. Cause I—I didn' tell her fo make one fourt' page. I had di-is. I—I was waiting fo her, but den she—she didn' teu me when she finish. (". . . I didn't tell her to go on to the fourth page . . .")	Commands t., explains, complains.
A: She made da yellow circu for me.	Counter-complaint against M.
t: Okay! . . . why don't we start this one over again.	Suggests resolution.
M: N-o! Don'! You canno'. Cause if you made a mistake you have to turn the paper ova. [as if reciting]	Interdicts A, thus contradicting t, cites rule.

continued

Example 10.1. *continued*

| Text | Comments |

Text	Comments
t: Okay turn the paper over and start all over.	Command to A, agreeing with M.
M: Wait! <u>Wait</u>! No-o! Wait! I gon check my cards see if I have dat.	Interdicts A, in effect contradicting t again.
t: How didju make that thing, Anna? Did she tell you?	Requests information.
A: No, but I <u>know</u>. I know what <u>card</u>.	Denies that she would have to be told.
M: But you not spose to make it if I don' teu you to, das why.	Corrects A, citing rule.
A: [inaudible] [Teacher moves away]	
M: . . . Den get one <u>red</u> crayon and make one triangle. [irritated tone] (". . . Then get a <u>red</u> crayon and make a triangle.")	Command, instructs.
A: . . . make da <u>papa</u>.	
M: Spose to make it on <u>dis</u> side, not that side.	Corrects
A: So-<u>o</u>!? It doesn't matter which side you make it on.	Challenge, cites another rule, implying that she has not erred.
M: Uh-huh, it <u>does</u>, too! As long as you saves. [about 1 minute and no turns later]	Contradicts, cites another rule: "[You have to use both sides] because it saves paper."
M: Hurry <u>u-up</u>, Anna! [sharply] If you don't make it now I go' tell the teacher . . . [pause]	Commands, complains, and threatens, specifying contingency.
M: Miss <u>Ho-owe</u>, she won't do what I'm tellin her to do an I hafta wait so <u>long</u>! [Teacher is not in view]	Complains.
A: I'm gonna wait until she tells me the whole thing, first.	Self-justification.
M: Huh <u>uh</u>, I gotta tell one bit at a time, dumby.	Contradicts, insults.
A: . . . uh spose to tell <u>all</u> den—<u>den</u> I spose to color. ("Huh uh, you are supposed to tell <u>everything</u> before I color.")	Counters by citing rule.
M: Huh uh, cause you might for<u>get</u>, so.	Contradicts, implying that A is incompetent.
A: Huh uh. [episode ends]	

While this has no more sequences than disputes recorded outside of school, it is at least as complex (see Example 6.8.). It is a good example of what happens when age peers attempt to relate hierarchically. The superior in this case was excessively bossy—even to the extent of interfering with the teacher's directives. The subordinate, who started out compliant, still insisted on doing things her own way, and asserting her own knowledge. The struggle escalated to insults. Arguments were introduced, even when they lacked relevance (e.g., ". . . as long as you saves.").

A novel behavior was frequently observed at KEEP, however. Children teased and disputed about who was ahead in school work. Such competition was not noted in the Aina Pumehana classroom, despite nearly 100 hours of observation. A possible explanation for this is discussed after illustrating it.

Example 10.2. (Second grade. Leila, a Caucasian, and Warren are doing exercises in their workbooks, Donnie is reading. L. has just failed to attract the teacher's attention)

Text	Comments
L: Ding Dong Bell.	Insult directed at t. for not paying attention to her.
D: You go copy, Ding Dong Bell. [W enters]	Turns insult onto L.
L: How come she doesn't come to me? Ding Dong Bell!	Complaint, repeats insult, ignores D.
D: You one Ding Dong Bell!	Repeats insult.
L: Oh, yer on the baby book.	Counter-insult.
W: [who has been observing them] You're on da ba-a-aby bo-o-ok.	Joins insulting, chants.
D: So.	Challenge, defends self.
L: Yer a baby. You don't even know times tables.	Further insult.
W: [looking at D's book] Eh! this one no mo time tables, eh? [later]	Allegation to support insult.
L: Donnie's on da ba-a-aby book [chanting]	
W: Ba-a-aby book. [points to it]	
D: I not on da ba-a-aby book!	
W: [points to D] You got the ba-a-aby bo-o-ok.	
L: Yeah, you got da ba-a-aby bo-o-ok. [D mumbles something]	

(This incident was first described by Martin 1975).

The children typically paid continuing attention to one another's progress in doing assignments, claimed to be ahead, and sometimes got into disputes about these claims. An example:

Example 10.3. (Second graders <u>M</u>illie, a Samoan; <u>D</u>ina; <u>S</u>herrie; and <u>W</u>ally are doing assignments in their workbooks)

[D says something to S, flips through her workbook and looks into M's book, comparing. S speaks to D, then stands and leans toward her]

Text	Comments
D: I passed her! I passed her. [flips through her book] [to M] I passed you. [S points with her pencil to D's and M's places in workbooks]	Claim.
M: [looks up a bit irritated and then resumes work] [About 1½ minutes and no turns later]	Refuses to respond.
D: [to M] Eh, look! She stay with me! Aye! [W flips through pages of his workbook, glancing at M, who is working]	Expression of concern.
W: [to himself] I pass . . . [resumes work] [pause]	Claim, unfinished sentence, soliloquy.
M: [to W] You neva pass me, eh?	Challenge.
W: [reaching over to flip page in M's book] Whea?! I pass you! [indignantly, chin out]	Counter-challenge, counter-claim.
M: [shakes head "no", pouting]	Contradicts, timidly.
W: You on dis, you on dis?	Invites response, requests information.
M: [looks at W, says nothing] [W nervously beats his book with pencil as he waits for response]	Does not respond.
D: [leaning toward M and pointing to her work] Look, I pass her, I go pass her, yeah? [taps her book and M's with pencil]	Claim.
W: [leans across table staring at M's book, ignores D] Oh, no, no. [D goes back to work]	Invites response again, denial.
W: [resumes seat, looks at M] Eh, she can—I—she pass me. She damn well pass me, eh!	Admits he is behind, exclaims.
M: [nods head affirmatively]	Agrees timidly.
W: [head cocked toward M] You neva pass me. [unemphatically]	Repeats initial challenge, but de-escalates.
M: [has resumed work, looks up and nods affirmatively]	Contradicts, timidly.

Example 10.3. *continued*

Text	Comments
W: [leans toward her, shakes fist in front of her face, then with pencil clasped in fist, shakes it rhythmically 3 times, gradually pulling it closer to his face]	Ritual warning.
M: [looks up and then back down] [another boy stands up and pounds table, then relapses into chair] [episode is over]	Does not respond. Urges a fight.

Description taken from Martin (1975).

The ritualized nature of this dispute suggests that it has been practiced often, as numerous examples testify.

This appearance of disputing over who is ahead in school work is interesting, since the philosophy at KEEP has opposed individual competition. It is predictable from the hypothesis developed in Chapters 3 and 4, however, that children who are sensitive to assertiveness in same-age peers would dispute over any perceived claim to be ahead on assignments, if those assignments were important to them. It may be that the emphasis upon task completion (Tharp 1977; Jordan and Tharp 1979), added to the fact that students work in groups, promotes comparing of task completion, and this leads to disputing over who is ahead.

On the other hand, work in groups may also provide more experience in cooperating, and this, as suggested in Chapter 1, may provide opportunities for children the same age to discover ways of resolving disputes. The work of Jordan suggests some of the ways in which the children cooperate. She states that "peer teaching/learning interactions," both in and out of school, "take place in the context of ongoing attempts to perform an activity" and "are involved in the enterprise at hand." For instance, although children may freely insult one another, they do so while actually trying to do something. But a child who knows what to do will in school show another who is having difficulty performing, or actually perform the correct behavior for another (1977: 33–35). Jordan's observations are valuable because there was little of this "modelling" and "intervention" that was not rejected by other children in the tapes of center activity reviewed by the senior author. I was not searching for tapes in which it occurred, however, while Jordan was observing in order to find such incidents. Her observations, cited from K–1, are confirmed for grades 2 and 3 (Jordan, D'Amato, and Joesting 1981; Ignacio 1981). While there is no evidence at present that such cooperation increases over the 4 years that children attend KEEP, it would be reasonable to hypothesize that it does, given the increased opportunity for same age peers to cooperate there, as compared with home.

The children's drive to complete their official or self-assigned tasks, which so frequently clashed with the teacher's attempts to control their activities in the Aina Pumehana classroom, did not affect control of the KEEP classroom to the same degree. The explanation for this difference clearly lies in different class-room management systems. Through a training process which begins in kinder-garten, KEEP students are accustomed to move from one activity center to another at preset and known times. When they do so according to the rules, which are strictly monitored, they receive rewards. When they do not, they lose privileges.[33] This has the obvious result of linking their drive to complete work with the orderly pursuit of class routines. This result is a good example of the way in which a cultural pattern, in this case the habit of completing work on one's own, may be utilized in the classroom instead of combatted. The habit exemplifies an "accommodated element" which is characteristic both of home and KEEP, as well as some school cultures elsewhere (Jordan and Tharp 1979).

How has all of this affected learning to read? Overall, the system of classroom management, and the children's generally favorable reactions to it, may have been necessary for the dramatic improvement in reading ability which eventually occurred, but it was not sufficient, as Tharp has argued (1980). While the time spent by the children interacting with one another does not seem to prevent most of them from completing their assigned work, and that spent by teachers in actual instruction is much greater at KEEP than it was at Aina Pumehana, the crux of the matter, so far as reading is concerned, appears to be how reading instruction affects students' interaction with one another and the teacher over written mate-rials. In the next section, we examine a typical session using the method of teaching reading comprehension. The major argument to be developed is that the new technique introduced a rich social context for the act of reading which motivates students to participate in reading lessons and to practice reading on their own in order to feed back information obtained from reading into the lessons. This motivation is based, we believe, upon the resemblance between certain features of the reading lesson and talk-story sessions outside of school.

The structure of the reading lesson

Au (1980a: 101, 109; 1980b) has demonstrated that reading lessons which are regarded as good examples of the KEEP method for direct instruction of com-prehension (Tharp 1980) are characterized by "joint performance," i.e., se-quences of dialogue during which more than one child is likely to participate in response to a teacher's question with the approval of the teacher and the group, although not in unison. As she correctly notes, this is a major similarity between the reading lesson as a whole and talk-story narrative performance outside of school, as originally described by Watson-Gegeo (Watson 1975: 54–55). The analysis that follows suggests that joint performance also occurs in regard to the underlying routine, i.e., both teacher and students propose, corroborate, or argue one another's propositions in a way that resembles narrative performance among groups of children as defined and illustrated in Chapter 7. The analysis also proposes that the teacher helps to bring about such a result by using specific routines in two different phases of the lessons. An explanation is then offered for the children's motivation to participate so energetically while at the same time sticking to topics that the teacher wants to discuss.

The lesson described is the same one analyzed by Au (1980a). Four other lessons, two similar and two contrasting ones, have been analyzed by her also (1980b). The present lesson is atypical of a good lesson in only one feature, so far as known. That is, in most sessions the teacher spends only a few minutes discussing the children's experiences before moving on to silent reading and discussion of the reading, repeating the cycle several times in a session. In this instance the entire session has only a single period of silent reading.

Student time

"Student time" gets its name from the fact that students are free during this discourse to offer reports and narratives based upon personal experiences, rather than being limited to answering requests for specific information from the book. It corresponds to the "E" [Experience] phase of the lesson, as described by Au (1979). The author had no knowledge of this concept before analyzing the tape, however. The characterization of student time was based solely upon the children's behavior and the teacher's response to it. The phrase is borrowed by analogy from Bremme and Erickson (1977), who describe a type of event which resembles "show and tell" in many American classrooms. It differs from the latter, however, in that any topic is relevant in "show and tell," whereas only topics that are responsive to the teacher's questions are relevant in student time.

A second grade teacher at KEEP is conducting a reading lesson with four students. The story they are about to read is "Freddy Found a Frog" by Alice James Napjus (1973). To involve them in the reading and help them understand the story before they read it, the teacher asks a series of questions calling for personal reports and speculation relating to the story. To the question, "What would you do with a frog if you had a frog?" asked of Eli, a student responded:

Example 10.4. (Lokia, Marian, Cynthia, Eli, and Teacher. Group and Voice unidentified)
(Numbers indicate lines on transcript in McMillen, Boggs, and Au 1979)
(Note: Initials in this transcript have been changed to the pseudonyms above as follows: A=Lokia, L=Marian, C=Cynthia, and S=Eli)

Initiation	Reply	Evaluation
	45-6	
	L : Boy-y-y, he would drop it! I'd be scared to hold it!	
		47A
		T : You would be scared
	47B	to hold it.
	T : Why? What does it feel like when you hold it? [puts hand in front of	

continued

Example 10.4. *continued*

Initiation			Reply		Evaluation
			her body and gestures holding something, looks at E, rubs her hands together in front of her chest]		
		48-9			
		M :	Yucky((C: Slippery)).	50	
51				T :	Might feel slippery.
L :	It spits! Da ting	52			
	spit--	E :	Maybe		
53			you might wanna give it to somebody		
L :	It'll spit at you.		else.	54	
	[sits back and starts			T :	Oh, you think they
	to roll up pants	55-6			spit at you?
	leg]	G :	Ye-e-eh.	57	
58		E :	They do, they do.	T :	Oh-h-h. [softly]
M :	And goin' have warts				
	like this. [pulls	58-9			
	up pant leg, raises	G :	[look]		
	leg to table level]	T :	You get warts from touching frogs?		
		60-1,63			
		E :	Yah.	62	
			No-o+o	T :	Is that
			If they spit on		true? [looks at E]
			you, you get warts.	64	
65				T :	A-a-a-ah.
M :	Like right hea.	65			
	[points to leg]	G :	[look]	T :	[looks]

For an explanation of columns see Chapter 6 and p. 158 below. Overlaps are indicated by vertical brackets if on different lines or by horizontal brackets or (( )) if on same line.

In this passage the children are engaged in coreporting, collaborating to develop Lokia's proposition. The children, not the teacher, initiate the above sequence with their propositions; other students repsond with affirmation, corroboration, or in one case momentary contradiction. The teacher's role is limited in this portion to evaluations—one form of mediation—and responses in the form of follow-up questions. These clearly function to encourage the students to continue talking story.[34]

After inviting personal experiences or speculation, the teacher in student time usually affirms, or at least gives recognition to, all answers that do not contradict any group consensus, and are responsive to her questions; not just to one answer that she is looking for. Au refers to such behavior as the teacher allowing "breathing room" (1980a: 111). Thus, in the following instance the teacher asks for specific information about a personal experience, but Marian responds with a long narrative instead, which supports her earlier claim to have touched a frog.

Example 10.5. (same as Example 10.4)

Initiation		Reply	Evaluation
68-70			
T :	What did it feel like,		
	Marian?		
C :	Even S...		
	when I	wen--	
M :		My--my-my bro-	
	ther, you know uh--		
	across the street?		

Example 10.5. *continued*

Initiation	Reply	Evaluation
There--there's some ones and he wen down by the river	71	
72 and catch um tiny ones.	E : Oh, I nevah, [repeats 2x]	
an caught big ones and I wen try pick up the tiny one in my hand and --an everytime I wen try go squeeze um but, I couldn't cause it--uh --wa-was slippery and wen just wen fall out.	C,E,L: [look at her]	73
74 [gestures throughout]		T : A-a-a-a-h-h-h.
C : Even S..., she	75	
76 got	E : ye-e-s.	
T : What does it feel like? Is it hard? Is it		
77 s-o-o-ft?	78	
C : Yah, me an my fren-- me an my fren--	M : Soft.	
		79 T : It's s-o-o-ft.

The teacher gets the answer she is looking for eventually, but meanwhile she allows Marian her digression, and, thus encouraged, Cynthia tries and eventually tells her story too.

During student time, the teacher also bases her questions upon student replies, thus further encouraging the introduction of digressions. An instance occurred early in the session, when Cynthia surprised the students by stating that she would eat the legs of a frog:

Example 10.6. (Same as Example 10.4)

1-14 M:	Y a h? [turns towards C with surprise] You eat the legs?
1-15A T:	Okay [points to C].
1-15B	Cynthia might even eat it. [looks at M then back to C] Good. You can eat frog, can't you? [nods in agreement]
E:	Uck!
1-16 L:	Yah, ⌈da legs. [T looks at her, then back at C]
1-17A T:	⌊Cynthia, what—?
1-17B	How do you fix it? [rising intonation]
1-17C	Do you know how mommy fixes it? [rising]
1-18	[C shakes head "no"]
1-19A T:	No? [rising]
1-19B	What does it taste like?
1-20 C:	Chicken.
1-21A T:	That's what a lot of people say: frog tastes like ch-i-ck-e-n. [looks at L and M, sounds pleased]

The previous example also illustrates another means by which the teacher encourages personal experience reports and speculation: her animated style of responding and asking questions. Intonation is one element of this style. Another is "enactment," mimicking by gesture the act or event she is describing or referring to verbally. For example, here she is challenging Eli, who said that he did not know what he would do with a frog:

Example 10.7. (Same as Example 10.4)

Initiation	Reply	Evaluation

43A-C
T : You don't know what
   you would do with it?
   [returns eye contact,
   shakes head negatively]
   What if I came to school
   and I had a frog and
   I said, "Here, Eli,
   you can have it."
   [looks at M and C,
   gestures giving frog to
   E, looks back at him]
   What would you do
   with it?
	44
	E : (no reply)	

This led directly into Example 10.4 above. We think it no coincidence that the students immediately took over initiating and talking story, as indicated there.

Based upon the conclusions presented in Chapter 7, it seems likely that the teacher's invitation to talk-story, backed up by her intonation, enactment, and other dramatic features may suggest the behavior of a receptive parent who is acting in an egalitarian way. Children, who are always ready to talk-story with a receptive adult, therefore respond favorably to this behavior on the part of the teacher. As mentioned, similar sessions occurred spontaneously in the Aina Pumehana first grade classroom described in Chapter 9. Student time differs from talk-story out of school, however, in that it lacks the rich variety of verbal play and the contradicting routine that are so common there (see Chapters 6 and 7). In the entire reading lesson, only two or three simple contradictions and two bits of verbal play occur, and none are picked up. There may be several reasons for this difference. Because the children were not free to organize themselves and establish their own topics, they had no need to use verbal play as a means of relating. On the other hand, because of the teacher's inviting behavior they were not provoked to it in rebellion, as they frequently were in the Aina Pumehana classroom.

Thus, talking-story in student time is not too surprising. More surprising is what happens during the other type of discourse that characterizes the reading session. This is termed "book discussion."

Book discussion

In book discussion, the teacher requests specific information from the story which the children have just read during the same session. Unlike student time, personal experience reports and narratives are not called for, and are rarely given, as we shall see. In place of them, the teacher asks questions, the answers to which cue her as to whether they have comprehended details of the story as she has. This corresponds to the "T" [Text] portion of the lesson as Au describes it (1979), with the exception noted earlier. When she infers a difference in interpretation, she proceeds to correct the student's interpretation. The bulk of the discourse consists of such digressions from a straightforward recapitulation of the story. Without them, indeed, there would be little discussion. The major finding is that the resulting discussion has a basic structure consisting of the same underlying elements as talk-story in other settings. We term it "talking-story with a book," since it is not about personal experiences but about interpretations of information obtained from a book.

Several of the teacher's routines are entirely limited to book discussion, and thus help to frame it. Thus, by inviting speculation about information in the story before the students begin to read, she implies that such information is going to be discussed later.

Example 10.8.

1-115 T:	Where do you think Freddy's going to find his frog?
1-129 T:	Where does Freddy put his frog?

She also directs them to obtain specific information when they read:

Example 10.9.

1-157B T:	I want you to find out what Mr. Mays says he would do with the frog.

Whether or not these were answered by the students before they read, they were all asked during book discussion. Occurring beforehand, they functioned to announce the discussion to follow. She also initiates discussion about information from the book by simply looking down at the book. The effect that this has is indicated in the following:

Example 10.10. (same as Example 10.4)

2-57 E:	Just like in da book
	⎡ when George [E and T exchange eye-contact]
2-58 T:	⎣ How do you—
2-59 E:	—wen go use cake.
2-60 T:	Cake for bait?
E:	[nods "yes"]
T:	⎡ O-oh-h. [looks down at book, flips pages]
2-61 E:	⎣ George wen go use that.

By looking down at her book in the midst of a free-flowing discussion during student time (lines 2–49 to 2–56: McMillen et al., 1979: 21), the teacher causes Eli to limit his remarks, even though she has just paid positive attention to him. In other instances, the discussion tapers off in a similar way when she does this.

Unlike student time, the teacher in book discussion does not welcome and affirm all relevant and noncontradictory responses to her questions. Instead, she may interdict answers that do not agree with her interpretation of the story. Thus:

Example 10.11.

2-5 T:	Do frogs like to go fis⌐hing?
2-6 G:	⌊N-o-o-o.
T:	Cyn⌐thia do frogs
2-7 E:	⌊Y-e-e-es.
	[T raises open hand to E's face]
2-8 T:	like to go fishing?
	[pause]
2-9 M:	N-⌐o-o-o.
2-10 C:	⌊N-o-o-o.
2-11 T:	Why don't they like to go⌐fishing?
2-12 L:	⌊Cause they
	hate water.
	[T raises open hand to L's face, has an "intense surprise" look: mouth open and eyes wide]

Her first interdict, to Eli, would have happened in student time, because it contradicts the group's prior answer. She interdicts Lokia, however, because the answer reveals an interpretation of the story that differs sharply from the teacher's. That is, the teacher's interpretation of her question is: "Do frogs like to be taken fishing?" the answer to which is "no," because under the circumstances they would be used for bait. But Lokia, and others, interpret the question to mean "Do frogs like to fish?" Hence the intense surprise look on the teacher's face. During student time, such a speculation would have been welcome. Not here.

She also corrects answers that she considers incorrect. Thus:

Example 10.12. (same as Example 10.4)

Initiation	Reply	Evaluation
97A		
T : Cynthia, why did Freddy laugh?		
	C : (no reply) [looks at book]	
	98	
97B	L : Because	
T : ⌊Marian?	maybe he didn't--⌋	
97C	M : (no reply)	
T : Lokia?		

Example 10.12. *continued*

Initiation	Reply	Evaluation
	98 L : --maybe he didn't know that--[distracted by outside noise]--maybe he didn't know that he was going to use the frog.	
		100(A) T : No-o-o, he laughed for another reason.

Here the teacher is pursuing her interpretation of Freddy's thought that a frog could not fish, but most of the children were not clued into her interpretation. Subsequently, she explained as follows:

2-104 T: Mr. Mays said "I don't have a frog, but if I did, I'd take it fishing," and Freddy thinks, "Ha, going fishing with a frog—the frog's sitting with a fishing pole?" [enacts thinking and fishing pole on shoulder]

She also challenges misunderstanding of story detail:

Example 10.13 (same as Example 10.4. L is explaining why she thinks the frog felt sad.)

Initiation	Reply	Evaluation
	113 L : Because he--he was sitting and then --then when--when he said he would use him for bait, he jumped--the frog jumped in Freddy's pocket.	T : [gives surprised look and gazes at L mouth open]
	114 E : Not, he jumped out.	115A-B T : Is that what happened? Did it jump out of Freddy's pocket? 115C T : Don't think so.

(Other passages indicate that the teacher interpreted Lokia as saying that the frog jumped *into* Freddy's pocket, whereas it had jumped while *in* Freddy's pocket, which is what Lokia apparently had in mind.)

There is no reason for the teacher to correct misunderstandings in student time, because she is not trying to establish any particular interpretation. She does, however, interdict, challenge, and correct in student time, but only those answers that she regards as contradicting the expressed consensus, which are rare.

Likewise different is her handling of volunteered reports and narratives. She allows them in book discussion, but only after a wait, and then she does not affirm them enthusiastically, nor base follow-up questions upon them, as she does in student time. For instance, Marian told a speculative story based upon a picture that she had seen in the book during silent reading. After repeated unsuccessful efforts to gain recognition:

Example 10.14. (same as Example 10.4)

2-141B T: Marian?

2-142 M: This—this lady right hea, I think she might um—Freddy might ask her what would you do—do with a frog and she might say—she—she might cook the legs and—and
⌈ she said it [points to place in book, M and
⌊ T exchange eye-contact]

2-143 T: ⌊ Maybe

M: tasted good.

2-144 T: 'Kay, [looks down at book] how did Freddy find his frog in the first place? [looks up at L]

Here the teacher cuts Marian off with a neutral evaluation in order to return to discussion of the story read. The teacher wants no digressions at this point.

When a misunderstanding surfaces, however, the teacher responds by center-ing the ensuing discussion upon clarifying it. Such discussion occupies more time than exchanges which do not reveal misunderstanding to the teacher. An illustration:

Example 10.15. (Same as Example 10.4)

2-76 T: Why did he suggest using the frog for bait?

2-77 L: He couldn't ⌈ think of any-

2-78 C: ⌊ But Freddy laughed.

L: thing else.

2-79 T: O-o-o-h, that's the first thing
⌈ that came to his mind.
│ [raises both hands to shoulder level, palms
│ up, during "Oh," then points to her own head]

2-80 C: ⌊ But Freddy laughed.

2-81 T: Good. [looks at C]

2-82 C: But Freddy ⌈ laughed. [looks down at book]

2-83 M: ⌊ O-o-o-h [waves hand and stamps feet]

2-84 T: Did Freddy think it was funny? [looks at her book]

The dialogue that follows continues through Example 10.12, including the teach-er's explanation in line 2-104, centering on why Freddy laughed.

How does the discourse in book discussion resemble the underlying structure of talk-story set forth in Chapter 7? For the initial question or summons, there are the formal openers discussed above and illustrated in Examples 10.8 and 10.9. These occur only at the start of book discussion and when the teacher returns to it after an interlude of student time, as in Example 10.10. Her "okay," combined with looking down at the book, typically occurs then. What serves as the propo-sition? Here we have a choice. We could consider the student's reply to the teacher's question as constituting a proposition, but this way of viewing it overlooks the crucial role of the teacher's and students' interpretations of the story, which are prior to her questions. It is more revealing to see the teacher's questions as implicit propositions. Indeed, she sometimes states these when evaluating the students' answers (see column 3 in Transcript 10.2). The students' responses to her questions can then be viewed as corroboration or contradiction of her implicit proposition, which leads naturally to mediation: her evaluations, challenges, or corrections.

This in turn raises several interesting questions. Do the students ever propose? In student time, their reports and narratives are propositions, which the teacher invariably evaluates positively. But they also propose during book discussion, and do so without answering a question from the teacher. The reason it happens is that they anticipate the recapitulation of the story by the teacher. This was in fact what happened in Example 10.15. Cynthia was anticipating the point in the story where Freddy laughed, not responding to the teacher's question in line 2-76. The teacher, caught off-guard, looked at the book in front of her at that point (line 2-84) and subsequently engaged in the line of questioning indicated in Example 10.12.

Do students ever mediate the teacher's propositions? Clearly, they never evaluate the teacher's questions as she does their answers. But they do attempt to defend their responses when she challenges them, in effect turning them into counter-propositions. And, just as the teacher tells them to read a certain passage to settle a disagreement, so they read a passage in their own defense! During the exchange contained in Example 10.13, Eli proposed that the frog jumped out of Freddy's pocket, whereupon the following exchange occurred:

Example 10.16.

Initiation	Reply	Evaluation
		115B T : Did it jump out of Freddy's pocket? 115C T : Don't think so.
115D,117 T : Turn and look on page [pause] sixteen [pause]. 'Kay, okay, on page sixteen, see if you can find the sentence that says what--where Freddy's frog was. Lokia thinks that it's in his hand, Eli thinks it's--[is cut off]	118 E : "He ran down the street." [reading]	

(It turns out that it was Freddy, not the frog, who ran down the street, but Eli tried.)[35]

By proposing and arguing their propositions, the children contribute to the joint participation structure of book discussion. This resembles the joint construction of a narrative performance among themselves, as described in Chapter 7. Only here the teacher is included as a participant. More significantly, so is the book!

The interesting question is how and why the form of the session involves the children as it does. A related question is why the discussion is limited to the topics that the teacher wants to discuss. To provide tentative answers, we consider the framing function of student time and book discussion and the relationship of both to the kind of talk-story the children are familiar with. We then conclude with consideration of why the reading lesson is effective.

We suggest that students stick to different topics in student time and book discussion because of certain routines used by the teacher which frame, or provide a context for, the content of each type of discourse. Primary are her requests for reports and speculation based upon personal experience during student time, and for information and interpretations based upon the book during book discussion. Responses to these different types of request are reinforced in such a way over a number of sessions that the children come to know what is expected in each type of discourse. Specifically, the teacher's affirmation and reinforcement of any forthcoming answer or volunteered report or narrative during student time confirm that students' propositions are appropriate then. By contrast, the teacher's systematic interdicting, correcting, and challenging student interpretations during book discussion, together with her delayed and minimal response to volunteered reports and narratives not based upon the story read, reinforce the inference that the teacher's propositions, as implied by her questions, are appropriate during book discussion. These appear to be sufficient reasons for students limiting themselves to the topics that the teacher wants to discuss during student time and book discussion.

There are also functional relationships between the two types of discourse that need to be considered. Student time is typically interwoven with book discussion. This may well give the students an opportunity to get into the discussion what the teacher puts aside during book discussion.[36] This interweaving of their own stories with the information that the teacher wants to hear would also contribute to the students' perception of the reading lesson as a form of talk-story.

The children are motivated to participate in the reading lesson, we believe, because its underlying structure is that of an egalitarian mode of speaking. The same phenomena that make it a joint performance also make it an egalitarian mode of speaking when the teacher shares the functions of proposing, corroborating or contradicting, and evaluating propositions with the students. As argued throughout, and especially in Chapter 7, part-Hawaiian children respond positively to egalitarian speech events involving an adult. Such an explanation is consistent with Au's conclusion that student participation in these lessons is likely to be more productive when there is a ''balance of rights'' between teacher and students, such that neither controls all three dimensions of participation, i.e., topic, number of speakers, or turn-taking (1980b: 169).

The discussion in the reading lesson as a whole provides a vital sociolinguistic context in which the act of reading, and the content, can acquire immediate social meaning. It is this fact that makes it possible for the children to learn to read so well, we hypothesize. The close actual link between reading and discussion is indicated on more than six occasions in the sample lesson when children have to read and interpet what they read while simultaneously answering a question or arguing a point with the teacher. On five of these occasions, they read aloud from a passage as part of the conversation. While three of these (including Example 10.16) occur in response to the teacher's directives, two are volunteered. For instance, in the following exchange Eli conarrates with the teacher a detail from the story, reading the words without any directive to do so, and at least one other voice is also heard doing the same. This is literally talking-story with a book.

Example 10.17.

Initiation	Reply	Evaluation
		106B,108
		T : So Freddy laughs, he goes, "Tsk, frogs can't fish, they can't sit there with a fishing pole." [gestures
	F : [gazes at book]	toward E, looks at him] But Mr. Mays really meant, "Uh-uh [negative], I would use
107-8		that frog
	E : [reading] "The frog would	as--
	be my bait." ((G: "Bait."))	bait."

Au has presented convincing evidence based upon another four lessons at KEEP that students are engaged a higher percent of the time in reading and producing more ideas relevant to what they are reading during turns involving more than one child, and when there was a balance of rights between teacher and students, as defined above (1980b). We would point out that this motivation continues outside the assigned reading in the lesson. Thus, Marian's speculative story in Example 10.14 was based in part upon another part of the book that they were using. The children had also read ahead in this book (lines 1-102 to 107), so that when the teacher invited speculation about the reading to come they were prepared to respond. Because the teacher ostensibly reproves them for reading ahead, they have to do it surreptitiously, which no doubt adds to their motivation. They also introduce information from books read at another time into the reading lesson, as in Example 10.10 (see also lines 2-49 to 2-55 in McMillen et al. 1979).

The cultural significance of the KEEP reading lessons

The KEEP reading lesson, as described below, differs from lessons in a mainland classroom which Mehan has described (1979). In this section, these differences are presented in order to consider the question of whether or not the KEEP lessons are effective because they are congruent with Hawaiian culture, or because they represent good teaching such as that which would occur in mainland classrooms. The conclusion reached is that there are different kinds of good teaching, and that represented in the KEEP reading lesson is uniquely effective with these Hawaiian children because it enables them to participate without learning to recite.

Lessons, according to Mehan, are typically made up of sequences of social acts, jointly constructed by knowledgeable students and a teacher. The typical sequence consists of an "initiation" by the teacher—typically a request for information that determines the relevance of subsequent responses—followed by one or more appropriate "replies" by students, and concluded with an "evaluation" by the teacher which restates or clearly indicates the correct answer. The sequence may contain repeated attempts by the teacher, using prompts or corrections, to elicit a particular response if it is not immediately forthcoming ("extended sequences"). Sequences in turn are joined topically in sets, which are usually initiated by the teacher. In this way, the teacher controls each step in the unfolding of a lesson, the goals of which exist in her mind, and not, presumably, in the minds of the children (1979: Chapter 2).

Such a structure seems to be emic, as Mehan claims it to be. In this book it is referred to as "recitation." It is argued here that the KEEP reading lesson, while resembling recitation in its most general features, is not perceived as such by the children, but rather is reacted to as if it were talk-story, and that it succeeds not because the children are knowledgeable in recitation, but because the teacher does some things which allow the children to contribute as they would to talk-story. This analysis is confirmed by certain observed differences between the KEEP lesson and the lessons described by Mehan.

In the two transcripts presented below, utterances by the teacher and students at two points in the sample lesson have been categorized in accordance with Mehan's concepts whenever applicable. The result is clearest in Transcript 10.2 (lines 2-89B to 141A), where it can be seen that the teacher initiates each sequence, students reply, and the teacher alone appears to evaluate—which follows Mehan's model. In the first transcript (lines 1-41 to 85), however, students initiate sequences, while the teacher replies, thus reversing the usual roles in recitation. Initiation and reply are used here in the same sense as defined in Chapter 6. We are not claiming that the students' initiations are not occasioned by any of the teacher's prior remarks, nor that students control topical relevance, but only that specific sequences occur in which there is no immediate prior utterance by the teacher on the same topic, whereas the teacher's subsequent utterance is relevant and predictable as to topic given the student's utterance. Examples follow.

As described earlier, the KEEP reading lesson consists of two different events, "student time" and "book discussion," which differ primarily in terms of topical relevance. Since the former appears to depart most from Mehan's description, it is examined first. The particular set of exchanges begins with line 41: "T: Eli, what would you do if you had a frog?" and ends with line 85, following which the teacher frames a transition, saying "O-k-a-y," and looking down at her book (see Transcript 10.1, which is taken from McMillen et al., 1979). It consists of three topically related sets of sequences in Mehan's terms. In the first, the teacher tries to elicit responses to the question of what you would do with a frog. The second set comprises a discussion of what happens to you if you touch a frog. It is clearly introduced by a student, as follows:

51,53

L: It spits! Da ting spit—It'll spit at you.

In the third set, the teacher attempts to return to her earlier question by asking:

68

T: What did it feel like, Marian?

The students at this point, however, want to tell stories about catching frogs:

69

C: Even S . . . —(see lines 74–75ff for continuation)

70

M: My—my—my brother, you know [etc.].

85

C: You know me an my fren huh [etc.]

Transcript 10.1. (lines 1-41 to 85 of KEEP reading lesson arranged in accordance with Mehan's categories: McMillen et al., 1979: 5–9)

Initiation		Reply		Evaluation
41 T :	Eli, what would you do if you had a frog?	42 *E :	[pause] I don't know.	
43A–C T :	You don't know what you would do with it? What if I came to school and I had a frog [etc.] What would you do with it?			
		44 *E :	(no reply)	
		45–6 L :	Boy-y-y, he would drop it! I'd be scared to hold it!*	47A T : You would be scared to hold it.
		47B T :	Why? What does it feel like when you hold it?	
		48–9 M :	Yucky ((C: Slippery*)).	50 T : Might feel slippery.

continued

Transcript 10.1. *continued*

Initiation	Reply	Evaluation
51 *L : It spits! Da ting spit--	52 E : Maybe you might wanna give it to somebody	
53 L : It'll spit at you.	else	54 T : Oh, you think they spit at you?
	55-6 *G : Ye-e-eh.	
58 M : And goin' have warts like this.*	*E : They do, they do.	57 T : Oh-h-h.
	58-9 G : [look] T : You get warts from touching frogs?	
	60-1,63 E : Yah. No-o-o If they spit on you, you get warts.	62 T : Is that true? [looks at E] 64 T : A-a-a-ah.
65 M : Like right hea.*	65-66A G : [look] T : Why, did you touch a frog on your leg? *M: [nods "yes"]	
66B-C T : How many of you have touched a frog? Can you raise your hand if you've touched one?	67 *E,M: [raise hands] *C: [shakes head "no"]	
68-70 T : What did it feel like, Marian? C : Even S... when I wen-- *M: My--my-my bro- ther, you know uh-- across the street? There--there's some ones and he wen down by the river		
72 and catch um tiny ones an caught big ones and I wen try pick up the tiny one in my hand and --an everytime I wen try go squeeze um but, I couldn't cause it--uh --wa-was slippery and wen just wen fall out.	71 E : Oh, I nevah, [repeats 2x] C,E,L: [look at her]	
74 [gestures throughout]		73 T : A-a-a-a-h-h-h.
*C: Even S..., she 76 got--	75 E : Ye-e-s.	
T : What does it feel like? Is it hard? Is it 77 s-o-o-ft?	78 M : Soft.*	
C : Yah, me an my fren-- me an my fren--		79 T : It's s-o-o-ft.
80 C : Me an my fren--	81 M : Feels oogie.*	82A T : And it felt oogie.
82B-3 T : Was it cold when you ((*C: Mrs. A)) touched it?	84 L : O-o-oh-h, feels yucky.	
C : Mrs. A, Mrs. A.		
85 *C: You know me an my fren huh [etc.].		

* indicates nomination by teacher before or after speaking, according to placement.
  (For nonverbal indications of nomination see McMillen et al.)

Note: See footnote 37.

As a consequence of this difference in goals, the teacher ends up competing with the student to initiate sequences throughout the third set, instead of initiating each sequence herself as typically happens in Mehan's data. This shows up graphically in the initiation column of the transcript.[38]

One can see that, overall, the three sets of sequences just described resemble a typical single sequence as characterized by Mehan above. But each sequence in the KEEP sets does not produce a replica of the answer that the teacher expects, nor is every one a reply to her initiation. This contrasts with Mehan's data, as he reports that more than 90 percent of the sequences in the lessons he analyzed were teacher initiated (1979: Table 2.3).

This happens because of a difference in the way each teacher achieves the goals of the lesson. Consider these facts. Sequences in the mainland classroom were structured by a turn-allocation procedure so that only one student would be talking at a time, at least until the teacher received the answer that she was looking for. In order to accomplish this, the teacher indicated who was to speak and negatively sanctioned students who spoke out of turn (Mehan 1979: 81–111). While the teacher in the KEEP lesson does nominate specific speakers before they speak on occasion (indicated by * before the turn on the transcript), she never reproves students verbally when they speak out of turn, even when they overlap her own speech (Au 1980a—contrast Mehan 1979: 99–100, 101). Rather, in student time the teacher appears to use a strategy of encouraging and inviting participation from several at once. This is illustrated in the third topical set of Transcript 10.1 and by her frequent eye-contact, inviting or incorporating several students simultaneously (see Au 1980a and McMillen et al., 1979, for evidence). She then subsequently reaffirms and builds upon those contributions that fit her own topical goals. Thus, instead of specifically directing topically related sets of sequences step by step, she allows the students to respond within a set of logically related alternatives, and to take the initiative in doing so (see Baird and Bogert 1978). The result, we argue, is a dialogue that can be perceived by the students as talking story, even while it resembles the overall structure of recitation at a higher and more inclusive level. Student time thus represents a synthesis of cultural features.

"Book discussion" on first examination appears to resemble more closely the individual sequences described by Mehan (see Transcript 10.2). But the more one analyzes it, the more different it also appears. To begin, "book discussion" resembles recitation in that the teacher is clearly looking for answers to her questions that agree with her interpretation of details of the story in context. She is not content with just any relevant reply or comment, as is the case in "student time" (for an example, see line 102A). As a result, the sequences are all "extended" in Mehan's terms: i.e., she repeats her founding question after a negative evaluation, or gives a series of prompts (which Mehan classifies as evaluation) until all, or in some instances a certain student, agree with her statement. Let us now look at a set of exchanges that illustrate these points.

Transcript 10.2. (lines 2-89B to 141A of KEEP reading lesson arranged in accordance with Mehan's categories: McMillen et al., 1979: 24-29)

Initiation	Reply	Evaluation
89B T : Cynthia, why did you say Freddy laughed? 89C T : Okay, read that part that you s-sid when Freddy laughed.	*C: (no reply) 90 *C: "I would take it fish- ing, Freddy laughed." [reading] *C: (no reply) 92-3 E : Mr. Mays.* V : Mr. Mays. 95	 91 T : 'Kay, who says, "I would take it fish- ing"? 94 T : Mr. Mays.
97A T : Cynthia, why did Freddy laugh? 97B T : Marian? 97C T : Lokia?	E : Because frogs-- *C: (no reply) 98 L : Because maybe he didn't-- *M: (no reply) 98 *L: --maybe he didn't know that--[distracted by outside noise]--maybe he didn't know that he was going to use the frog.	 100(A) T : No-o-o, he laughed for another reason.
100(B) T : Marian, who can read that?	101 *M: Because--cause Mr. Mays didn't know what to do with the frog. That's all he could think [etc.] That's why Freddy laughed. 103 E : Frogs can't fish.* 105 G : No-o-o-o-o. 107-8 E : "The frog would be my bait." ((G: "Bait.")) 110 *C: No-o-o-o	 102A T : Okay, wait--okay, wait a minute. That's not the reason Freddy laughed! 104,106A T : Right! Okay, Mr. Mays said [etc.] "...fishing pole?" That's pretty funny. 106B, 108 T : So Freddy laughs [etc.] "...I would use that frog as- bait." 109A,B T : Right, the frog would be his bait. And then, did Freddy laugh, Cynthia? 111A T : No-o-o, he didn't think that was too funny.
111B T : How do you think the frog felt when he heard, "hu-u-uh-- that--that-- --he wanted-- that he was gonna be used--	112 L : Sad. 113 L : Because he--he was sitting and then --then when--when he said he [etc.] the frog jumped in to Freddy's pocket.* 114 E : Not, he jumped out.*	 115A,B T : Is that what happened? Did it jump out of Freddy's pocket?

Transcript 10.2. *continued*

Initiation	Reply	Evaluation
		115C T : Don't think so.

115D,117
T : Turn and look on page
   --sixteen--
   'Kay, okay, on page
   sixteen, see if you can
   find the sentence [etc.]
   Eli--thinks its--
	118
	E : "He ran down the
	   street." [reading]*
		119
		T : Who, the frog?

	120-21 V : No.	
122 T : Marian?	C : No-o-o.	

124
T: Re-e-ea-a-d it to
  me honey [waiting]
	123
	*M: Uh--it says--
	   it says--	

	125
	*M: Um--"The frog gave a
	   jump in Freddy's pock-
	   et." [reading]
		126,128A,B
		T : O-k-a-y
		   the frog

	127 E : O-o-oh-h.* [T and E exchange knowing looks]	gave a jump in Fred- dy's pocket. Does it mean it jumped out of Freddy's
	129-31 G : N-o-o -o-o.	pocket? 132 T : No, it's inside [etc.] Who ran down the street?
	133-34 M : Freddy-y ((*G: Freddy-y))	134-35 T : Freddy-y-y. Freddy ran down

	136,138
	E : Because--
	   because
	   he didn't want
		the street.
		137
		T : O-k-a-y.

	140 E : Mr. Mays to make him a bait.*	141A T : Exactly right, Eli, good reading.

* indicates nomination by teacher before or after speaking, according to
placement. (For nonverbal indications of nomination see McMillen et al.)

These exchanges comprise two sets of topically related sequences. One is
focused upon "Why did Freddy laugh?" (lines 89B–111A) and the other on
"How do you think the frog felt?" (lines 111B–141A). Each set consists of two
extended sequences. At the first of each set, the teacher asks an interpretive
question (a "wh-question"). Students either do not reply, e.g., Cynthia following 89B and 97A and Marian following 97B, or they answer incorrectly from the
teacher's point of view, e.g., Lokia in 112–13. Each time, the teacher initiates a
second extended sequence in which she asks them to read a relevant passage.
Thus:

89C

T: Okay, read that part [etc.].

100(B)

T: . . . Marian, who can read that?

115D

T: Turn and look on page—sixteen—

117

T: 'Kay, okay, on page sixteen, see if you can find the sentence [etc.].

Following the reading in each instance, she prompts until they respond with the answer she is looking for. Thus:

109A, B

T: Right, the frog would be his bait.
       And then, did Freddy laugh, Cynthia?

109B

*C: N-o-o-o-o.

111A

T: N-o-o, he
       didn't think that was too funny.

Again:

126, 128A, B

T: O-k-a-y, the frog—
       gave a jump in Freddy's pocket.
       Does it mean it jumped <u>out</u> of
       Freddy's pocket?

129

V: N-o-o-o

132

T: No, it's inside— [etc.].

So far, the above description would apply to the lessons described by Mehan, with the minor difference that more of the sequences are extended. But "book discussion" has several features that are either very infrequent or lacking in Mehan's account. One is that the students frequently anticipate the teacher's questions, answering them before they are asked. This appears following:

95

E: Because frogs—

Here the teacher has just produced agreement that Mr. Mays said that he would take the frog fishing and reinstates the founding question, which was "Why did Freddy laugh?" (line 97A). *Before* she asks it, however, Eli starts to answer, "Because frogs can't fish." He holds up until line 103, however. Even then the teacher has not gotten around to rephrasing the question following Marian's incorrect answer in line 101. Eli anticipates again when an inspiration strikes him at line 127, which he subsequently utters at 136, 138, and 140. This instance is discussed further below.

He is not the only one to do this. Lokia in fact coinitiates the second set of topical sequences while the teacher is still formulating her question about how the frog felt:

111B
T: How do you think the frog felt when he
        heard, "hu-u-uh—   112
        that—|that—   L: Sad.|

        he wanted—   113
        that he was gonna be   L: Because he—he was|
        used—   sitting and then
                                                        [etc.]

Anticipation is seen most strikingly in the children's response to the teacher's prompts. Thus, explaining what Mr. Mays meant by saying that he would take the frog fishing, the teacher says:

                                                106B,108
                                                T: So Freddy laughs [etc.]
107   ". . . I would use that frog
   E: |"The frog would   as—|
       |be my bait." ((G: "Bait"))   bait."|

Anticipation in this instance leads to cospeaking, which in effect means joining the teacher in evaluation. This role is reserved to the teacher in all of Mehan's examples.

This sharing of a role is further illustrated by Eli when he supplements the teacher's point that Freddy, not the frog, ran down the street (correcting a mistake that he had himself made in line 118) by explaining:

136, 138, 140
   E: Because—because
       he didn't want
       Mr. Mays to make him a bait.

The teacher meanwhile was framing a change of topic, saying "O-k-a-y" (line 137). She interrupted herself to affirm Eli's point after allowing him to finish:

141A
   T: Exactly right, Eli, good reading.
       (sits back in chair while exclaiming, points to Eli)

Comparing this difference in participation with the mainland classroom, one can ask what allows such sharing of roles between teacher and children to happen. Mehan appears to argue that the teacher incorporates responses initiated by students into lessons because students learn when and how to insert them into recitation, i.e., the typical sequence characterized at the beginning of this section (see 1979: 159–160). The argument advanced here, on the other hand, is that such contributions in the KEEP lessons result from a cultural congruence. On the one hand, the teacher is prepared to stimulate and utilize these contributions, instead of attempting to control the form and content of the lesson at every step. On the other hand, the students are prepared to engage in talk-story. They have not become more expert in recitation. We have argued, in fact, that they are culturally resistant to learning how to recite. Joint performances require anticipating what is going to happen in a story, recapitulating, taking advantage of others' contributions—in short, not waiting to be asked specific questions to which there is only one correct answer. It is true that the teacher's prompts serve to guide them, with the result that they can join in her evaluations. But they also diverge at other points, as argued earlier in this chapter. The result resembles talk-story at the most fundamental level: i.e., the students' responses to her questions can be viewed as corroboration or contradiction of her implicit propositions, which lead naturally to mediation in which both parties participate. This hardly resembles recitation.[39]

This is an appropriate place to take up the question of why questions do not appear to inhibit participation in the KEEP reading lesson, as we have claimed questions generally do (Chapter 5). Our answer is that the questions are so adequately framed by the egalitarian mode of speaking in the lesson that they lose the negative connotation that they have in other settings. As argued in Chapter 9, individual answers during recitation carry the risk of being wrong before the whole class, while any inquiry into one's knowledge or actions may similarly put an individual on the spot if only that person is required to respond. Throughout most of the reading lesson described, the teacher allows any respondent to speak, whether nominated or not. In most of the remaining instances, the child had previously indicated a desire to speak. Thus, no child was required to reply to a question from the teacher (Au 1980a). Questions function as part of a hierarchical relationship during interrogation and recitation, while they function in a more egalitarian relationship during talk-story and throughout the great majority of the reading lesson. This makes quite a difference in the children's readiness to respond.

We turn now to the argument that lessons like the KEEP one could occur in a classroom anywhere, and be effective. We have argued, on the contrary, that certain features of the KEEP lesson are rare or lacking in the classroom described by Mehan, and that these differences are due to a convergence between the methods used by the teacher and the children's cultural readiness to talk-story. Would students lacking the cultural background described here respond in a similar fashion to the KEEP lessons? In my opinion, they would. It is not that students anywhere will not talk-story if given a chance. It is that teachers so rarely give them a chance. This is nicely illustrated in an article by Michaels and Cook-Gumperz. The first of several examples of discourse "produced collaboratively" by the teacher and two students during "sharing time" in a first grade classroom could be a narrative from student time at KEEP, i.e., it resembles talk-story on the children's part. The second example, however, is not even a narrative because, as the authors note, the teacher asks a series of questions that interfere with the story which the child was attempting to tell, so that it does not get told (1979).

As Jordan and Tharp have argued, "the accommodated school culture" at KEEP looks in many respects like the culture from which the students come and like schools elsewhere. Observers from schools on the mainland are likely to see little that differs markedly from examples that they know. Observers of part-Hawaiian children, on the other hand, are likely to see the similarities with the children's culture. But some aspects of the accommodated school culture are different from both (1979). This is particularly true of the reading lesson. Nothing exactly like it occurs in the children's culture, as Chapter 7 has indicated (see also Au 1980a for an excellent discussion of the differences). And nothing like it has been described for mainland classrooms, to the best of our knowledge.

So what then becomes of the argument that the KEEP lessons are particularly appropriate for Hawaiian students because of their cultural background? My answer is that it enables Hawaiian students to learn without first having to learn how to recite. Students of other cultural backgrounds do not have this difficulty to anywhere near the same extent. Other students can learn in other ways, even if they do not learn to recite. But the same is not true for the part-Hawaiians studied here. For these students, as we have argued throughout this book, talking story with an adult is a singular opportunity. It allows them to use existing sociolinguistic skills, their desire to speculate (see Chapter 8), and their positive response to egalitarian modes of speaking in classroom lessons, and to be reinforced for it instead of punished. To see why the KEEP lessons are so culturally significant, one needs to keep in mind all that talk-story means to a part-Hawaiian child. The cultural significance is not to be found in the specific skills involved in talking story alone, but in the speech economy of the Hawaiian culture, which gives particular meaning to talking story, as we have tried to portray throughout this book.

Other factors

A comparison of the KEEP and Aina Pumehana classrooms indicates that a total transformation in the children's culture is not necessary in order to improve the effectiveness of reading instruction. The children appear to have adapted to the KEEP system without causing their own routines and patterns of relating to suffer, so far as we can tell. This follows the principle of "least change" stated by Jordan and Tharp:

> In creating the accommodated educational culture for which KEEP aimed, we wished to effect only those changes in either school or child culture which would be necessary to produce the good learning desired. . . . (1979: 277)

Erickson has also given a statement of this principle, which calls for the kind of comparison of the reading lesson contained in this book (1977).

What remains unanswered is how much transformation in the classroom culture is necessary in order to make the new reading program work in a public school. There is a subtle quality at KEEP which is not indicated in the video-taped incidents transcribed above. On the teacher's part, there is an attitude that the children *can* learn—almost a Pygmalion phenomenon. On the children's part, there is a willingness to accept what is presented to them. Put more simply, the teachers accept the children and the children accept school to a much greater degree than occurred in Aina Pumehana, even in the first grade. The mitigation of the struggle for control of the classroom, and the coincident synthesis of cultures, may have had a lot to do with this mutual acceptance. If this speculation is valid, the KEEP system of classroom management may be essential to success of the reading program. Clearly, the reading lessons cannot even be installed without some form of effective classroom management. But is any one form necessary?

As the KEEP techniques are disseminated, two extreme outcomes are possible. One is that *this* system of classroom management is not necessary, and the reading program can succeed on its own with any satisfactory system of classroom management. Another extreme possibility is that classroom management techniques and the method of reading instruction together may not be enough to change the attitudes of some teachers and administrators towards the children, particularly if successes with the reading program are not immediate. More likely than either extreme, however, is an outcome in which classroom management techniques will vary, while the method of teaching reading may not be fully implemented. In such a case, the results will be ambiguous. It is for this reason that further studies and comparisons are needed. For it must be determined whether classroom management, the method of teaching reading, or some other factor is at fault in case of failure. An unexplained failure cannot be allowed to occur. Too much is at stake.

Methods Used in Recording at Home

The purpose of the project which produced the home recordings was to determine which phonological and syntactic features kindergarten children who were speakers of Hawaiian Creole English used in surroundings most familiar to them, as compared with those they used in a formal interview with a strange adult. Since this dialect has been undergoing change in the direction of decreolization (Day, Boggs, Gallimore, Tharp, and Speidel 1975), it seemed likely that some features of standard dialect might be in common use at home, and it was considered important to discover this, since one hypothesis current at the time was that incompetence in standard dialect contributed to confusion in learning to read (see Labov 1967, for instance). At issue was a decision to undertake instruction in standard dialect, as well as the knowledge necessary to do this, if it should be undertaken. The conventional wisdom was that such instruction should be provided. As a consequence of research that grew out of the project sketched here, a decision was made not to teach standard dialect. Subsequent findings over more than 5 years have indicated that such instruction was not necessary in the context of the KEEP project (see Gallimore and Tharp n.d.).

In order to accomplish the purpose just indicated, the mothers of five children who were of kindergarten age were engaged to participate in the study. All of them lived in the central Honolulu area of the KEEP school and had household incomes that qualified them to receive Aid to Families with Dependent Children. Fathers were present in four of the five families. Of the three families referred to in this book (see Note 4), two included five children below the age of 6 years, while a third included at times six children who ranged in age from an infant to a 13 year old. After being contacted by a member of the KEEP staff, a community worker, or a mutual acquaintance, these five agreed to participate in a series of training sessions. They were paid a modest amount for the training and subsequently for completing 2 hours of recording. Several agreed to participate, however, without realizing that they would be paid. One of those whose recordings appear in the book continued to record after turning in her assignment. None dropped out. In general, there was much evidence from our many discussions with them that they were motivated by inherent interest in their children's speech. This interest grew during the training and recording. This method of collaboration demonstrated great promise in light of these results.

The mothers, like most people raised in Hawaii, were interested in "good speech," i.e., standard dialect, but also shared the view that you should speak in a way (use whatever lect) that made you and others feel at ease, i.e., equal, and not putting on airs or talking down. Thus they readily understood why we were interested in their children's speech patterns. Since we did not want to heighten their awareness of pidgin for obvious reasons, however, we stressed that we were looking for normal everyday speech events, and not for a particular style of speech. After illustrating concretely what we meant, a series of conversations was conducted privately with each mother at home, the purpose of which was to identify with her typical speech events in which her child of kindergarten age participated. Only one of the mothers labelled a speech event in advance. She reported that, during dinner, her children often engaged in "sarcastic" speech, which she illustrated as: "I beat you, you punk." "No, you never (sic), you punk." (This we categorized as the contradicting routine, see below, Appendix 2.) All of the mothers, however, gave good descriptions of verbal behavior that we could subsequently recognize in their recordings, even though they did not label them. After defining speech events in this way, the mothers were encouraged to pay attention to times of day and circumstances in which the children were usually most talkative, and to practice turning on the recorder at such times. In one case, we had to correct the assumption that we were only interested in speech involving the mother and other adults. In all cases, we cautioned strongly against trying to get children to talk by asking them questions. Despite this, one mother did so, with the results presented in Example 5.9.

Each mother then decided when and under what circumstances to record. One recorded while playing with her children, listening to their questions, and preparing them for school, and generally left the recorder running when she was available for interacting with them. Another recorded almost entirely when the eldest, 5 years old, was baby-sitting the younger ones, while they were eating, before they fell asleep, and in general when she was not around them. The third recorded almost exclusively when the children were engaged in dramatic play together (see Appendix 2). As a consequence of these separate strategies, recordings of comparable situations were not made in each family, with a few exceptions which constitute the bulk of the home data reported in the book. As noted, only routines that occurred at least once in each family, or which have been observed elsewhere, have been included.

After recording, the mothers were asked to listen to each tape, and write down as many utterances as they could understand and identify each speaker in those instances. Two of them did this despite the fact that they were not accustomed to writing anything. The third had not completed enough schooling to do this, and instead dictated to a staff member when she could comprehend what was on the tape. We had planned to listen to all of the tapes with each mother in order to compare our hearing with theirs, but several obstacles prevented this. With five young children to care for and no child-care assistance, it was impossible to schedule the time. We also discovered that they rapidly tired of trying to hear an utterance in more than one way (see below).

There were several interesting features in the mother's transcriptions. Generally, enough was transcribed to get the sense of the exchange, although not every utterance that was interpretable was transcribed. Sometimes the mother would label the utterance, rather than transcribe it: e.g., "teasing sister." Often, of course, the mother wrote down what would be expected in a given routine, rather than what was actually said. On other occasions, she would write a phrase that sounded like that on the tape even though it made no sense. In general when a mother and staff member listened to a tape together, however, the mother found it impossible to hear an utterance in more than one way, whether it made sense or not. Apparently, linguistic training does make one more flexible in perceiving speech.

In general, less than half of the speech on the tapes was included in the mothers' transcripts. Despite this, their transcriptions were invaluable, for they often suggested an interpretation or hearing that would not have occurred to me without the mother's intimate knowledge of circumstances, history of the interaction, and their children's speech (particularly distortions, see Appendix 2 and Chapter 7). Lacking behavioral notes on accompanying activity made much of the recordings uninterpretable, since the speech was referencing actions or circumstances that were not explicitly mentioned or implied by specific sounds on the tape.

Summary of Speech Events and Routines Occurring in Recordings Made at Home, in the Community, and in Non-instructional Circumstances at School

1.0 Routines involving adults.

1.1 Free and entertaining.

    1.1.1 Talking to baby. Word and name play, chanting, singing, exclamations of greeting, and suggested dialogue. Related to joy of *aloha: 'a'a* (see Chapter 2). Examples: 7.1, 7.2, 7.3, 7.4.

    1.1.2 "Laughing it up with kids" (mother's gloss). Taunting, playful threats, challenges, and mock fighting, interposed with teasing contradicting (see next) and word play. Examples: 3.8, 6.3.

    1.1.3 Teasing contradicting. Initiated by a parent with a patently false statement, threat, or insult, or by a child provoking a parent to make a statement that the child then contradicts. Respondent replies with outright contradiction, which is exchanged numerous times. Referents for teasing are hypothetical actions or personal attributes, unlike disobedience, which involves clear and present action. Examples: 6.1, 6.2, 6.3.

    1.1.4 Word play. Deliberate distortion of speech, including punning, alliteration, elision, rhyming, and cospeaking. Distortion of parent's speech by child suggests teasing or accusation of nonseriousness of parent. Also engaged in by children with one another, often derogatorily. Examples: 7.5, 7.7, 7.8, 7.13.

    1.1.5 Name play. Same as word play, applied to personal names. Also engaged in by children with one another. Examples: 7.6, 7.13, 7.14.

1.2   Discussing. Children request information and offer opinions. Parent responds appropriately, even proferring explanations. (Limited to two episodes in a single family.) Example: 5.4.

1.3   Telling/showing children what to say/do.
   1.3.1   Naming body parts. Parent sings names for body parts while touching own body, children imitate word and touch own body.
   1.3.2   "Make X" (mother's gloss). Parent says this while demonstrating a nonverbal gesture, such as raising eyebrows to greet.
   1.3.3   Demonstrating name play. See 1.1.5. Also engaged in by children. Example: 7.5.
   1.3.4   Conversing over telephone. Parent arranges call and addressee, gives lines to child without regard to what addressee says.

1.4   Initiating interaction with adults.
   1.4.1   Asking for information. Questions requesting information directed to parent, usually repeated. Speculative answers to own question may be provided by child. Child waits patiently for a reply which is rarely forthcoming. Examples: 5.1, 5.2, 5.3.
   1.4.2   Requesting and coaxing, "nagging" (mother's gloss). Included are need statements (naming object desired with unique pitch suggesting an appeal to pity, or "I like X"), and hints (predicting desired outcome). Usually repeated with ellipsis and declining urgency. Parental reply is likely, occasionally with explanation for refusal, unlike direct requests for information which in this context are likely to bring refusal, challenge, and unrelated commands that function to remind child of his/her status. Examples: 5.3, 5.5, 5.6.
   1.4.3   Reporting on siblings. Report of behavior by a sibling or siblings that violates parental injunction or may bring negative parental attention in the future. Offered confidently and not rebuffed by parent; unlike other routines in this category (1.4). Common, although no examples given.

1.5   Ordering children to do something. Parent calls child's attention and utters imperative, which is typically repeated after an interval during which the child ignores or responds with verbal compliance only. Parent escalates with verbal emphasis, complaints ("grumbling"), and routinely delivered threats, but ignores noncompliance otherwise. Genuine anger is not expressed until 1.6.1 begins. Examples: 3.2, 3.3, 3.4, 5.7.

1.6   Interrogation and punishing.
   1.6.1   Punishing, "checking," or "tuning up" (mother's gloss). Parent begins by expressing genuine anger, specifies concretely the time and circumstances in which punishment will be meted out, and then confronts, if child has not complied with prior command (see 1.5). Confrontation calls for specification of command that was violated,

accusation, presentation of evidence (often nonverbally), insult (optional), and physical chastisement or scolding. Incriminating evidence is typically elicited by means of a direct question. Children must reply minimally to such a question or not at all, and look downcast throughout the confrontation. To do otherwise is to "talk back," which will increase the severity of punishment. Examples: 5.8, 5.10.

1.6.2   *Interrogating children.* Questions by parent requesting information about a given child's whereabouts, activities, etc. Child replies cautiously and minimally, as in 1.6.1. For this reason both routines are put in the same category. Example: 5.9.

2.0   Routines among children.

2.1   *Dramatic play.* Routines intended to represent or enact situations which are not actually occurring. In each of the following, children claim roles, and may either describe their actions or accompany them with noises intended to represent them.

2.1.1   *Playing house.* Doing chores, leaving children, visits by relatives, and sending children to the store are enacted, among other events. Mother role, the most popular for girls, typically consists of commands, often accompanied by explanation; assertion of authority whenever a child complains; and ignoring of requests. When requests are escalated, "mother" reproves, refuses, and asserts her authority. Child role consists of requests for explanation, claiming of tasks, complaints about being selected to do something, and requests for various things. Babies use baby-talk, act inappropriately, lack understanding, and get their way in disputes with siblings. Mother's lieutenant role informs mother, requests information and advice in carrying out mother's orders, and transmits commands to children. Example: 3.1.

2.1.2   *Playing store.* Making purchases, giving and counting change, figuring out if one has enough money, and requesting right to make own purchase are enacted. Common, although no examples given.

2.1.3   *Playing hospital.* Receiving shots, making arrangements to take a new baby home, taking medicine, and giving instructions for regimens are enacted. Common, although no examples given.

2.1.4   *Playing school.* Teacher role consists of commands and corrections. Dumb student role is enacted by boy. Students conspire to make teacher think that they are ill when they are not. No example given.

2.2   *Talking story.* The interweaving of narration, verbal play, and conversation along with any of the following.

2.2.1   *Narratives.* With rare exceptions narratives are not told in the absence of adults. Nevertheless, adults are not typically joint performers in children's narratives. A minimal narrative consists of two or more clauses that indicate a sequence of events or actions in the past. Expanded narratives also contain orientation and mediation (see Labov and Waletzky 1967; Watson 1973). Narratives among peers are typically joint performances (see Chapter 7). Examples: 4.7, 4.8, 4.9, 4.16, 8.1, 8.6. Note that many of these are excerpts and not whole narratives.

2.2.2 *Reports.* These differ from narratives in referring to only a single event with orientation as to where, when, etc. They may or may not contain mediation. Examples: 4.1, 8.5.

2.2.3 *The Name Game.* Sharing knowledge of the personal name of a parent with another child while withholding it from another. Used to recruit allies and influence others. Guessing, pretending to know, challenging, name play (see above), and outright prevarication are components. No examples given.

2.2.4 *Jingles.* Rhymed verses, frequently focused upon obscenities, often used to insult or derogate their target. Examples: 7.9, 7.15.

2.2.5 *Sex jokes/teasing.* Allegations of sexual attributes, acts, or relationships made about (a) target(s). Usually exchanged, rather than contradicted. Often contain idioms unique to sex joking. Friendly or insulting, depending upon prior relationship with speaker, intonation, and context. Examples: 7.10, 7.11, 7.14, 7.16.

2.2.6 *Situational joking.* Exaggerated threats, interdiction, word play, allegations, sharp rejoinders, and buffoonery, which cause general laughter. Compare with 1.1.2. Examples: 4.11, 4.12, 6.11, 6.12.

2.2.7 *Genre jokes and riddles.* Standardized jokes of American origin, told as narratives, and riddles, involving a battle of wits with one member of the audience, are reminiscent of *ho'opāpā* (see Chapter 2), except that they are not serious contests. Example: 7.12.

2.3 Disputing, contradicting. Beginning with an assertion, claim, or allegation, disputes tend to escalate through outright contradiction (including "Not!") to supporting argument/allegation/appeal to authority, challenge, insult, counter-insult/threat/trial with interdiction appearing when a participant is unable to produce an adequate reply. Disputes may begin with any of these subroutines, and skip any. Contrasts with 1.1.3 in seriousness, as well as elaboration of subroutines. Examples: 4.2, 4.3, 4.4, 4.6, 6.4, 6.5, 6.6, 6.7, 6.8, 6.9, 6.10.

2.4 Making an apology. Following an interpersonal conflict, offender offers an apology, while group leader and others accuse the culprit, offer reparation, joke, express sympathy with the offended, and call attention to his or her feelings, not necessarily in that order. Example: Boggs 1978a. Observed on one occasion only at KEEP.

2.5   *Taking care of younger siblings.* Older child, usually a girl, commands
      by issuing imperatives, directs, corrects, demonstrates, and provides
      information and explanation to younger sister; also addresses commands
      to whole group. Younger sister acts as a lieutenant, informs older sister,
      and requests information and advice. Compare with 2.1.1. Example:
      3.9.

Appendix Tables

Appendix Table 1. Sources and Amount of Data.

Place	Age	Number of children	Number of hours	Period of recording	
Honolulu/home	3–5	9 (3 fams.)	7.5	'72–'73	(3 months)
KEEP/kindergarten	4–5	10 plus	1.25	'72–'73	(1 month)
Aina Pumehana 1st–3d grade	6–8	32 plus	30	'66–'68	(18 months)
4th–6th grade	9–12	unknown	1	'70–'71	(24 months)
Ngh and camp	10–12	26 boys, 6 girls (2 fams.)	17	" "	" "
Home and ngh	13–16	unknown	10	" "	(3 months)
Nāpua Team	5–7	55	8	" "	(10 months)

Appendix Table 2. Dimensions of Verbal Routines. (See below for Definition of Dimensions.)

Routine	Rate of Initiation		Rate of Success		Escalation/ Mediation		Directives, Parents
	Parents	Children	Parents	Children	Parents	Children	Parents
Order/punish-	10/11*	1/28*	—	—	18/30	1/29	19/30
ing %	91	04			60	03	63
(N=3)							
Questioning	10/13*	2/22*	8/10	1/2	0/14	4/28	0/14
(N=1) %	77	09	80	50	0	14	0
Requesting	0/3	4/12	0/0	4/21	1/14	9/38**	1/14
(N=4) %	0	33	—	19	07	24	07
Discussion	0/6	7/16	0/0	7/8	6/12	1/18	1/12
(N=1) %	0	44	—	88	50	06	09
Contradicting	3/11	2/19	3/3	2/3	3/14	1/20	3/14
with %	27	11	100	67	22	05	22
parents							
(N=2)							

continued

Appendix Table 2. *continued*

Routine	Rate of Initiation		Rate of Success		Escalation/ Mediation		Directives, Parents
	Parents	Children	Parents	Children	Parents	Children	
Contradicting with peers % (N=11)	—	14/83 17	—	14/20 70	—	35/115 30	—
Joking with peers % (n=4)	—	8/31 26	—	8/11 73	—	9/43 21	—
Requesting & Contradict- % ing (N=1)	0/6 0	5/15 33	0/0 —	5/8 63	4/10 40	0/18 0	3/10 30
Narrative with peers % (N=3)	—	10/26 38	—	10/10 100	—	13/35 37	—

Rate of initiation = Number of successful initiations ÷ number of successful initiations + responses/replies.

Rate of success = Number of successful initiations ÷ number of all initiations.

Escalation/mediation = Number of escalations/mediations ÷ number of turns.

Directives = Number of directives ÷ number of turns.

*All initiations combined.

**8 of these were children taken mother's role.

Source: Appendix Table 3.

Appendix Table 3A. Frequency of Sub-routines in Cited Data.

Type of Routine and Location of Example	Parents/Adults					
	Number of Turns	Attempted Initiation		Number of Responses/ Replies	Number of Escalations/ Mediations	Number of Directives
		Unsuccessful	Successful			
Order/punishing:						
Ex. 5.7	8	0	6	0	2	7
Ex. 5.8	18	3	1	1	12	12
Ex. 5.10	4	0	0	0	4	0
Questioning:						
Ex. 5.9			See Appendix Table 2			
Requesting:						
Ex. 5.1	2	0	0	0	0	0
Ex. 5.2	1	0	0	0	0	0
Ex. 5.3	8	0	0	1	0	0
Ex. 5.6	3	0	0	2	1	1

Appendix Table 3A. *continued*

Type of Routine and Location of Example	Parents/Adults					
	Number of Turns	Attempted Initiation		Number of Responses/ Replies	Number of Escalations/ Mediations	Number of Directives
		Unsuccessful	Successful			
Discussion:						
Ex. 5.4			See Appendix Table 2			
Contradicting with parents:						
Ex. 6.1	3	0	1	1	1	1
Ex. 6.2	11	0	2	7	2	2
Requesting con-tradicting:						
Ex. 5.5			See Appendix Table 2			

Appendix Table 3B. Frequency of Sub-routines in Cited Data.

Type of Routine and Location of Example	Children					
	Number of Turns	Attempted Initiation		Number of Responses/ Replies	Number of Escalations/ Mediations	Number of Directives
		Unsuccessful	Successful			
Order/punishing:						
Ex. 5.7	12	0	0	11	1	
Ex. 5.8	14	0	1	13	0	
Ex. 5.10	3	0	0	3	0	
Questioning:						
Ex. 5.9			See Appendix Table 2			
Requesting:						
Ex. 5.1	2	2	0	0	0	
Ex. 5.2	1	1	0	0	0	
Ex. 5.3	19	9	1	8	1	
Ex. 5.6	16	5	3	0	8	
Discussion:						
Ex. 5.4			See Appendix Table 2			
Contradicting with parents:						
Ex. 6.1	4	0	0	4	0	
Ex. 6.2	16	1	2	13	1	
Requesting and contradicting:						
Ex. 5.5			See Appendix Table 2			

continued

Appendix Table 3. *continued*

Type of Routine and Location of Example	Number of Turns	Attempted Initiation		Number of Responses/ Replies	Number of Escalations/ Mediations	Number of Directives
		Unsuccessful	Successful			
Contradicting with peers:						
Ex. 4.2	9	0	1	3	5	
Ex. 4.3	8	0	1	7	1	
Ex. 4.4	8	0	1	5	4	
Ex. 4.5	4	0	0	3	1	
Ex. 6.4–6.6	9	0	1	7	2	
Ex. 6.7	10	0	1	6	4	
Ex. 6.8	23	1	2	13	8	
Ex. 6.9	9	2	1	3	4	
Ex. 6.10	5	0	1	4	1	
Ex. 6.11	14	0	1	10	4	
*	16	3	4	8	1	
Joking with peers:						
Ex. 4.11	11	1	2	4	4	
*	8	0	2	4	2	
Ex. 5.12	18	2	3	11	2	
*	6	0	1	4	1	
Narrative with peers:						
Ex. 4.7	18	0	6	8	6	
Ex. 4.8	11	0	2	5	4	
Ex. 4.9	6	0	2	3	3	

Sub-routines do not add up to number of turns because one turn may contain more than one sub-routine; likewise parents frequently do not reply, but are counted as having a turn each time a child made a request.

*Text not shown.

Footnotes

[1]For a well-documented test of the congruence hypothesis in an Odawa Indian classroom, see Erickson and Mohatt (1982).

[2]Ogbu (1978) has criticized the cultural difference hypothesis, which is similar to the match–mismatch hypothesis, as inadequate for explaining the failure in school of children belonging to caste-like minorities, that is, those minorities like Blacks and Mexican-Americans who are denied employment in many occupations because of their ethnic status alone. He proposes that the fundamental cause of such failure is disillusionment with the value that education has had for social mobility in the historical experience of such minorities. He further argues that life circumstances explain why such minorities retain certain cultural patterns and develop patterns of behavior in their children which differ from mainstream U.S. culture (op. cit.: Ch. 6). There is evidence to support these hypotheses in the case of the population described in this book, but it is beyond the scope of the book to evaluate it. The argument developed here is that, when cultural differences are taken into account, and a program of classroom management and reading instruction is based upon them, significant improvement in academic achievement results. It is important to be able to do something about cultural differences, whatever their ultimate origins.

[3]Princess Bernice Pauahi Bishop, a granddaughter of Kamehameha the First, willed the income from her vast personal estate, consisting entirely of lands, in perpetuity for the welfare and education of the "children of Hawaii," and to support a school for boys and a school for girls. Recently the Hawaii Supreme Court, overseer of the will, has given its approval for expenditure of funds for educational purposes outside the walls of the Kamehameha Schools. The KEEP program was set up pursuant to this ruling.

[4]This occurred when Watson-Gegeo told me about the discussion of verbal routines that had occurred in John Gumperz' seminar at Berkeley in 1972–73. When I wrote to her describing some of the routines which appeared in my recordings, she was able to reply with a mass of comparable examples from her data observed in the third community mentioned above, which she had not analyzed up to that point.

[5]For details of work with the mothers, see Appendix 1.

[6]Hawaiian words throughout the text are in italics, except for those in common English usage. An exception is made here in order to remind the reader of the Hawaiian origin of the word "aloha."

[7]It is puzzling that our principal source contains no extended discussion of obedience and respect for authority. Obedience is likewise missing from the report of the *Kūpuna* Conference.)

[8]Compare the identical meaning of *namanam tekia* in Truk (Marshall 1979: 150) and Mead's discussion of "acting above one's age" in Samoa (Mead 1928).

[9]The studies reviewed here include three monographs (Gallimore and Howard 1968; Gallimore et al. 1974; and Howard 1974) and three unpublished reports (Heighton 1971; Rosco 1977; and Alu Like 1976). The monographs were all based upon ethnographic observations and interviews conducted over a 2-year period (in some instances longer) in a community on the leeward coast of O'ahu. The samples were extensive and reasonably representative of this community, while the methods of data collection were systematic and varied. Further descriptions can be found in the sources. Heighton's dissertation is noteworthy because it offers in one chapter the most comprehensive overall ethnographic description of the culture of this community that we have, the others being more specialized. His seven principal informants past 40 years of age were all raised elsewhere, several on other islands. Rosco's paper is based upon intensive interviews of ten informants within a single family. All lived on O'ahu, although they were raised on another island. Altogether, the informants in these studies represent families from every island and district in Hawaii, the Alu Like study having been carried out in a representative sampling of households throughout the State of Hawaii.

[10]The dialogue was recorded by an overhead microphone. Research procedures, carried out with the understanding and approval of the parents, involve periodic monitoring of teacher and student interactions by means of sound and video tape. While the children are familiarized with the apparatus, they usually ignore it because it is omnipresent and they do not know when it is in operation. I am indebted to Violet Lui for making this recording.

[11]A similar style of appeal has been reported for Norwegian children of all ages by Hollos and Beeman (1978).

[12]Michael Mays first called my attention to the former use. Watson-Gegeo has pointed out the function of distracting (personal communication 2/3/1979).

[13]Hollos and Beeman (1978) report an identical sequence for Norwegian children, whereas Hungarian children increase the stridency of their demands under similar circumstances.

[14]A point which I am grateful to Karen Watson-Gegeo for making explicit.

[15]Watson-Gegeo has recorded her induction into a playful performance of this routine by a 6 year old girl, even though the former had no understanding of what was happening (Watson-Gegeo and Boggs 1977).

[16]Labov has reported the same thing for Black English speakers when "sounding" (Labov et al. 1968), and Lein and Brenneis (1978) for Fijian Indian children.

[17]From a linguistic perspective, it is worth noting that one way of contradicting is by grammatically incorporating and negating another speaker's clause. Examples of this are:

(1) M: Ge' one hole in da back . . .

    F: <u>Not</u> get one hole in da back!   (Example 6.10.)

(2)   <u>Not</u> + ju get black heya!   In this instance speaker negates what another thinks has been
           <u>You</u> get black heya!   said.

(3) K: You two <u>dd</u>u know.   (<u>dd</u> is a trill)

    D: Not, "you <u>dd</u>u know" . . .   (Example 6.14 below.)

Negating and incorporating in this way changes the primary stress in the sentence in the first two of these examples: normally in Hawaiian Creole English, primary stress is on the last stressed component. A shift in stress to the "Not", such as occurs here, Odo (1973) refers to as "focusing." I am indebted to Mike Forman for pointing this out. In the last sentence above, the speaker not only contradicts, but also mimics another's speech in order to correct it (see below). I have used quotation marks in text throughout only when vocal mimicry, pause, or pitch changes indicate that imitation is intended.

[18]It was incorrectly reported (Boggs 1978b) that "almost the same boys and girls were involved" in both age categories. This is true so far as the same school classes and friendships are concerned. But only 4 of 26 identified individuals were identical.

[19]Watson-Gegeo has used the term "contrapuntal" (Reisman 1970) to refer to this entire pattern because there is, she claims, "a related but distinct melody to the intonation contour (which) accompanies each part of the routine." Thus, the corroboration or response to a proposition may be actualized verbally or provided nonverbally, but tonally there is a place for it in the joint performance (ibid.). Perkins has suggested that this tonal pattern may be related to traditional speaking style in Hawaiian (Watson-Gegeo, personal communication, February 3, 1979). Unfortunately, we have not analyzed the data for tonal and breath group patterns. Therefore, we are avoiding the term "contrapuntal" in this book, so as not to confuse the tonal pattern with the underlying structure or the joint performance feature, even though all may be cooccurring. For further comment on the need to describe the tonal pattern, see Erickson (1977).

[20]Compare the treatment of the effect of "adjacency pairs" upon selection for next turn in Sacks et al. 1974: 716–717.

[21]In general, this supports the generalization in Sacks et al. (1974) that one party talks at a time, but this is culturally somewhat variable. There are significant exceptions in Lein and Brenneis (1978).

[22]Compare Gallimore et al. 1974: 171, cited in Chapter 2, for similar instances of adolescent humor.

[23]Mediations cannot be compared with escalations, since different rules of interpretation apply. Thus, a second supporting argument counts as a mediation in narrative, but not as an escalation in contradicting.

[24]As pointed out by Watson-Gegeo (personal communication, February 3, 1979), all of the local stories, whether based upon sex or other themes, are part of the folklore that the children are exposed to, and differ in style of performance and structure from European fairy tales.

[25]By the mid-'70s, the rate of turnover had been reduced considerably. But the basic problems described here are still observable.

[26]Little attention has been given to the tendency for Hawaiian culture to predominate in communities of mixed local populations. While mainland American culture affects all strata to some degree, its effects are greatest in the socio-economic upper and middle classes. Hawaiian life-style, by contrast, strongly influences those who are not in these classes in both rural and urban areas where Hawaiians and part-Hawaiians exceed 20–25 percent of the population.

[27]See Howard (1973) where a similar point was made about recitation on the basis of data provided in Boggs (1972).

[28]The classification scheme is modified from that used by Mitchell-Kernan and Kernan (1977). It was introduced by Ervin-Tripp (1976, 1977).

[29]This behavior was also used to obtain help from the teacher. See Green (1970), cited in Gallimore et al. 1974: 216.

[30]I am indebted to Watson-Gegeo for reminding me of this parallel.

[31]I am greatly indebted to the following for the written descriptions and transcriptions of the tapes used in this chapter: Kehau C. Lee, Doug Doi, Kathy H.P. Au, and Georgia McMillen, all of whom also contributed valuable interpretations. Lee and Doi worked many hours as unpaid volunteers before funds were found to compensate them.

[32]In addition to the sources cited, this description is based upon my own observations and communication with Kathy Au and Alice Ignacio.

[33]During the early years, points were given to individuals and groups. Recently, various privileges and praise have been awarded or withheld instead, but based upon strict attendance to contingencies. See Tharp (1980).

[34]The problem posed by the children's favorable response to questions here is discussed in the next to final section of this chapter.

[35]While Eli's statement constitutes a proposition, it is also a response to the teacher's directive to find the sentence. Not all propositions are initiations. Thus, the teacher often proposes during evaluations—see column 3 in Transcript 10.2 below.

[36]I am indebted to Gisela Speidel for this suggestion.

[37]Note that the teacher's prompts and evaluations both appear in the evaluation column. This follows Mehan's procedure. Teacher's comments in lines 47B, 59, and 66A are placed in the reply column because they are replies to students' utterances, even though they function simultaneously to initiate replies by students. Mehan does not indicate what he would do in such an event. See footnote 38 on "reflexivity."

[38]The teacher's positive response to these volunteered reports and narratives is, of course, what makes them initiations. If the teacher ignored, dismissed, or otherwise negatively evaluated them while reiterating her initial question, they would appear in Mehan's scheme as incorrect replies to her question. Likewise, the teacher would not be categorized as replying, as I understand Mehan's examples. This is a prime example of the reflexivity discussed by Mehan (1979). Teacher and students together by their social acts construct a discourse that is either recitation or something else.

[39]Au points out that the "R" [Relationship] sequences in the lesson "involve negotiation about the interpretation of story events which can be shared by all— teacher and students" (personal communication, March 24, 1980). As noted above, being unaware of the R concept when analyzing the transcript, we categorized this portion of the lesson as an interweaving of student time and book discussion. During one of these, interestingly (lines 2-268 to 283), the teacher argued for her proposition against the discrepant views of several students, whereas it is the students who argue for their view when challenged during book discussion, or T sequences. See McMillen et al. 1979.

References

Alu Like, Inc. (1976). Social and Economic Patterns of Hawaiians. *In* Needs Assessment Survey. Honolulu: Alu Like, Inc. Unpublished manuscript.

Ames, Louise Bates. (1966). "Children's stories." Genetic Psychological Monographs 73, 2: 337–396.

Apoliona, Haunani. (1979). Lecture to Anthropology 486, Feb. 13. University of Hawaii at Manoa.

Ashton-Warner, Sylvia. (1963). Teacher. New York: Simon and Schuster.

Au, Kathryn Hu-pei. (1979). "Using the Experience-Text-Relationship Method with minority children." Reading Teacher 32: 677–679.

————. (1980a). "Participation structures in a reading lesson with Hawaiian children: analysis of a culturally appropriate instructional event." Anthropology and Education Quarterly 11: 91–115.

————. (1980b). A test of the social organizational hypothesis: relationships between participation structures and learning to read. Unpublished doctoral dissertation, University of Illinois at Urbana-Champaign.

Au, Kathryn Hu-pei, and Cathie Jordan. (1977). "Teaching reading to Hawaiian children: finding a culturally appropriate solution." *In* C. Jordan, R. G. Tharp, K. H. P. Au, T. S. Weisner, and R. Gallimore, A Multidisciplinary Approach to Research in Education: the Kamehameha Early Education Program. Honolulu: Kamehameha Early Education Program, Technical Report #81.

Baird, Lynn A., and Karen Y. H. Bogert. (1978). The teaching of comprehension skills; a workshop for teachers. Honolulu: Kamehameha Early Education Program, Working Paper.

Beckwith, Martha Warren. (1932). Kepelino's Traditions of Hawaii. Honolulu: B. P. Bishop Museum.

————. (1970). Hawaiian Mythology. Honolulu: University of Hawaii Press. (Orig. 1940.)

Berko-Gleason, J., and S. Weintraub. (1976). "The acquisition of routines in child language: 'Trick or Treat.' " Language in Society 5: 129–136.

Bernstein, Louise. (1969). Humor as an indicator of social relationships among twenty Hawaiian children. Unpublished honors thesis, Department of Anthropology, University of Hawaii at Manoa.

Bettelheim, Bruno. (1943). "Individual and mass behavior in extreme situations." Journal of Abnormal and Social Psychology 38: 417–452.

Bickerton, Derek, and Carol Odo. (1976). General Phonology and Pidgin Syntax, Vol. 1. Honolulu: University of Hawaii at Manoa, Dept. of Linguistics, Final Report on NSF Grant No. GS-39748.

Bilmes, Jack, and Stephen T. Boggs. (1979). "Language and communication: foundations of culture." *In* A. Marsella, T. Ciborowski, and R. Tharp, eds., Perspectives on Cross-Cultural Psychology. New York: Academic Press.

Boggs, Stephen T. (1972). "The meaning of questions and narratives to Hawaiian children." *In* C. B. Cazden, V. P. John, and D. Hymes, eds., Functions of Language in the Classroom. New York: Teachers College Press.

———. (1977). The meaning of 'āina in Hawaiian tradition. Unpublished manuscript.

———. (1978a). "From the mouths of babes: Reflections of social structure in the verbal interaction of part-Hawaiian children." *In* K. A. Watson-Gegeo and S. L. Seaton, eds., Adaptation and Symbolism: Essays on Social Organization. Honolulu: East-West Center Press.

———. (1978b). "The development of verbal disputing in part-Hawaiian children." Language in Society 7: 325–344.

Boggs, Stephen T., and Ann M. Peters. (1980). An ethnographic-linguistic study of child language. Proposal to Linguistics Program, National Science Foundation, June, 1980.

Boggs, Stephen T., and R. Gallimore. (1968). "Employment." *In* R. Gallimore and A. Howard, eds., Studies in a Hawaiian Community: Na Makamaka O Nanakuli. Pacific Anthropological Records #1. Honolulu: B. P. Bishop Museum.

Boggs, Stephen T., and Karen Ann Watson-Gegeo. (1978). "Interweaving routines: strategies for encompassing a social situation." Language in Society 7: 375–392.

Bremme, Donald W., and Frederick Erickson. (1977). "Behaving and making sense: some relationships among verbal and nonverbal ways of interacting in a classroom." Theory into Practice, Vol. 16.

Brenneis, Donald, and Laura Lein. (1977). " 'You fruithead': a sociolinguistic approach to children's dispute settlement." *In* S. Ervin-Tripp and C. Mitchell-Kernan, eds., Child Discourse. New York: Academic Press.

Bruner, Jerome S. (1978). "The role of dialogue in language acquisition." *In* A. Sinclair, R. J. Jarvella, and W. J. M. Levelt, eds., The Child's Conception of Language. New York: Springer-Verlag. Appendix.

Cazden, Courtney B. (1979). Peekaboo as an instructional model: discourse development at home and school. Stanford Papers and Reports on Child Language Development 17: 1–29.

Cazden, Courtney B., Vera P. John, and Dell Hymes, eds. (1972). Functions of Language in the Classroom. New York: Teachers College Press.

Chall, Jeanne S. (1979). "The great debate: ten years later, with a modest proposal for reading stages." *In* L. B. Resnick and P. A. Weaver, eds., Theory and Practice of Early Reading, Vol. 1. Hillsdale, NJ: Erlbaum.

Cole, Michael, and Sylvia Scribner. (1974). Culture and Thought. New York: John Wiley and Son.

Conference. (1980). The Voice of the Kupuna: Report of a conference of native Hawaiian elders held May 29–31, 1980, at the Kamehameha Schools. Reprinted in the Native Hawaiian, Vol. 4, No. 6.

Day, Richard R. (1974). "Can Standard English be taught? or what does it mean to know Standard English?" Florida FL Reporter 12, 1–2: 71–76; 102–103.

Day, R., S. Boggs, R. Gallimore, R. G. Tharp, and G. E. Speidel. (1975). The Standard English Repetition Test (SERT): a measure of Standard English performance for Hawaii Creole English-speaking children. Technical Report #15. Honolulu: Kamehameha Early Education Program.

Doo, Wayne Wai. (1978). Paper presented to Anthropology 486, University of Hawaii, Manoa, spring semester.

Edwards, A. D., and V. J. Furlong. (1978). The Language of Teaching: Meaning in Classroom Interaction. London: Heinemann.

Elkins, Stanley M. (1968). Slavery. Chicago: University of Chicago Press. (Orig. 1959.)

Erickson, Frederick. (1977). "Comments." In C. Jordan, R. G. Tharp, K. H. P. Au, T. S. Weisner, and R. Gallimore, A Multidisciplinary Approach to Research in Education: the Kamehameha Early Education Program. Honolulu: Kamehameha Early Education Program, Technical Report #81.

Erickson, Frederick, and Gerald Mohatt. (1982). "Cultural organization of participation structures in two classrooms of Indian students." In George Spindler, ed., Doing the Ethnography of Schooling: Educational Anthropology in Action. New York: Holt, Rinehart, and Winston.

Ervin-Tripp, Susan. (1976). "Is Sybil there? the structure of some American English directives." Language in Society 5: 25–66.

———. (1977). "Wait for me, Roller Skate!" In S. Ervin-Tripp and C. Mitchell-Kernan, eds., Child Discourse. New York: Academic Press.

———. (1978). "Adult-child dialogues from two to three." Language in Society 7: 357–374.

Fillmore, Lily W. (1976). The second time around: cognition and social strategies in second language acquisition. Unpublished doctoral dissertation, Stanford University.

Firth, Raymond. (1957). We, the Tikopia: a Sociological Study of Kinship in Primitive Polynesia. London: Allen and Unwin. (Orig. 1936.)

———. (1973). Symbols, Public and Private. Ithaca, NY: Cornell University Press.

Fornander, Abraham. (1969). An Account of the Polynesian Race. Rutland, VT: Tuttle. (Orig. 1878.)

Gallimore, R., J. W. Boggs, and C. Jordan. (1974). Culture, Behavior and Education: A Study of Hawaiian-Americans. Beverly Hills, CA: Sage Publications.

Gallimore, Ronald, and Alan Howard. (1968). Studies in a Hawaiian Community: Na Makamaka O Nanakuli. Pacific Anthropological Records #1. Honolulu: B. P. Bishop Museum.

Gallimore, Ronald, and Roland Tharp. (1971). "Proposal." Reprinted in R. Tharp and R. Gallimore, A Proposal to Build an Education and Research Program: A Kamehameha Early Education Project Proposal. Honolulu: Kamehameha Early Education Project, Technical Report #3 (1975).

———. (n.d.). What do sentence repetition tests measure? Unpublished manuscript, University of California, Los Angeles, Dept. of Psychiatry and Biobehavioral Sciences.

Goldman, Irving. (1970). Ancient Polynesian Society. Chicago: University of Chicago Press.

Graves, Nancy B., and Theodore D. Graves. (1978). "The impact of modernization on the personality of a Polynesian people." Human Organization 37: 115–135.

Green, Laura. (1970). Nonverbal attention-seeking among Hawaiian children. Unpublished master's thesis, University of Hawaii at Manoa.

Gumperz, John J., and Eleanor Herasmchuk. (1972). The conversational analysis of social meaning: a study of classroom interaction. In Roger Shuy, ed., 23d Annual Roundtable, Sociolinguistics: Current Trends and Prospects. Washington, DC: Georgetown University Press.

Handy, E. S. C., and M. K. Pukui. (1972). The Polynesian Family System in Ka'u, Hawaii. Wellington, New Zealand: The Polynesian Society. (Orig. 1953.)

Handy, E. S. C., E. G. Handy, and M. K. Pukui. (1972). Native Planters in Old Hawaii: Their Life, Lore, and Environment. Honolulu: B. P. Bishop Museum.

Heath, Shirley B. (1980). What no bedtime story means: narrative skills at home and school. Paper prepared for the Terman Conference, Stanford University, November 20–22

———. (1982). Questioning at home and at school: a comparative study. In G. D. Spindler, ed., Doing the Ethnography of Schooling: Educational Anthropology in Action. New York: Holt, Rinehart, and Winston.

———. (1983). Ways with Words: Language, Life and Work in Communities and Classrooms. Cambridge: Cambridge University Press.

Heighton, Robert H., Jr. (1971). Hawaiian supernatural and natural strategies for goal attainment. Unpublished doctoral dissertation, University of Hawaii.

Hollos, Marida, and William Beeman. (1978). "The development of directives among Norwegian and Hungarian children: An example of communicative style in culture." Language in Society 7: 345–356.

Homans, George C. (1950). The Human Group. New York: Harcourt, Brace.

Howard, Alan. (1971). Households, families and friends in a Hawaiian-American community. Working Paper No. 19. Honolulu: East-West Center Population Institute.

———. (1973). "Education in 'Aina Pumehana: the Hawaiian-American student as hero." In S. T. Kimball and J. Burnett, eds., Learning and Culture. Seattle, WA: American Ethnological Society, University of Washington Press.

———. (1974). Ain't No Big Thing: Coping Strategies in a Hawaiian-American Community. Honolulu: University Press of Hawaii.

Howard, A., R. Heighton, C. Jordan, and R. Gallimore. (1970). Traditional and modern adoption patterns in Hawaii. In V. Carroll, ed., Adoption in Eastern Oceania. Honolulu: University of Hawaii Press.

Hymes, Dell. (1962). "The ethnography of speaking." In Anthropological Society of Washington, ed., Anthropology and Human Behavior. Washington, DC: Anthropological Society of Washington.

———. (1971). "On linguistic theory, communicative competence, and the education of disadvantaged children." In M. L. Wax, S. Diamond, and F. O. Gearing, eds., Anthropological Perspectives on Education. New York: Basic Books.

———. (1972). "Introduction." In C. B. Cazden, V. P. John, and D. Hymes, eds., Functions of Language in the Classroom.

———. (1974). "Ways of speaking." In R. Bauman and J. Sherzer, eds., Explorations in the Ethnography of Speaking. London: Cambridge University Press.

Ignacio, Alice J. (1981). Paper presented to Anthropology 480D, University of Hawaii at Manoa, fall semester.

I'i, John Papa. (1959). Fragments of Hawaiian History, trans. by M. K. Pukui. Honolulu: B. P. Bishop Museum.

Iwamura, Susan J. (1980). The Verbal Games of Pre-school Children. London: Croom Helm.

Johnson, William P. (1977). A study of the missionary effort to "civilize" the Hawaiian. Unpublished master's paper, University of Hawaii, Manoa.

Jordan, Cathie. (1977). "Teaching/learning interactions and school adaptation." In C. Jordan, R. G. Tharp, K. H. P. Au, T. S. Weisner, and R. Gallimore, A Multidisciplinary Approach to Research in Education: the Kamehameha Early Education Program. Honolulu: Kamehameha Early Education Program, Technical Report #81.

Jordan, Cathie, John D'Amato, and Ann Joesting. (1981). "At home, at school and at the interface." Educational Perspectives 20: 31–37.

Jordan, Cathie, and R. G. Tharp. (1979). "Culture and education." In A. Marsella, T. Ciborowski, and R. Tharp, eds., Perspectives in Cross-Cultural Psychology. New York: Academic Press.

Kamakau, Samuel M. (1961). Ruling Chiefs of Hawaii, trans. by M. K. Pukui. Honolulu: Kamehameha Schools Press.

———. (1964). Ka Po'e Kahiko: the People of Old, trans. by M. K. Pukui. Honolulu: B. P. Bishop Museum.

Labov, William. (1967). Some Sources of Reading Problems for Negro Speakers of Non-Standard English. Champaign, IL: National Council of Teachers of English.

Labov, William, Paul Cohen, Clarence Robins, and John Lewis. (1968). A Study of the Non-Standard English of Negro and Puerto Rican Speakers in New York City, Vol. 2. New York: Columbia University. C.R.P. Report No. 3288.

Labov, William, and Joshua Waletzky. (1967). "Narrative analysis." In June Helm, ed., Essays on the Verbal and Visual Arts. Seattle, WA: American Ethnological Society, University of Washington Press.

Lein, Laura, and Donald Brenneis. (1978). "Children's disputes in three speech communities." Language in Society 7: 299–324.

Luomala, Katherine. (1979). Hawaiian oral arts. Lecture at the Kamehameha School, March 15.

Malo, David. (1951). Hawaiian Antiquities, trans. by N. B. Emerson. Honolulu: B. P. Bishop Museum. (Orig. 1898.)

Marshall, Mac. (1979). Weekend Warriors: Alcohol in a Micronesian Culture. Palo Alto, CA: Mayfield Publishing Co.

Martin, Laura. (1975). A study of body movement behavior in contradicting routines of Hawaii Creole English speaking children. Paper presented to ESL 360 and 660, University of Hawaii at Manoa, spring semester.

McMillen, Georgia, S. Boggs, and K. H. P. Au. (1979). A discourse-annotated transcription of a model KEEP second grade reading lesson, Teacher: Claire Assam. Honolulu: Kamehameha Early Education Program, Technical Report #94.

McNamee, Gillian D. (1979). "The social interaction origins of narrative skills." The Quarterly Newsletter of the Laboratory of Comparative Human Cognition 1: 63–68.

Mead, Margaret. (1928). Coming of Age in Samoa. New York: Morrow.

Mehan, Hugh. (1979). Learning Lessons. Cambridge, MA: Harvard University Press.

Michaels, Sarah, and Jenny Cook-Gumperz. (1979). "A study of sharing time with first grade students: discourse narratives in the classroom." Berkeley Linguistics Society 4: 1–14.

Mitchell-Kernan, Claudia, and Keith T. Kernan. (1977). Pragmatics of directive choice among children. In S. Ervin-Tripp and C. Mitchell-Kernan, eds., Child Discourse. New York: Academic Press.

Nakuina, Emma Metcalf. (1893). "Ancient Hawaiian water rights and some of the customs pertaining to them." Thrumm's Hawaiian Annual for 1893: 79–84.

Napjus, Alice James. (1973). "Freddy found a frog." In L. Evertts, L. C. Hunt, and B. J. Weiss, People Need People. Holt Basic Reading System. New York: Holt, Rinehart, and Winston.

Odo, Carol. (1973). "Focusing and defocusing in Hawaiian English." In C.-J. N. Bailey and R. W. Shuy, eds., New Ways of Analyzing Variation in English. Washington, DC: Georgetown University Press.

Ogbu, John U. (1978). Minority Education and Caste. New York: Academic Press.

O'Neal, Karen, and Karen Bogert. (1977). Classroom organization for the language arts teacher: a system for meeting learner needs through the use of work areas and small group instruction. Honolulu: Kamehameha Early Education Program Technical Report #78.

Perkins, Leialoha Apo Mark. (1978). The aesthetics of stress in ōlelo and oli: notes toward a theory of Hawaiian oral arts. Unpublished doctoral dissertation, University of Pennsylvania.

Philips, Susan U. (1972). Participant structures and communicative competence: Warm Springs children in community and classroom. In C. B. Cazden, V. P. John, and D. Hymes, eds., Functions of Language in the Classroom. New York: Teachers College Press.

Pukui, M. K., E. W. Haertig, and C. A. Lee. (1972). Nānā I Ke Kumu (Look to the Source), Vol. 1. Honolulu: Hui Hanai, Queen Liliuokalani Children's Center.

Reinecke, John E. (1969). Language and Dialect in Hawaii. Honolulu: University of Hawaii Press.

Reisman, Karl. (1970). Contrapuntal Conversations in an Antiguan Village. Penn-Texas Working Papers in Sociolinguistics No. 3. Austin: University of Texas Press.

Rosco, Rona Dale. (1977). The existence of the 'ohana in contemporary Hawaii. Unpublished master's paper, University of Hawaii, Manoa.

Sachs, Jacqueline. (1977). "Talking about the there and then." Stanford Papers and Reports on Child Language Development 13: 56–63.

Sacks, Harvey, Emanuel A. Schegloff, and Gail Jefferson. (1974). "A simplest systematics for the organization of turn-taking for conversation." Language, 50, 4: 696–735.

SB Honolulu Star-Bulletin newspaper, issues of 11/29/79 and 12/3/80.

Scollon, Ron, and Suzanne B. K. Scollon. (1979a). Thematic abstraction: a Chipewyan two-year-old. In R. Scollon and S. B. K. Scollon, eds., Linguistic Convergence: An Ethnography of Speaking at Fort Chipewyan, Alberta. New York: Academic Press.

————. (1979b). The literate two-year-old: the fictionalization of self. Unpublished manuscript, University of Alaska, Fairbanks: Alaska Native Language Center.

————. (1980). "Literacy as focused interaction." Quarterly Newsletter of the Laboratory of Comparative Human Cognition 2: 26–29. (Orig. 1979.)

Sinclair, J., and M. Coulthard. (1975). Towards an Analysis of Discourse: The Language of Teachers and Pupils. Oxford: Oxford University Press.

Stoel-Gammon, Carol, and Leonor S. Cabral. (1977). "Learning to tell it like it is: The development of the reportative function in children's speech." Stanford Papers and Reports on Child Language Development 13: 64–71.

Sutter, Frederic K. (1980). Communal versus individual socialization at home and in school in rural and urban Western Samoa. Unpublished doctoral dissertation, University of Hawaii at Manoa.

Tharp, Roland G. (1977). Peer orientation, industriousness, and learning to read: experiments with the Hawaiian child. In C. Jordan, R. G. Tharp, K. H. P. Au, T. S. Weisner, and R. Gallimore, A Multidisciplinary Approach to Research in Education: the Kamehameha Early Education Program. Honolulu: Kamehameha Early Education Program, Technical Report #81.

————. (1980). The direct instruction of comprehension: description and results of the Kamehameha Early Education Program. Paper presented to the American Educational Research Association meeting in Boston.

Tharp, Roland G., and Ronald Gallimore. (1976). The uses and limits of social reinforcement and industriousness for learning to read. Honolulu: Kamehameha Early Education Program, Technical Report #60.

Turner, Victor W. (1968). The Ritual Process: Structure and Anti-Structure. Chicago: Aldine-Atherton.

Vygotsky, L. S. (1978). Mind in Society: The Development of Higher Psychological Processes. Cambridge, MA: Harvard University Press.

Watson, Karen Ann. (1972). The rhetoric of narrative structure: a sociolinguistic analysis of stories told by part-Hawaiian children. Unpublished doctoral dissertation, University of Hawaii, Manoa.

————. (1975). "Transferable communicative routines: strategies and group identity in two speech events." Language in Society, 4: 53–72.

Watson-Gegeo, Karen Ann, and Stephen T. Boggs. (1977). "From verbal play to talk-story: the role of routines in speech events among Hawaiian children." In S. Ervin-Tripp and C. Mitchell-Kernan, eds., Child Discourse. New York: Academic Press.

Name/Subject Index

Italics indicate bibliographic citations.